What You Sow Is a Bare Seed

What You Sow Is a Bare Seed

A Countercultural Christian Community during Five Decades of Change

CELESTE KENNEL-SHANK

WIPF & STOCK · Eugene, Oregon

WHAT YOU SOW IS A BARE SEED
A Countercultural Christian Community during Five Decades of Change

Wipf & Stock
An Imprint of Wipf and Stock Publishers
199 W. 8th Ave., Suite 3
Eugene, OR 97401

www.wipfandstock.com

PAPERBACK ISBN: 978–1-6667–7107-7
HARDCOVER ISBN: 978–1-6667–7108-4
EBOOK ISBN: 978–1-6667–7109-1

08/02/23

Dedicated to every person
who made up the Community of Christ in DC,
especially my father, Duane Shank (1952–2022),
who was curious about this unusual small band of Christians
while talking with David Anderson
on the sidelines of their children's neighborhood soccer game.
Because of that, my life changed immeasurably for the better.

Contents

Acknowledgments

THIS BOOK IS THE latest in a long line of collective creations by the Community of Christ. I authored it, but any talent I possess would be nothing without the candor of all of the people I interviewed. They engaged in the kind of rigorous self-examination that was a hallmark of the Community. I am grateful to each person who trusted me with their stories, the ones that appear in these pages and the ones that do not. A few people went above and beyond. David Anderson and Larry and Nyla Rasmussen read and commented on the whole manuscript, asking thoughtful questions along the way. Another advisor on the project as a whole was Amanda Huron. Sandra Wojahn made sure I had all of the documents and photos I needed, helped me connect with members from earlier periods in the Community, and offered essential feedback and support.

I dedicated this book to everyone who was part of the Community during its fifty-one years, many of whom I did not know. Additional gratitude is due to all of the people who were part of the gathered Community in the 1990s. My mother, Ellen Kennel, has often told me, "I knew I needed a village to help raise you." In my childhood and teenage experiences of worship and Community gatherings, I always felt safe and cared for in our building and in the homes of Community members. That is something everyone deserves and yet so many do not have.

I am exceedingly grateful to have received a Pastoral Study Project grant from the Louisville Institute. Everyone there has been wonderful, along with the other grant recipients with whom I was part of a conversation group in winter 2021.

With my particular love of libraries, I was thrilled to spend several days at the Swarthmore College Peace Collection, where the Community of Christ archives are located, and I'm grateful to the curator and staff.

I want to offer special thanks to a few of the colleagues and friends who listened to me talk about this book and gave input. Elizabeth Palmer encouraged me as I was beginning to think about taking on this project.

I'm grateful for walks and talks along the way also. Justin Skolnick, a dear friend, shared his thoughts from research on mid-twentieth-century American Christianity. Sister Janet Ryan helped me to trust my sense of call to write this book. I'm honored by Jennifer McBride's support of this book, and I'm lucky to call her my friend. My life and work are greatly improved by the friendship of Russell and Charissa Johnson. I am counting on them placing this book on their shelves between the Holy Bible and a book about garlic as promised. Steven P. Miller was a fantastic editor, helping me turn my news experience writing first drafts of history into authoring a finished historical narrative. Alison Casella Brookins has been a kindred bivocational colleague along with my clergy women's writing group—Melissa Earley, Elizabeth Felicetti, Heidi Haverkamp, Meghan Murphy-Gill, and Teri McDowell Ott—who offered fabulous feedback on questions big and small. Elizabeth even read my whole draft manuscript. Her comments made me feel like a standup comedian when all of her jokes land.

Thank you to my housemates Andres, Beth, Miguel, and Remedios for living with this project along with me for the past eighteen months—and extra thanks to Miguel for expert assistance in making historical photos publishable. My beloved, Josiah, offered many forms of support. To name a few: he celebrated his fortieth birthday in eastern Pennsylvania so that I could go to the archives at Swarthmore College, and he listened many times when I flopped on the couch, saying I was done for the day, and then kept puzzling over some aspect of this project. Writing this book would have been a lot harder without his companionship.

Lent 2023

Introduction

STANDING IN THE CHECKOUT line at the grocery store near my home in Chicago, I opened a cloth bag to get ready to fill it. Inside I saw a flash of yellow and chartreuse. I pulled it out and discovered it was a card made by Sally Hanlon, with a calligraphy message: "Love's Life Tasks: Trust God. Serve Neighbor. Tend the *Garden. *aka: Creation.— Rudy Wendelin." A smile creased my cheeks. I can't get away from these reminders of the Christian community where I grew up in Washington, DC. Nor do I want to.

In her 1952 book *The Long Loneliness*, Dorothy Day wrote of founding the Catholic Worker Movement with Peter Maurin, and the work of confronting injustice, nurturing Christian community, and seeking to shape a new society "where it is easier for people to be good."[1] Their challenge was to make people want to live that way. "It would take example, and the grace of God, to do it,"[2] Day wrote. I agree. That is why I want to share the stories of the people who were examples to me. People such as Sally and Rudy. I cannot think of what it means to be a Christian or to live a faithful life apart from thinking about them and many others from the Community of Christ.

The people who formed me became even more extraordinary to me as I have chosen a career—two, in fact—that has me reflecting daily on those questions. Beginning as a reporting intern at Religion News Service fresh out of college, I have written and edited stories about the changing religious landscape in the past two decades. I've interviewed hundreds of religious leaders. In the United States and in several countries in the global South, I've been to Christian, Jewish, Muslim, Buddhist, and interfaith services. I've spent many hours in conversation with people starting new congregations and with those trying to revitalize established ones. As a pastor I've worked at some of those efforts myself. In all of this, data and statistics have their place—such as the rising percentage of people in the United States with no religious affiliation, aka the nones, or those fed up with organized

1. Day, *Long Loneliness*, 280.
2. Day, *Long Loneliness*, 226.

religion, the dones. Yet numbers can be numbing without stories of people behind them.

A characteristic that drives my work as a journalist and a pastor is the desire to engage the stories of people's lives: their struggles, joys, and concerns. True stories told well have transformative power without being prescriptive. Social-justice-oriented communities and activists have shown me that we are often relearning the same lessons that others learned before. Granted, there are some things we all have to learn for ourselves, but I believe we're better able to do that when reflecting on concrete examples. Our own context may not be as different or new as we think.

I was in my thirties before I met the Community's founding pastor, John Schramm, or read *Dance in Steps of Change: The Story of the Community of Christ, Washington, D.C.'s Answer to the Tensions That Challenge the Church Today*, the book he wrote with longtime lay leader David Anderson about the Community's first five years, published in 1970. I was amazed at how the Community's central ideas played out over decades and yet stayed consistent. I absorbed them in my childhood and youth through what older adults said and, more importantly, what they did. In contrast to many of my peers, who have moved away from the religious tradition they grew up with, I found the Community's convictions even more potent because of my work and life experience.

I know now that the adults who shaped my childhood experiences were not the superheroes they sometimes seemed to be, yet they were extraordinary. Among them was David Hilfiker, a physician who was one of the founders of Christ House, which provided time, space, and care for men who were homeless to recover from medical crises.[3] Christ House is connected to the Church of the Saviour, which influenced the early Community of Christ. Its current ministries are a short walk away from my childhood home and the building the Community owned. We volunteered to help provide meals at Christ House as well as connecting with the Church of the Saviour in other ways. Hilfiker writes in *Not All of Us Are Saints*, "If each of us has to invent the wheel all over again, our journeys become naive, solitary, narrow. The experiences of each of us in moving closer to a just lifestyle are of value to others who want to do likewise."[4]

In that spirit I tell the stories and overarching story of the Community of Christ, one group of people who sought to live out their commitments to justice, peace, and the life of faith. The Community's life and times can't be fully understood without some of the wider context of the history of US

---

3. Hilfiker, *Not All of Us Are Saints*, 13.

4. Hilfiker, *Not All of Us Are Saints*, 115.

cities, US politics, and American Christianity—with all three colliding in church engagement in urban areas in the post–World War II era. Some of the people who were drawn into the Community I have never met. Others are among the dearest people to me, in the world and now in the cloud of witnesses. I want to show you these beloveds in all their glorious messiness. I want to show you why they matter at a time when divisions tear Christians apart across the United States and around the world, as people who found a way to challenge the worst excesses of their culture and live into new possibilities for their faith tradition. By refusing to blur their differences, they found often-elusive common ground.

Among them, my faith formation was as an ecumenical Christian. Anyone who is familiar with the word *ecumenical*—being from the whole world of Christianity, or at least multiple traditions within it—knows that it doesn't make sense at some level to say that. I'm not quite a cradle ecumenical Christian, since my family didn't join our community until I was seven years old. But from that point on, my faith formation happened within a community made up of Christians who came from different denominational traditions and who continued to embrace those traditions and blend them together in the life of the congregation.

In junior high, because of my one ardently evangelical friend—and by that I mean that I had only one; together the two of us were the only Christians in our friend group—I learned that there was such a thing as a nondenominational church. And I learned to distinguish my own congregation from it. "The Lutherans are still Lutheran, and the Catholics are still Catholic, and my family is still Mennonite," so my explanation went.

But it wasn't until twenty-five years after my family joined that ecumenical group, when the Community of Christ ended its time as a congregation and sold its building, that I better understood what a rare gift we shared. I could see how unusual it was for me and my few peers in the Community to have been formed in the crucible of multiple Christian traditions interacting with each other every week as one body.

A few months after the Community's final Sunday worship, I went to the Lutheran School of Theology at Chicago for a service in which the school returned a ninth-century New Testament manuscript to the Greek Orthodox Church. The seminary president in 1920 purchased it from a European book dealer without knowing it had been stolen. Seeing the return of the codex I found myself deeply moved, as I imagine many in the room were. But I also found myself thinking how right it felt to be among Christians of many traditions, singing psalms together and hearing Isa 40:1–8: "Then the glory of the Lord shall be revealed, and all people shall see it together." The Orthodox archbishop called it an act of ecumenism, transcending dialogue.[5]

The Community of Christ witnessed and took part in acts of ecumenism weekly if not daily for five decades. Amid the messiness and brokenness of our lives, the glory of God was revealed, and all of us saw it together. The congregation started as a "package mission" of the American Lutheran Church in 1965. During a decade when some of my relatives were returning from overseas missionary work, the Community of Christ saw its mission as engaging everyone in a square mile in an inner-city neighborhood. Among them were people who had come to the city for graduate school or to start their careers. The label "yuppies"—coined decades later to describe young urban professionals—would fit, pejorative though it often is. Some of these twenty- and thirty-somethings would also now fit in another category created more recently by sociologists of religion called "spiritual but not religious."

My parents were among those folks—though nearer to forty when they joined the Community. They were attracted to it because it offered a faith community with many of the good qualities of the churches they had been raised in, but without the strictness. Our family had attended the neighborhood Unitarian church for a while, but they wanted Jesus in their lives as something more than a good teacher. With people from backgrounds such as the Lutheran Church–Missouri Synod, the Roman Catholic Church, or conservative plain-dressing Mennonites in my parents' case, the Community of Christ created a place where I as a child always felt free to let faith and doubt intermingle, to let questions and convictions coexist.

I was baptized in the Community of Christ by my grandfather Luke Shank, an ordained Mennonite minister who was visiting for the occasion, and Phil Wheaton, an Episcopal priest from the Community of Christ who was also a dear family friend. I read from 1 Cor 13 about how we prophesy only in part and see as through glass, darkly, and a prayer from Saint Francis of Assisi that God is our source of humility, patience, inner peace, joy, and justice. I said: "I seek God today in gratitude for the joy in my life, and for the compassion and faith in me shown by others. I offer myself as a companion to all people and creation in the world to serve others. In my life, I know little, and wish to make no prophecies, only to keep an open heart and work radically for justice and always treat others with compassion."

My father, Duane Shank, an activist and organizer who was a central lay leader during the second half of the Community's life, called my baptism "an example of ecumenism in action—not just words, but action." He had

5. Kennel-Shank, "U.S. Lutheran seminary," 14–15.

been part of a great deal of ecumenical and interfaith dialogue in his activism against war and economic injustice. Though I was only beginning to understand it at seventeen, I embraced being baptized not only into one congregation but into the global church. It was the beginning of learning how we are bound into the mystical body of Christ, in solidarity with people around the world, some we will encounter and some we will not.

Today, there is a cohort of about two dozen of us who spent all or most of our childhoods in this peculiar manifestation of Christian community. At our final retreat, reunion, and 50th anniversary celebration—all rolled into one weekend—I talked with those who grew up with me and those who had grown up in the Community of Christ a decade before me. I felt a kinship with all of them, even those I had only met in passing before that weekend. We had a common refrain: "I've never been able to find another church like this. I don't feel fully at home anywhere else." One peer said, "It was just a really neat way of growing up." Beyond our cohort, she hasn't encountered anyone else with a similar experience. "If I wanted to look for a church now, it would be hard to find a church that meets those expectations—I have high ones."[6]

The Community was not perfect, because it was created by human beings. Yet its core people taught me that Christian love and grace extended toward one another again and again can be the stuff of real life, and not only something to sing about around a campfire.

I came to believe that the best way to tell the Community's story is through its people. And the people who passed through the Community in its fifty-one years were among the most fascinating I've ever encountered—and I say that putting on my best news reporter hat. They included Mary Catherine Bateson, a linguistics scholar and anthropologist who wrote one of the Community's litanies. She asserts in *Composing a Life* that "continuity is the exception in twentieth-century America," and by accepting that we can look for constants. "What is the ongoing entity of which we can say that it has assumed a new form?"[7] In times of great change, "by setting a number of life histories side by side, we will be enabled to recognize common patterns of creativity that have not been acknowledged or fostered."[8] This book does that with examples of the life of faith and the community that was their collective creation.

Larry Rasmussen, a social ethicist, saw the Community as an example of the kind of communities that are essential to his vision for church and

6. Lindsey Pohlman, in discussion with the author, November 2021.
7. Bateson, *Composing a Life*, 14–15.
8. Bateson, *Composing a Life*, 4–5.

society. After fourteen years in the Community, he published his book *Moral Fragments and Moral Community.* When Community members read it and he came to speak about it with them, people teased him: "This book is all about us. Why didn't you say so?" David added, "You only mentioned us once, and that was a footnote!" Larry said, "I realized in talking with the Community at that time that it is all about the Community." His proposal for strengthening civil society was not merely abstract but based on his experiences in the Community.[9]

These communities are sacred places where people share power in an egalitarian way of life, deliberating the most controversial issues together, and creating "a genuine sanctuary," Larry wrote.[10] "They are havens for the people who belong to them, but they are not havens to get away from the world, but where you can risk things together with some joy and some adventure because you feel safe with one another."[11] Further evoking the Community of Christ, these communities are made up of "pastoral people present to one another in time of trouble and joy" who offer to each other "havens of refreshment and of celebration around simple gifts. They are places of song, dance, and not a little silliness. They know how to do feasts, and they know how to pray and be quiet and be merciful to one another."[12]

Such communities are essential for democracy. Participatory communities like the Community of Christ practice democracy on a small scale,[13] but the practice nurtures "communities that have a sense that even though they're small, they're important," Larry said. "They have some good news for the wider world." As his thinking has evolved over his decades as a social ethicist, he now calls these groups "anticipatory communities: communities that are very self-conscious of who they are. They are self-conscious about their values. They choose their values rather than assuming the wider culture's unwritten ethic.[14] These communities can also engage in critique of themselves because they know that the gospel of grace means they can make mistakes in their efforts to live an ethical life.[15] This is a task for individuals as well as for the community as a whole.

9. Larry Rasmussen, in discussion with the author, November 2022.

10. Rasmussen, *Moral Fragments*, 150.

11. Rasmussen, in discussion with author, November 2022; Rasmussen, *Moral Fragments*, 163.

12. Rasmussen, *Moral Fragments*, 164.

13. Rasmussen, *Moral Fragments*, 197.

14. Rasmussen, in discussion with the author, November 2022.

15. Rasmussen, *Moral Fragments*, 15, 111–23.

Loyalty is a further quality that could be set as a minimum requirement defining a community instead of mere association, Larry wrote. "Loyalty is faithfulness and a studied commitment to take others seriously in season and out." This allows a community to hold divergent views, "even fight with one another," Larry wrote, "without forsaking community."[16] That was certainly true of the Community of Christ.

ð

When I began this project in 2020, I contacted the email list and social media group for people who were part of the Community. I told them I was seeking "to tell a thorough-but-not-definitive version of the Community's history." Receiving no objections to my taking on the project, I conducted more than fifty interviews with former Community members who are still living, as well as people who were interested observers of the Community—neighbors, friends, family members. I had a sense of urgency as many members had already died and several more died or stopped being able to communicate as I was working on this project. While I felt deeply those lost opportunities not only for myself but for my readers, I was grateful for autobiographical writing published by several of them.

Written documents, including in the Community's extensive archives, helped to flesh out memories and fact-check names, dates, and many of the accounts shared in interviews. Other recollections lack a written record, and later events often reshape memories for us all. Unless I found documentation that something was incorrect, or feared it would be misleading, I let the story stand as told to me. In some instances, there were multiple memories of the same event, sometimes divergent. In those cases, I tried to let the various perspectives sit side by side. In this way they may become like pieces of colored glass in a kaleidoscope, together forming a multifaceted image, more striking than each could create on their own.

NOTES ON NAMES AND EDITORIAL CHOICES

This book is about the Community of Christ in Washington, DC, which was affiliated with the American Lutheran Church and, after a denominational merger, the Evangelical Lutheran Church in America. It had no relationship to the denomination headquartered in Independence, Missouri, that

16. Rasmussen, *Moral Fragments*, 129, 131.

in 2001 changed its name from the Reorganized Church of Jesus Christ of Latter Day Saints to Community of Christ.[17]

After the first reference, Washington, DC will be shortened to DC, because that is how DC natives and long-time residents most often refer to the city.

For personal names, I use the name a person called themselves at the time that I interviewed them. For people who were not part of the Community, I follow the custom of long-form journalism and historical narrative to use last names after first reference. For people who were part of the Community, however briefly or sporadically, I use their first names subsequently. My primary reasons for doing this were because many people's last names changed over the course of the years covered by this book, and because I often interviewed several members of the same families. The Community also tended toward an informality and familiarity that made such a decision natural in most cases.

I wrestled with it when it came to people I never met, who were deceased or too ill to communicate by the time I started this project. This was especially the case for Rosemary Radford Ruether and Mary Catherine Bateson, each active in the Community for a portion of its early years, who achieved prominence as scholars and authors. I do not take it lightly that women are often called by their first names in professional settings where men are referred to with their titles of Dr. or the Rev. For the sake of consistency, I use first names in this case. However, I hope the tone and substance of my writing conveys respect for each woman and for all of the subjects of this book.

I capitalize *Black* and *Indigenous*, but not *white*, following the current Associated Press style.[18] (The Chicago Manual of Style allows such an approach, recognizing varying contexts.[19]) *Black* and *Indigenous* describe cultural identities worth honoring, as with names for diverse European ethnicities, while *white* is a term created to construct and uphold an unjust system. Leaving *white* lowercase is a way to acknowledge whiteness in discussing race while not giving it additional power. There are plenty of thoughtful responses to this question. This is the approach that made the most sense to me. I also noted that this was the style used in many articles in *Stance*, the Community's self-published journal.

Finally, this book's citations are in the style of the publisher, Wipf & Stock, adapted from the Chicago Manual of Style. Some readers will want

17. Community of Christ, "Our History: W. Grant McMurray," para. 35.
18. Associated Press, "Explaining AP Style."
19. University of Chicago, *Chicago Manual of Style*, 476.

to flip back to the bibliography often for additional publication details, while others may wish to ignore the footnotes while continuing through the narrative.

1

"A Church That Wants to Be in the City"

WATER FORMS THE FIRST of the concentric circles at Dupont Circle's iconic gathering space near downtown Washington, DC. It fills a fountain centered by classical sculpted figures who appear to have emerged from the pool itself. Around the fountain a stone wall forms a continuous circular bench. A walkway encircles it and benches encircle the walkway. Beyond the benches, pathways lead to large sections of grass, ample enough for a few picnics or lawn games. At night the grass sometimes becomes a bed, though unless a person is truly exhausted it's difficult to fall asleep with all of the light and activity on the circular sidewalk that surrounds the grass and the traffic circle forming the outermost layer.

Dupont Circle's affluence rose and fell and rose again like tides. The West End part of the neighborhood was a lower-income integrated area of small farms and businesses until the 1870s when it gained streets, utilities, and sidewalks. In the following decades those who amassed extravagant wealth during the Gilded Age built mansions for embassies and private homes. A couple were dubbed castles: one owned by the first senator from Nevada turned real-estate magnate, and another by a German immigrant who made his fortune in brewing. After World War I, the economic tumult of the Great Depression caused many of the upper class to sell their homes. The wealthy moved out and commercial buildings started moving in. Dupont Circle gradually became a mixed-income neighborhood, the location of several embassies as well as a rooming house that was possibly the largest in the city at the time.[1]

---

1. Asch and Musgrove, *Chocolate City*, 189–91; DeFerrari, *Lost Washington*, 91.

Moving from the suburbs into the inner city, John and Mary Schramm, a white couple in their thirties with four children, came to the West End of Dupont Circle in 1965. Seven years earlier, John planted Hope Lutheran Church in 1957 in Annandale, Virginia, when he was twenty-six years old and fresh out of seminary. He joined a Lutheran mission committee for the metro area, and every time he heard his peers talk about urban congregations, it was about the problems. "It was always a church in trouble, a big building to maintain," John said.[2]

With the support of lay leaders in the Annandale congregation, John decided it was time to flip that script.[3] He made a pitch to the American Lutheran Church's board of missions within the US. "Every time we talk about starting a new church it's always in the suburbs," John said. "Why don't we start a church that wants to be in the city from the very start?"[4] John set out five principles for a new church:

1. that the church would see one square mile in the inner-city as its parish,

2. that the pastor would live within that parish and

3. gather people for worship there,

4. that the congregation wouldn't own a building, and

5. that it would strive to be financially self-sufficient.

The mission board took a chance on this congregation that saw itself as making a commitment to be in the city when so many other congregations were abandoning it. The board offered church plants a $30,000 subsidy spread out over three years with the plan that it would be self-supporting by the end of that time. The Community of Christ became package mission no. 256 of the American Lutheran Church.[5] Before the meeting with the mission board, John didn't have his mind set on a particular neighborhood. In the course of conversation, they determined that Dupont Circle in Northwest DC wasn't closer than a mile to any other Lutheran churches, he said. "All the other Lutherans said, 'Oh, good, we'd never go in there in a hundred years.'"[6]

2. John and Mary Schramm, in discussion with the author, May 2020.

3. John Schramm, in discussion with the author, August 2022.

4. Schramm, in discussion with the author, May 2020.

5. Schramm and Anderson, *Dance in Steps of Change*, 15–16; John Schramm, in discussion with the author, May 2020; Schramm and Hayden, "Community of Christ," presentation at Holden Village; Schramm, "Community of Christ," 15.

6. Schramm, in discussion with the author, May 2020.

෫෯

Dupont Circle was already home to another Christian community that challenged traditional assumptions about church. The Church of the Saviour had its headquarters in a twenty-five-room, 12,000-foot building that had once been a grand house. They were determined not to own a traditional, steepled church but tired quickly of borrowing space. Gordon Cosby, Mary Campbell Cosby, and Elizabeth-Anne Campbell founded Church of the Saviour in 1946. Serving as chaplain of an airborne infantry regiment during World War II made denominational differences seem arbitrary to Cosby. He wanted to start an ecumenical church located in DC. He wrote a prospectus with this vision and mailed it to Mary and Elizabeth-Anne, sisters he had known since childhood, asking if they felt called to start this church with him.[7]

This style came to be one of the key elements of the Church of the Saviour, with a person testing a sense of mission with one or two others, and each of them deciding what their mission was. When they overlapped, they carried it forward together. As the church grew, Cosby developed a reputation for his sermons, which drew from an understanding growing at the time at the edges of the church and in liberation theologies that the "real Jesus" was socially and politically engaged and especially concerned with the oppressed.[8] Elizabeth O'Connor, who joined the Church of the Saviour a few years in, extended its influence beyond DC through her writing. Through books such as *Call to Commitment* and *Journey Inward, Journey Outward*, she shared the Church of the Saviour's vision of the spiritual life.[9]

Members promised to strive to mature as Christians at any cost of time, energy, and money. That kind of Christianity affected relationships with all people. The description *ecumenical* was important to them during a period before the term was widely known, and they participated in the local, national, and world Council of Churches. Members pledged themselves to disciplines as a response to the unearned grace of God. At a minimum, they were to engage in daily prayer at a set time, read Scripture daily, grow in love for all people, worship weekly, actively participate in a small group, give away at least 10 percent of their income, and admit their failings in order to invite help. In addition to Sunday worship, there was the School of Christian Living, offering instruction in areas such as Old Testament, doctrine, and

---

7. McClurg, "Introduction," ix–x; O'Connor, *Call to Commitment*, 6–7, 10, 13–14.

8. Cosby, *Seized by the Power*, 94.

9. Devers, "Introduction." Several interview subjects told the author they learned about the Church of the Saviour first through books by O'Connor.

ethics. It was a kind of seminary training in the midst of the congregation, though many participants did not join the church.[10]

When membership grew to about sixty, they divided into fellowship groups, each of which met once weekly on a weeknight. O'Connor wrote of the groups, "In one sense each of the nights was a church in itself."[11] Elton Trueblood, a theologian and educator who served as chief of religious policy under Eisenhower, wrote of the Church of the Saviour's model, "To remain small when growth is possible is mystifying and faintly un-American. The very conception of making membership genuine rather than nominal, and therefore difficult, is bitterly resented by some, who rightly see this conception as an implicit criticism of their own superficial standards of membership."[12]

Annually, members took time to reflect on whether they could reaffirm their commitment to each other. They asked themselves if they were growing as Christians as a result of their common life. O'Connor wrote that—paradoxically, perhaps—this self-examination was collaborative. "It is easy for the religious to become closed and unyielding" without such a practice in community.[13] This required, Cosby reminded them, more than conditional commitment that allowed people to easily withdraw.[14] Cosby said in a sermon, "We arrive with our exit strategy already prepared. As soon as we start to see the community in all its immaturity and brokenness, we will have decided already on some good reasons to leave." Yet everyone needed a discipleship community as "part of that broken people marching into God's future."[15]

The point of this inward journey was to enrich one's ability to engage with the world, to turn outward towards others beyond the church. Mission groups held the inward and outward together, forming the core of the church. The mission groups had a minimum of two and a maximum of fifteen people, some focusing on an area internal to the congregation, such as its library, and others focusing on outreach and service. Each group focused on only one area, a task God gave to them as part of their larger experience of being grasped by God.[16]

10. O'Connor, *Call to Commitment*, 25–27, 34.

11. O'Connor, *Call to Commitment*, 47.

12. Trueblood, "Introduction," ix.

13. O'Connor, *Journey Inward, Journey Outward*, 10–11.

14. O'Connor, *Journey Inward, Journey Outward*, 24–25.

15. Cosby, *Seized by the Power*, 18.

16. O'Connor, *Call to Commitment*, 49–50; O'Connor, *Journey Inward, Journey Outward*, 28–32; Study on the Church of the Saviour, based on discussions with Community, 22 November 1970, in Community of Christ Papers.

From the mission groups grew the idea for Potter's House coffee shop and gallery. It opened in 1960 in a lively commercial stretch in the Adams Morgan neighborhood, a forerunner among hundreds of church-sponsored coffeehouses in the following decade. Unlike many of those, Potter's House displayed no religious symbols, though some neighbors knew that a church managed it. In the basement, artists offered courses such as ceramics, textile design, and weaving. On Sunday mornings there was worship. Church of the Saviour members volunteered as staff and entered into conversations as the opportunity arose, O'Connor wrote, some of them on "the ferment that is going on in the churches and the quest for forms that will make the church relevant and enable it not only to address the world, but be addressed by it."[17]

The Church of the Saviour embraced change as a trait of Christian community and did not seek its own continuation. Adapting to be true to its mission in its time is always necessary, as any congregation can find a sense of safety in a way of being it once adopted as new and daring. "No person or group is forever free from the temptation to settle down into mediocrity," O'Connor wrote. The patterns of their life together changed year to year, and "while the church of Christ must endure," O'Connor wrote, "the institution of the Church of the Saviour" might not. Since many congregations get stuck in forms that served another time, when a church explores new ways of being, "it has often been called an experiment. We would say that the church of Christ is never an experiment," O'Connor wrote.

Whether or not they liked the description "experimental," ministries like the Church of the Saviour and the Community of Christ cropped up by the dozens in the post-war period, especially during the mid-1960s. The National Council of Churches surveyed them in 1968, contacting 350 "in a wide variety of activities and locations, the majority urban oriented," and most receiving the bulk of their financial support from established denominations.[18] The Church of the Saviour was one of the earlier ones, and an influence on many others.[19]

For the Community of Christ, the proximity was not only in affinity but in geography. The Church of the Saviour headquarters, what it had starting in 1950 instead of a steepled church building, was a third of a mile from where the Community started on N Street NW. John Schramm had several conversations with Gordon Cosby as he was forming his ideas about planting a church in Dupont Circle. John and others attended courses in the

17. O'Connor, *Journey Inward, Journey Outward*, 62–67, 77; O'Connor, *Call to Commitment*, 118.

18. Wild, *Renewal*, 192.

19. Wild, *Renewal*, 38; Webber, *Congregation in Mission*, 47.

School of Christian Living. Several of the Community's early practices came from the Church of the Saviour, such as having groups that met for worship and study on a weeknight.[20] In a report to the denomination in 1967, John described the Community as being on "an inward journey and an outward journey," in its common life of worship and in its witness and service to its neighbors.[21]

It was also from the Church of the Saviour's influence that the Community focused on encouraging members to discover their unique gifts and to take risks in sharing them with the world—and even to be willing to fail. A primary way this was expressed was in mission groups. Among those in the Community were Focus on Youth, Church and the Arts, and the Square Mile group.[22] The Community learned from the Church of the Saviour the idea that "there are diverse missions that can be run by different people, and it's a good idea to be creative and think up a mission," said Dunstan Hayden, an early Community member. In the Community's groups, however, Dunstan said, "the missions were floating. They could start. They could stop." *Nonchalance* was one of John's favorite words. Dunstan said, "That clearly distinguished us from the Church of the Saviour. They were much more serious people there: you've signed up and you put your name down and, by God, you better do what you promised to do."[23]

The Community respected the level of commitment that the Church of the Saviour expected, but that approach did not lend itself to the practices of the people who made up the Community. The Community had a different style.[24] Margaret Thomas and her husband, David, were a young couple looking for a new church. They met John Schramm and decided to try the Community, Margaret recalled. "We said, 'How do you join?' They said, 'Paint your name on a cup and hang it on a hook.'" Adding your personalized coffee mug to the set of them in the fellowship space, that was the only membership ritual.[25]

Another characteristic that was crucial to the Community—the parish model—came from a different stream of thinking at that time. The

20. Schramm, in discussion with the author, May 2020.

21. John E. Schramm to the members of the Eastern District Mission Committee of the American Lutheran Church, Summary report for 1966, in Community of Christ Papers.

22. Schramm, *Gifts of Grace*, 34; O'Connor, *Call to Commitment*, 90; Minutes of Community meeting, 7 May 1967, Community of Christ Papers.

23. Dunstan Hayden, in discussion with the author, May 2021.

24. David Anderson, in discussion with the author, March 2021.

25. Margaret Thomas, in discussion with Christina Nichols and Martin Johnson, September 2016.

Church of the Saviour worked mainly in several DC neighborhoods where it owned property, but it did not have a geographical focus.[26] George Webber's 1964 book *The Congregation in Mission*, read and quoted from often in the Community's early years, elaborates on two points that dovetailed with John and Mary's ideas: a Christian community choosing to be in the city, and a neighborhood as their central concern. In 1948, Webber and his Union Theological Seminary classmates Don Benedict and Archie Hargraves founded the East Harlem Protestant Parish,[27] believed by some to be "the most significant experiment in American Protestantism in the 20th Century."[28] Benedict said, "We wanted to return Protestantism to the idea of serving everyone in a given geographical community rather than staying with the concept of church as the central place of worship attracting like-minded people from anywhere."[29]

At that time the postwar demographic changes were underway for white Protestants in most major US cities. White Protestants had begun leaving city neighborhoods when Catholic and Jewish immigrants arrived in earlier decades, and the flight accelerated when African Americans began moving to northern and western coastal cities during the Great Migration. A study by the National Council of Churches found that from 1955 to 1965, two-thirds of new churches opened in the expanding suburbs. Thus, what looked like a church-planting heyday wasn't the result of successful evangelization so much as mass relocation.[30] Webber lamented how "as a group, white, middle-class Protestants have fled the city as though it had the plague." He confronted his co-religionists on their "pervasive dislike of cities" and white-picket-fence version of the good life.[31]

East Harlem Protestant Parish's founders, like other renewalists who were forerunners and contemporaries of the Community of Christ, had among their building blocks the idealism of the earlier Social Gospel movement, through which clergy and laity engaged in politics and other public spheres considered secular. Another, more chastened influence was neo-orthodoxy and Reinhold Niebuhr, as evident when renewalists eschewed the idea that their goals could be fully accomplished by humans in this life. Niebuhr, in his neo-orthodox view, "distrusted human

26. Study on the Church of the Saviour, based on discussions with Community of Christ, 22 November 1970, in Community of Christ Papers.

27. Community of Christ Papers, Swarthmore College Peace Collection; John and Mary Schramm, in discussion with the author, March 2021; Wild, *Renewal*, 43.

28. "Rev. Dr. J. Archie Hargraves."

29. Livezey, "Church as Parish," 1176.

30. Wild, *Renewal*, 30–32.

31. Webber, *Congregation in Mission*, 36.

institutions (including the church) but encouraged Protestants to work with them anyway."[32]

Dietrich Bonhoeffer, an even more influential theologian for this stream of socially engaged Christians, articulated what the church could be for the Community and like-minded congregations.[33] Bonhoeffer came from an upper-class family with several prominent members,[34] yet he critiqued Christians choosing their own comfort in "bourgeois existence" and seeing "their own personal goodness guaranteed."[35] Yet he trusted that critical reflection in small communities of those following Jesus could allow them to risk public action without knowing the outcome.[36] His book about his time in such a community, *Life Together*, served as a touchstone for Christians in the decades following his execution in 1945 as part of the German resistance to the Nazis. The Community chose it for an early text study; it was required reading for all who joined the Church of the Saviour. He believed that God calls us to act decisively in history. This involves costly solidarity with the world (where one doesn't explicitly work as a Christian or the church, or insist on controlling it), and finding a community to sustain oneself when the institutional church is assimilated to dominant culture. The Community was an expression of Bonhoeffer's idea of being religionless, as conventional religion was not relevant to its context.[37]

Likewise, Webber's *The Congregation in Mission* declared the political implications of the lordship of Christ. This creates tensions, but "a church that is not in tension with its culture is no church at all."[38] That idea shaped the Community, as well as that of a one-square-mile area of involvement, which was central to John and Mary's vision. The parish model was an antidote to becoming "an exclusive club or some other perversion of the Church."[39] This approach differed from what Mary remembered growing up as a pastor's daughter, with the idea that the task was winning souls for Christ, not shaping disciples or emphasizing justice and social responsibility.

John and Mary were energized by what Webber wrote about pastors who thought they were bringing Christ to Harlem and learned that Christ

32. Wild, *Renewal*, 15, 21–22.

33. Wild, *Renewal*, 22; O'Connor, *Journey Inward, Journey Outward*, 16, 19, 67.

34. Bethge, "Bonhoeffer's Family," 2–4.

35. McBride, *Church for the World*, 135.

36. McBride, *Church for the World*, 140.

37. O'Connor, *Call to Commitment*, 30; International Bonhoeffer Society, "Statement," para. 10–11; Bethge, "Bonhoeffer's Family," 26; Rasmussen, *Dietrich Bonhoeffer*, 59–62; Anderson, "Our Thing in the City," 38.

38. Webber, *Congregation in Mission*, 46.

39. Schramm, "For Love of Children," 1, 6.

had been there a long time.[40] Taking the incarnation seriously, Webber wrote, requires "being truly present in the world. If God is at work in the world, then clergy and laity must join fully in the life of the world and in that context discover what they are called to do. Too often, eager Christians have insisted in the world that they brought to the situation ready-made answers to the complex problems of society."[41]

The Lutheran mission board bought a house for the Schramm family around the corner from the rented worship space. A young middle-class couple, Bob and Kathleen Keating, left northern Virginia with their two children and moved in across the street. The first worship service of the Community was on February 2, 1965, with four adults and six children gathered around the Schramm family's dining room table. The first person to join them was the babysitter for the Schramms, a George Washington University student named Marilyn Hoff.[42]

As the Schramms and Keatings reversed the trend for white families at the time by leaving the suburbs for the inner city, many of their peers, both adults and children, thought they were deeply misguided.[43] A playmate of six-year-old Mike Schramm responded to the news of the family's upcoming move out of northern Virginia: "Don't go to DC. There's just a bunch of n____s there." That was Mike's only expectation for the move. It didn't make him afraid, and he knew that his parents did not use racial slurs. Mike was mostly curious.[44]

When they first arrived, Mark, the oldest, was seven, Karen was five, and Kathy was three. They all found pleasures in city living: going to the corner store for soda and gum, sitting on the front steps on hot summer nights and talking with neighbors, walking to the zoo and museums and galleries, riding their bicycles on the streets and alleys, playing hopscotch on the sidewalks, and watching the sun set between buildings, sometimes appearing like an enormous orange ball resting on the pavement at the end of the block.[45]

Among their neighbors, perhaps the most transient group was the countercultural young people who by the mid-1960s were beginning to

40. John and Mary Schramm, in discussion with the author, March 2021.

41. Webber, *Congregation in Mission*, 139.

42. Schramm and Anderson, *Dance in Steps of Change*, 16; John and Mary Schramm, in discussion with the author, May 2020; Anderson, "Marilyn's Gone," 2.

43. Schramm, "Shared Word," 6.

44. Schramm, in discussion with the author, March 2021.

45. Karen Martin-Schramm, Kathy Schramm Falk, and Mark and Mike Schramm, in discussion with the author, March 2021; Schramm and Schramm, *Things That Make for Peace*, 101.

be called hippies, sometimes with disdain. Many of these countercultural young people became disillusioned as they learned about the discrepancies between the rhetoric and reality of their childhoods in the 1950s. After the United States emerged from World War II as the most-powerful nation globally, the government sought to maintain its pre-eminence economically and militarily. The United States furthered the interests of corporate agribusiness and multinational corporations, using anti-communism as a smokescreen for replacing family farms in the United States and in nations where it exerted its influence. The government spoke of making the world safe for democracy and yet—among other examples—overthrew the democratically elected president in Guatemala and replaced him with an authoritarian who disenfranchised a large segment of the population. The US also interfered with a transition to democracy from colonial rule in Vietnam, preventing a vote because it deemed the candidate who would have won to be contrary to US interests.[46]

For those growing up in that era, the Cold War and threat of nuclear annihilation shaped their childhood and youth spiritually. One historian wrote that "the bluster, the militaristic stand, the desperate concern for being number one made no sense to a generation that had to cower under school desks in civil defense drills in helplessness and fear." The future was open to those young people (mainly white ones) whose families had benefited from the post-WWII boom, yet some asked: "Why work hard for a respectable career when in nuclear war even the spectacular glass office buildings would be reduced to rubble?" People needed community, a life of meaning, and a sense of place, and instead newly powerful advertisers in glossy magazines and on television screens peddled a vision of the life marked by families in their separate homes, surrounded by the latest models of appliances.[47]

Alongside their political disillusionment, many hippies had the same struggles as homeless youth in any era. Some ran away from home because of conflict with their parents, some sought escape in illegal drugs. Many in DC were attracted to Dupont Circle. The neighborhood had an entry point to densely wooded Rock Creek Park, which stretches for miles north into Maryland. Some of the hippies camped or hung out along the water's edge in the park as well as near the fountain in Dupont Circle, playing bongo drums and guitar on warm nights.[48] A Presbyterian church the Community often partnered with, the Church of the Pilgrims, started a ministry to the runaways, allowing them to use the church bathroom and call their families

46. Jezer, *Dark Ages*, 64–65; Eisenhower, *Mandate for Change*, 372.
47. Jezer, *Dark Ages*, 234–37.
48. Schramm, in discussion with the author, May 2020; Smith, *Captive Capital*, 10.

on the phone. The associate pastor started a coffeehouse in the church basement where they could gather.[49] Whenever that pastor met "somebody that he didn't know exactly what to do with," he sent them a few blocks away to John. "I knew that none of them were probably going to ever join a church," John said. But he could offer clothes or food, or a listening ear.[50]

One young man arrived as the Schramm family was sitting down to dinner, and he joined them. "He told me that he had a mission and he was going to visit every county in the United States and get a map of that county and we were to be the place where he stored all of his maps," John said. "So our basement had all of these county maps and he would call me—collect, of course—with the question, 'Reverend Schramm, I'm on the border of Minnesota and Wisconsin. Should I do Minnesota first and then Wisconsin or Wisconsin first and then Minnesota?'" John told him it made no difference. Periodically he would come back to DC seeking more conversation and hospitality. "He was not typical of the runaways," John said.[51]

David Earle Anderson, a college student in the early 1960s, had a hippie sort of disillusionment about society and the church. (He also had long hair and at times wore a necklace with a large peace sign.) He saw the church as becoming suburban and corporate, focusing on numerical growth and self-preservation. To his mind, it became "a kind of spiritual filling station to make middle-class folk feel good about themselves." In 1965, he had returned from Montgomery and the Selma-Montgomery civil rights march when a Lutheran program called the Prince of Peace Volunteers recruited him to be a presence on a university campus and observe what was happening. When David arrived in DC in August 1965, he was twenty-four years old, "pretentious, pompous, naïve," he said. "But having just witnessed the Selma march, seeing the budding of the student movement that would also blossom into the streets, I was convinced that the church—especially an urban church—had to find the proper way to support [justice movements] and yet maintain its own identity as church."[52]

Through the Prince of Peace program, he worked with John in the Community as well as on the American University campus. David had been married for one year to Margaret Elsie, who was twenty-one years old when they arrived. "Back in Minnesota people would tell us that we should be

49. "Rev. A. Thomas Murphy Jr.," para. 20.

50. Schramm, in discussion with the author, May 2020.

51. Schramm, in discussion with the author, May 2020.

52. David Earle Anderson, email message to author, August 23, 2020.

afraid to go to DC," she said. But staying with the Keatings "was just like having relatives welcome you home."[53]

Trying to extend that sense of family to neighbors, the Community organized a Thanksgiving meal in the basement borrowed from the Church of the Pilgrims, aptly named for the occasion. The Community used its mimeograph machine to copy signs with drawings from the children, shared widely in their one-mile parish area. "Anyone who is alone, has no place to go or who wants to share Thanksgiving with others," they welcomed, Mary Schramm wrote. Instead of a meal served by church members to a line of grateful recipients holding out their plates, they would all sit down together. Each household in the Community prepared a turkey dinner and dessert and brought it. They decorated the tables with linen, flowers, and their best dishes and silverware. The Community families then sat down to see who would come.[54]

Neighbors trickled in. "The variety was typical of the racial and economic mix of the neighborhood," Mary wrote, including "a runaway girl and a foreign student from a nearby rooming house. As we looked around the room, the variety was repeated at each table." They didn't require sobriety for people to enjoy the holiday meal. Among their guests were "an inebriated man we had often seen slumped in our alley," and a mother with two young children and "a teenager spaced out on drugs." People began to share the food and get to know each other, Mary wrote. "It didn't take long for the awkward silence to give away to the gentle hum of normal table conversation." Community members caught a glimpse of themselves as "part of a much larger family."[55]

ﾞ❧

The Community did not imagine that it was going to solve all the problems of society or the church. The Community claimed disregard for institutional self-preservation as an opportunity. It sought as a congregation, with its budget and programs, to be shaped by the theology of the cross. This meant, John said in a talk on urban ministry, that they were about giving their lives for their neighbors rather than building up their own institution.[56] They saw many other middle-class white Christians who remained in the city treating it as a duty, an expiation of "guilt for past omissions." In contrast,

---

53. Margaret Elsie Pearson, in discussion with the author, April 2021.

54. Schramm, *Gifts of Grace*, 100–101.

55. Schramm, *Gifts of Grace*, 100–101.

56. Schramm, "Theological Issues," 4–5.

the Community sought to approach urban ministry guided by a sense of freedom, John wrote.[57] The Community wrote in an early brochure, "The Community seeks to *be* mission, not merely to engage in mission work."[58]

Mary clarified that somewhat opaque statement: the best witness is engaging in ministry as one's whole self. To merely do what someone else said is necessary breeds resentment, she wrote. "There is no one more depressing to be around than a fanatical, humorless Christian." It was one more way Christians could be hypocrites in the eyes of their neighbors, preaching good news without there seeming to be anything good about it. "Few pay attention to the Christian message if it is not embodied in lives that radiate joy (not a plastic Christian smile, but real joy!). It is easy to distinguish these people from those enduring a life filled with ought-ness."[59]

In addition to Webber's *The Congregation in Mission*, they read William Stringfellow's *A Private and Public Faith* and *The Secular City* by Harvey Cox. All three had common themes: far from being godforsaken, the city bore witness to the power of God as much as anywhere, and it was the Christian's task to notice God's presence. In the 1960s, many saw the forces of secularization and urbanization as dehumanizing. More, to some the city was a place where God was not and where Christians brought salvation to lonely and wicked people. To Cox, secularization and urbanization could be positive, negative, or neutral: "The forces of secularization have no serious interest in persecuting religion. Secularization simply bypasses religion and undercuts religion and goes on to other things."[60] The less that Christianity was assumed to be the water people swam in, the more that being Christian became "a conscious choice rather than a matter of birth or inertia."[61] To be authentically Christian was to live out the gospel in communities distinct from the culture around them. The form that a congregation's life takes was determined by its mission, and some forms were disposable.[62]

The Community moved forward with the idea that its shape would come from the experience of the people. John told a *Washington Post* religion reporter that the Community's goal was to aid each member in becoming better able to "do his or her own thing in the neighborhood."[63] The

---

57. Schramm, "Community of Christ," 15.

58. Schramm and Anderson, *Dance in Steps of Change*, 18; "Community of Christ," brochure, 1965–67, in Community of Christ Papers.

59. Schramm, *Gifts of Grace*, 64.

60. Cox, *Secular City*, 156–57.

61. Cox, *Secular City*, 109.

62. Cox, *Secular City*, 150, 187.

63. Paka, "Churchless Congregations Growing," C21.

Community focused on the inner city without harboring illusions that this was the only place or best place to practice the work of engaging with the needs of its neighbors. For mission to be the core of the church required that Christians radically give themselves away—not necessarily as saints or martyrs, but as people engaged in the messiness of the real world and its problems.[64] John said it pithily in one of his succinct homilies: "Yes, you should put all of your eggs in one basket." Margaret Elsie remembered it long afterward, and she "took it in terms of the gospel. You have to choose and you have to put everything in."[65]

John's sermon was especially concise on Easter Sunday 1967 when the Community paraded out to Dupont Circle for worship. John preached: "Many things say no. But Easter says yes." John later elaborated that this "yes" affirms the value and worth of each person. "Easter is radically inclusive and freedom-oriented," he and David wrote about the Community's vision and life together. This "yes" stands in contrast to street-corner evangelists lining up no after no-no focused on personal, private sin. As Jesus made Mary Magdalene the first apostle on Easter morning, so Christ sends the church into the world, into the streets, with a task of spreading this collective, liberating "yes."[66]

They chose the name Community of Christ to avoid the word *church* while keeping Christ. "We got a lot of people who had a residual longing for a faithful expression of the Christian faith and were turned off by churches," John said.[67] One such person, Daphne DenBoer, wrote, "For some of us participation in the Community is a last affair with Christianity, a desperate attempt to prove, finally, that we need not associate with Christianity only what is distasteful to us." Like many more-institutional urban churches, they connected faith with public expression of their political concerns for civil rights, nonviolence, and economic justice. God called some to be martyrs, and some to a more ordinary life, she wrote. The Community was a place to go deeper in spiritual practice, to learn to pray without petition, as an act of contemplation. DenBoer continued in her description of participants like her: "We have accepted somewhat rigorous disciplines and in many respects we have learned to be audacious Christians; to be fools for Christ's sake."[68]

64. Schramm and Anderson, *Dance in Steps of Change*, 20–21.

65. Pearson, in discussion with the author, April 2021.

66. Schramm and Anderson, *Dance in Steps of Change*, 10–12; John 20:11–18.

67. Schramm and Anderson, *Dance in Steps of Change*, 16–17; Schramm and Hayden, "Community of Christ."

68. DenBoer, "That Last, Best Prayer," 1.

Contemplation was a prerequisite for action. It takes away illusions clouding reality. John and Mary wrote, "We have accepted so many illusions about life, the world, values, ourselves. To be dis-illusioned is to begin to see things as they really are." This causes one to confront urgent problems and to challenge basic assumptions. Before seeking to unmask the world's illusions, one needed their own vision cleared by a daily discipline of prayer.[69]

The Community was set up without most of the traditional trappings of what church had come to be in the mid-century United States. "When people hear the word 'church' their first question is often 'Where is it?'" the Community wrote in an early brochure describing itself. "When we say the Community of Christ we hope you will rather ask 'Who are they?' The Community is a fellowship of people, not a place. No church building will be constructed."[70] Echoing Elizabeth O'Connor's words about the church never being an experiment, John didn't see the Community as experimental, he said. "That sounds like you're going to try it, and if it works, you'll have a real one."[71]

Instead of a church building, even a rented one, they met in homes and in a basement with a sign on the door displaying the fish symbol used by early Christians. Their neighbor Ruth Schumm allowed them to meet rent-free in the bottom apartment of one of the properties she owned on N Street. Ruth got involved in the Community and invited a few of her tenants.[72] One was Anna Mae Patterson, a twenty-two-year-old recent college graduate, who lived downstairs from Ruth. One February evening while Community members were painting the basement worship space at 2107 N Street, Anna Mae took them a pan of muffins. She attended an Episcopal church but gradually became immersed in the Community, "a bunch of people who were absolutely committed to the gospel and to social justice at the same time."[73] Anna Mae summarized her observations of the first few years: "What's important about the Community is that here is a group of people, no matter how varied their theological interpretations or life styles, who are willing to bear the name of Christ—no matter how tenuous their commitment to the ideological content of Christianity, and to find the celebration of the Eucharist the pivotal point of their weekly life."[74]

69. Schramm and Schramm, *Things That Make for Peace*, 85–95.

70. "Community of Christ," brochure, 1965–67, in Community of Christ Papers.

71. Schramm, in discussion with the author, May 2020.

72. Anna Mae Patterson, in discussion with the author, May 2021; Linda Wells, in discussion with the author, November 2021; Schramm, "Community of Christ," 16.

73. Patterson, in discussion with the author, May 2021.

74. Anderson, "Our Thing in the City," 39; Anna Mae Patterson, email messages to author, August 6 and 16, 2022. The article quoted an unnamed young woman. Patterson

They agonized about how to define community and whether they had it. They finally decided that community is a gift. You can create the conditions in which community can be given, but you can't create community.[75] "There is a level of radical hospitality, where people are welcome to be who they are and yet to change," Anna Mae said. Having grown up the daughter of Presbyterian mission workers who served in multicultural settings in the United States, Anna Mae was familiar with and attracted to the Community's approach to "ministry as something involving the whole neighborhood and everybody in the neighborhood: Black, white, conservative, liberal."[76]

said that it sounded like her, and the author's extensive research determined Patterson was the likeliest person to have said it.

75. Anderson, "Quest for Community," 1, 6; Schramm, "Community of Christ," 19; Patterson, in discussion with the author, May 2021.

76. Patterson, in discussion with the author, May 2021.

2

"Part of the Old Order and Hoping for the New"

IT IS LOST TO time precisely how a group of linguists heard about the new Christian community in the basement of a Dupont Circle rowhouse. Charles Ferguson—who founded the Center for Applied Linguistics in 1959 to work at the intersection of language, politics, and policy—joined the handful of people who faithfully attended the Community of Christ's compline services, prayers for the end of the day. Allene Guss also lived near the Community's worship space. She may have come first and told the others. Dora Koundakjian wove herself into each of these young groups in a matter of months. Since immigrating to the United States from Lebanon seven years earlier, she lived in the segregated South to complete a bachelor's degree and in New England for a master's in linguistics before coming to DC. In each place, Dora observed the dynamics in US society and refused to stay on the sidelines.[1]

The one-square-mile area that the Community chose as its parish provided plenty of opportunities to be engaged. There was lots of poverty and neighbors had pressing needs of many kinds—for better housing, for help with addictions, for caring relationships deeper than casual acquaintance. There were also myriad forms of diversity. There were Black families who had been in DC for generations. There were newcomers of all backgrounds,

---

1. Center for Applied Linguistics, "Our Founder," para. 4; John Schramm, in discussion with the author, May 2020; Community of Christ Papers, Swarthmore College Peace Collection; Alicia Koundakjian Moyer, in discussion with the author, February 2021.

both born elsewhere in the US and in countries around the world.[2] Unlike many of the others born abroad, Dora was not a diplomat. "I am an office worker," she said one Sunday. "I belong to that blurred crowd that disappears into tall buildings every day, and much of what I do has little impact in any major way on public policy, on issues of justice and peace, or the state of the world in general. I think the work I do is important, but then it might not be. . . . I am also a Christian—the brand that thinks and firmly believes that one's beliefs should be reflected in all I do."[3]

❧

It was no surprise Dora chose linguistics as her field. Languages filled her ears and leapt off her tongue from Dora's earliest years. She was born in 1937 in Beirut. At home, Dora's family spoke Armenian speckled occasionally with Turkish. Among her neighbors and classmates in the cosmopolitan city, she learned Arabic, French, and English. Dora and her brother, Philip, bickered in Arabic.[4]

Beirut was a beautiful city in the eyes of their mother, Yevnige Berejiklian Koundakjian, who came for nursing school at age eighteen. She met Dora's father, Albert, also a survivor of the Armenian genocide during World War I. Dora's family moved between Lebanon and Syria during her childhood for high school teaching jobs that Albert held. For several years, he worked at a Quaker boarding school in the mountain town of Brummana, where wealthy people had their summer homes and vacationers came to visit the cool mountains near the sea. The school had an elegant hotel attached to it. Many British families stayed there and in the surrounding area. They lived on campus, where Albert was in charge of buildings and grounds. Yevnige served the guests tea, among other acts of hospitality.[5]

When family friends came to visit Brummana in the summer, trading the heat of Beirut for the coolness of the mountains, Dora was impressive and even a bit intimidating to the younger children. She read novels in English with hundreds of pages. She'd take her younger cousins on hikes without telling them where they were going. They followed her anyway.[6]

2. "Excerpts from the Statement," 2, 4.
3. Johnson, shared word in the Community of Christ, 6.
4. Yevnige Berejiklian Koundakjian, in discussion with Zoryan Institute, April 1989; Anie Khachadourian, in discussion with the author, March 2021.
5. Koundakjian, in discussion with Zoryan, April 1989; Khachadourian, in discussion with the author, March 2021; Grace Hyslop, in discussion with the author, March 2021.
6. Khachadourian, in discussion with the author, March 2021; Hyslop, in discussion

During World War II, everything was rationed in French-controlled Lebanon and Syria. Families had limited amounts of goods such as flour and cones of brown sugar. Sometimes there was sand mixed in. German airplanes would fly overhead and at times drop bombs. Lebanon became an independent nation during the war but was quickly plagued by conflict. In the post-war reshaping of territory, Turkish nationalists took over the area where Brummana was located. For the second time in their lives, Albert and Yevnige left home for the sake of safety.[7]

Yevnige spent her early childhood in an idyllic setting, where one of her grandfathers grew pistachios and both sides of the family owned land and had stables of horses. As the Ottoman Empire fell apart, nationalist groups rose up, including one called the Young Turks. When Yevnige was five or six years old, militants began training nearby. In 1915, the family received deportation orders and had fifteen days to gather as much luggage as they could carry with a donkey and a horse. The rest of the horses had been confiscated by the government. Armed men boarded them into luggage cars on a train to Aleppo. Yevnige's family and the families with them were fortunate—others had to walk. Some Turkish people risked their own safety to help the victims of violence perpetrated by nationalists among their people. A Muslim man devised a way for the men in Yevnige's family to fulfill the requirement to go to the mosque without compromising their Christian faith.[8]

Albert's mother died during childbirth. His father, who was a Protestant minister, caught typhus while building a church in the Ottoman territory that is now Syria. Albert was raised by his grandmother and uncles and fled with them during the genocide. Dora and her brother heard their parents' accounts so many times that they could finish them. They absorbed their mother's message: Do not forget your heritage. Be proud of being Armenian and that we have survived.[9]

When Dora was a teenager, the family returned to Beirut. She went to a British high school. She spoke fluent English with the accompanying accent. The family lived in a second-floor apartment, above another family, nestled among other homes above or between shops, grocery stores, and jewelers. Their home had a veranda and a spacious living room.[10]

---

with the author, March 2021.

7. Koundakjian, in discussion with Zoryan, April 1989; Hyslop, in discussion with the author, March 2021.

8. Koundakjian, in discussion with Zoryan, April 1989; Kifner, "Armenian Genocide of 1915."

9. Khachadourian, in discussion with the author, March 2021; Koundakjian, in discussion with Zoryan, April 1989.

10. Hyslop, in discussion with the author, March 2021; Khachadourian, in

Most of their neighbors were Muslim or Druze, but the Armenian Christian families didn't think much about being different. There weren't tensions in the Ras Beirut neighborhood, where there was also a Protestant Armenian church and an Orthodox church attended by some of the Arab Christians. Dora's friend Grace, the daughter of one of Yevnige's nursing school friends, lived in the neighborhood and attended the Protestant church. Dora's family also belonged to that tradition, but they didn't go to church often.[11]

Dora was drawn to some of the missionary groups who came to the Middle East. "She became very religious, kind of fanatic," her cousin Anie Khachadourian recalled, more so than her parents and her cousins. "She always was connected to some kind of religious group."[12] While they were students at the Beirut College for Women, Dora and Grace went together to Sunday afternoon gatherings at a church that welcomed students.[13]

At the same time, Dora was a wild woman, Anie said. "She had the reputation of everything an Armenian woman shouldn't be: she smoked, she wore red lipstick, she hung out with Muslims, Arabs, and would go with them to the beach."[14] Dora's parents were more lenient with her going out than other Armenian parents such as in Grace's family.[15] Dora spoke her mind in a way that was uncommon. Albert was also "a very strong-minded person," Anie said. Albert and Dora often butted heads.[16]

Before Dora had finished a bachelor's degree, she came to the US for further study in the fall of 1958, to a small college in Lexington, Kentucky. Moving to the US was expected for many Armenians, who had long-standing connections to American groups working in the Middle East. During the Armenian genocide decades earlier, churches and humanitarian groups had raised money for food and other relief. In Kentucky, one woman looked at Dora and said, "You don't look like a starving Armenian to me."[17]

On campus, Dora was surrounded by southern belles, with their white gloves and genteel manners.[18] "I had left a civil war behind me; I was wor-

discussion with the author, November 2022.

11. Khachadourian, in discussion with the author, March 2021; Hyslop, in discussion with the author, March 2021.

12. Khachadourian, in discussion with the author, March 2021.

13. Hyslop, in discussion with the author, March 2021.

14. Khachadourian, in discussion with the author, March 2021.

15. Hyslop, in discussion with the author, March 2021.

16. Khachadourian, in discussion with the author, March 2021.

17. Khachadourian, in discussion with the author, March 2021; Hyslop, in discussion with the author, March 2021.

18. Moyer, in discussion with the author, February 2021.

ried about my parents; I was broke, and I hated being where I had found myself!" she wrote. She counted the days until she could leave.

Kentucky was a segregated state. Shortly after Dora arrived in Lexington, she heard rumors about activists seeking to integrate a pharmacy chain store. After a trip to Main Street, her roommate warned Dora about going there, "because there was trouble and I could be taken for 'colored.'" Something changed inside Dora. "Was it anger? Was it an old story of my people? Was it excitement?" Dora saw no alternative "for a person who called herself a Christian" but to march downtown and walk into that Walgreens. "I told the Black kid who was sitting in the booth to move over."[19] Dora had seen that white people had power, and that though she was an immigrant, she had some of that power. She had found her approach to activism, to watch what was going on among the people around her, and then act.[20]

❧

Avenues radiate from Dupont Circle like spokes on a wheel. Along the side streets are row houses of varying sizes. In one section of the neighborhood, three-story homes line streets named with letters of the alphabet, with two-story buildings on cross-streets. A developer seeking to create a segregated enclave attracted residents for many of the larger homes. Poorer residents lived in shacks in the alleys, and eventually in apartments on cross streets. In 1965, many of the wealthy white residents were gone, but Black families still lived in many of the two-story homes.[21]

Many early Community members joined the first two families in moving into homes in the blocks surrounding their worship space. For the Black families in the area where the Community of Christ was worshiping, the only white men who normally knocked on their doors were bill collectors or someone looking for a way to rip them off. Yet John went door to door, including on the majority-Black streets such as Newport Place, inviting their neighbors to worship services.[22] Community members learned that neighborhood children "called us 'pretties,' a slang term for whites, one step below the insult of 'do-gooder.'"[23]

19. Dora Johnson, untitled selection in *Lenten Booklet 1990*, April 5.

20. Moyer, in discussion with the author, February 2021

21. Asch and Musgrove, *Chocolate City*, 189–90; Schramm, in discussion with the author, May 2020.

22. Schramm, in discussion with the author, May 2020.

23. Schramm and Anderson, *Dance in Steps of Change*, 15.

Yet some of the neighborhood children came to worship. One Sunday six Black boys chose to sit in the front row, remaining quiet and attentive during the service.[24] As the Schramm children played with their neighbors, they found that many knew that their father was a pastor. Others among the Black children thought John was the same dad as on the television show *Dennis the Menace*, since the actor was one of the few other white people they saw regularly. While the children played outside, they saw the full diversity of Dupont Circle, marked by how people were dressed: some with the flowing garb of hippies, some pushing against gender norms, others in suits and ties. "Kathy and I would be doing double Dutch rope outside and these business people would drop their briefcases and jump in our rope," Karen said.[25]

John and Mary's children went to the local public school, where each of them was often the only white child in a classroom (despite the schools having been desegregated a decade earlier). The teacher who taught first and second grade and served as onsite principal taught all four of the Schramm children to read. In addition sharing the work of starting the Community, Mary "poured herself into our school to try to make it better," Karen said. There was little music or art instruction and no parent-teacher association. There was no library, so Mary started one.[26]

It was an expression of their desire to care for all in their square mile, as it was when the Community asked several other churches to help with a summer program in 1965, serving children from the local public schools. It had elements of Christian education but was not a Vacation Bible School. After that, they started an afterschool tutoring program. They had about forty children, most of them from the same school that the Schramm children attended. For these activities, Mary and others collected children's books and then realized they depicted only white children. So they extended their effort to include more books showing Black and brown children. The Community tutors watched as one eight-year-old Black boy, Eric, paged through the new books. After it registered that the children in the book looked like him, he declared that they were dumb and that he didn't like the book. He slammed it shut.[27]

24. Anderson, *Thoughts, Faith, and Friends*, 12.

25. Karen Martin-Schramm, Kathy Schramm Falk, and Mark and Mike Schramm, in discussion with the author, March 2021.

26. Mary Schramm, *Gifts of Grace*, 65; Martin-Schramm, Falk, Schramm, and Schramm, in discussion with the author, March 2021.

27. Anderson, "Group Ministry, Lay Style," 11; Runck, "Community of Christ Tutoring Program," 3; Schramm, "Scattered and the Gathered," 5; John E. Schramm to the members of the Eastern District Mission Committee of the American Lutheran

Mary reflected on trying to avoid paternalism while seeking to help children such as Eric overcome the violence society did to him already by age eight. That injustice was becoming more widely known after the 1954 Supreme Court decision that ended school segregation, *Brown v. Board of Education.* Expert testimony in that case included psychologists Kenneth and Mamie Clark describing the scientific study they had done into the racial perceptions of children three to seven years old. They found that by a young age African Americans already had absorbed negative associations with people who shared their skin color and had formed low self-esteem.[28]

The Schramms acquired a reputation in the area for their political views. Some of their white neighbors who initially "welcomed with open arms the new preacher and his family who moved into their block" pulled those arms back and crossed them over their chests after learning that the Community supported civil rights and an end to the war in Vietnam. John and Mary wrote, "At one time two petitions were circulating around the neighborhood—one to get rid of the rats and the other to get rid of our congregation."[29]

A particular point of contention was that John and Mary taught their children about their convictions. It "incensed a few of the white neighbors" that the Schramm children played with children of all colors. One woman told Mary, "When I see your little girl playing with those Black children, it makes me vomit."[30] Another warned them that their children would get infected with "all kinds of diseases."[31] She may have heard the idea from members of Congress who presented it as an argument against integrated schools in DC during hearings on the topic.[32]

On their block, the Schramms witnessed a police confrontation with students headed to the White House to protest. John and Mary wrote, "The police were coming down 21st Street in waves, brandishing clubs, shouting through bullhorns, trying to disperse the crowd." The students turned over trash cans and compact cars. The police beat the students bloody in front of the Schramms' row house. The family watched with emotions on edge. After the students were arrested and taken away in vans, a woman living across the street shook her fist in Mary and John's faces. "What kind of parents are you," she hissed, "allowing your children to watch this." John and Mary

Church, Summary report for 1966, in Community of Christ Papers.

28. Schramm, *Gifts of Grace*, 102–3; "*Brown v. Board* and the 'Doll Test,'" paras. 2–3.
29. Schramm and Schramm, *Things That Make for Peace*, 16–17.
30. Schramm and Schramm, in discussion with the author, May 2020.
31. Schramm and Schramm, *Things That Make for Peace*, 16–17.
32. Asch and Musgrove, *Chocolate City*, 317.

thought about the woman's words and their choice not to shield their children from the protest. "Our kids know how we feel about the effects of war," John and Mary wrote. John and Mary had been raised with a Lutheran just-war position. They had been taught to support US military involvement in World War II and Korea. As they learned more about just-war criteria, they felt the war in Vietnam did not meet those standards. John and Mary found it ironic that church leaders who focused on sexual morality, drinking, and smoking were silent about "issues that are literally life and death—war, justice, racism, oppression."[33]

≥∙

The Community grew to thirty or forty people in the first two years, drawn together for a variety of reasons. Even as they held the ideal of welcoming everyone in their parish, it was challenging in reality. Mary wrote, "In the Community of Christ we struggle so much with this aspect of our Christian life and wonder if it is possible to experience the gift of community with the diversity we find in our neighborhood."[34] People came from various walks of life: a young Black attorney, a white bus driver, an engineer, university professors. One Black woman who joined in 1966, Grace Flenoy, earned the nickname Amazing Grace from Newport Place. Grace told other worshipers that she prayed for each person daily by name, and she hoped they were praying for her as well. She was generous in supporting worship and outreach, with no small gifts. She provided the Community with its piano.[35]

Grace also secured a home in upper northwest DC to be a group house for teenage boys as part of the For Love of Children ecumenical group that the Community joined in its first year as a congregation. The Church of the Saviour issued a call in spring 1965 to fifteen hundred churches in the metropolitan area: to empty the city's overcrowded Junior Village for children who were removed from their families.[36] The children were often abused and to varying degrees traumatized by the institutional environment. In 1965, Junior Village was the largest such institution in the United States, with a population of 900 children as young as six months.[37] Volunteering

33. Schramm and Schramm, *Things That Make for Peace*, 9–13.

34. Schramm, "Letter to Jenny Moore," 14.

35. Schramm and Anderson, *Dance in Steps of Change*, 73; Schramm, "Scattered and the Gathered," 5.

36. "Community Notes" (September 1967), 6; McNaughton, "For Love of Children," 1, 4. O'Connor, *Journey Inward, Journey Outward*, 144–46.

37. Bernard, "It Was Created," para. 4.

there and meeting the families of those children "awakened us to what white America had done" to Black people in DC, wrote Elizabeth O'Connor of the Church of the Saviour. "Things do not have to be as they are; laws can be changed and dehumanizing structures overthrown." They saw For Love of Children as joining God's work in the world.[38]

As For Love of Children began receiving children released from Junior Village—ultimately finding homes for about three hundred—the campaign combined advocacy for different policies with grassroots work to reunite families who had been separated when evicted or were at risk of that happening, to find them homes, and to recruit foster parents. In 1967 they adopted a model from the local child and family services agency to create group foster homes. Community volunteers were among the few dozen people who stepped up to be house parents for twenty-eight homes with 102 of the children. Norman and Ann Tucker offered a house to rent for one small group home; the house that Grace bought became another.[39] Dora was one of the Community members who volunteered as a part-time house mother for a group of teenagers, balancing supervision with the adolescent need for some measure of privacy.[40] Beyond such direct relationships, the campaign inevitably involved confronting the city, Dora wrote. Dora hoped that "there will be a group of people who will take it upon themselves to deal with the problems that create Junior Village, for as much as we try to empty out the institution it will be filled over and over again."[41] It took eight years of advocacy and research about alternatives in other cities—as well as embodying those alternatives in DC—before the city government agreed to stop placing children in institutional settings.[42]

While engaging in multiracial partnerships, the Community's gathered group was mostly white. In part, John attributes this dynamic to the Black power movement in the late 1960s and the call for Black people to have their own spaces. It was the contemporary iteration of a trend that had been established around the turn of the century, after the ending of Reconstruction's policies moving toward equity for DC's substantial Black population. The next generation of leaders, such as Frederick and Anna Douglass' son Charles and educator-activist Mary Church Terrell, "advocated a strong

38. O'Connor, *Journey Inward, Journey Outward*, x.

39. Bernard, "It Was Created"; Maney, "Story of FLOC," 16; O'Connor, *Journey*, 142–45, 158.

40. Johnson, "FLOC's Half-Way House," 1, 5; "Community Notes" (December 1967), 6.

41. Johnson, "House on Montague Street," 6.

42. Maney, "Story of FLOC," 16. Junior Village closed in 1973. For Love of Children still exists: https://floc.org/.

sense of racial pride" and channeled their education and ambition into building autonomous institutions rather than depend on those owned and controlled by white people. By the mid-1960s, a constellation of Black schools, cultural centers, and churches of many denominations were well established in DC.[43]

The Community also wondered if its humble space was a mark against it for many lower-income people. They might prefer to worship somewhere beautiful, with traditional church hallmarks. In contrast, the Community appealed to people who had been part of established congregations and were "turned off at some point by the church when they split over whether the carpet was red or blue or some such thing," John said. Leaving traditional churches made them free to decide what they did and didn't need. The people who shaped the Community's culture found it refreshing to dress casually, worship in a fifteen-by-forty-foot basement, and sit on metal folding chairs, however uncomfortable they could get at times.

The Community rented the space from Ruth Schumm, a white woman in her forties who invested in real estate. A Dallas native who retained her Texas accent, she moved to Washington in 1944 as a journalist reporting on government affairs. She then became an aide to Lyndon Baines Johnson as senator and vice-president, and a Peace Corps staff person. Ruth saw groups spend heaps of time talking about a problem and little or no time doing something about it. As she got to know the Community, she was intrigued by its assertion that it existed for mission. She had an idea for a ministry, and the Community helped her start it.[44]

Ruth knew that many of their neighbors paid high rents for low-quality housing. Across the city, Black people of all classes faced unfair treatment in jobs and housing, paying as much as 50 percent more than white people did for comparable units.[45] Many families struggled to save up for a down payment. To address this, Ruth began Home Buyers in 1967. She garnered support from several local churches, created a nonprofit corporation in her living room, and began lending money for a down payment to buy homes. It raised funds through the crowd sourcing of that time, debentures, or unsecured loans to be paid back if the effort succeeded. Lower-income families entered into a "rent-with-the-option-to-buy" agreement with Home Buyers. Usually, this amount was close to what they paid in rent for overcrowded

43. Asch and Musgrove, *Chocolate City*, 210–11.

44. Linda Wells, in discussion with the author, November 2021; Anna Mae Patterson, in discussion with the author, May 2021; Schramm, in discussion with the author, May 2020; Schramm and Anderson, *Dance in Steps of Change*, 83–86; "Ruth Schumm Dies."

45. Asch and Musgrove, *Chocolate City*, 335.

housing.[46] Except with Home Buyers, each month the family received a statement showing that their payment covered the mortgage, taxes, insurance, and a portion of what Home Buyers initially invested. Once the family paid Home Buyers back, they took the title to the house. Up to that point, they also had access to support services in home maintenance and budgeting. Ruth wrote, "We are not giving them a patronizing handout, but a chance to make it on their own."[47]

The first family lived in an apartment near the Community with two parents, a grandmother, and four children in one room, a kitchen, and a back porch. The father worked sixteen hours a day in two jobs. With assistance from Home Buyers, they moved to a home with three bedrooms and a fenced-in backyard with a peach tree. The two other families who took part in Home Buyers in its first year also came from their square-mile parish, though the homes they found were in other parts of the city. The three families were reunited with seventeen children whom city authorities put in Junior Village when it deemed their prior housing unsafe.[48]

Home Buyers expanded quickly, and Ruth quit her government job to devote herself to it. Over the next few years, Home Buyers bought thirty-five houses for families, most of them Black or multiracial, to make their own. In one instance, Ruth rose to the challenge of finding a home for sale to fit a family with ten children. Home Buyers also created a support network for furniture, repair assistance, and volunteers to help with the move. Ruth followed up to see how families were doing. In one check-in call, Ruth asked if the house's furnace was functioning well. The person replied, "Nobody ever asked us before if we were warm enough."[49]

As Ruth's efforts with Home Buyers continued in their area and beyond, other Community members jumped into work with the integrated neighborhood association. Across DC since the late 1800s, exclusively white groups had organized themselves into citizens associations. Black people—already a third of the DC population by the turn of the century—created their own groups with *civic* in the names. Neighborhood groups of all kinds became a form of democratic representation after DC lost home rule in 1874 and was controlled by Congress for a century.[50]

46. Schumm, "Home Buyers, Inc.," 1, 5; Aaseng, "House for 10 Children," 2.

47. Schumm, "Home Buyers," 5.

48. Schumm, "Home Buyers," 5; Schumm, "Home Buyers' President Says," and Schumm, "Introducing Our First Family," 1.

49. Aaseng, "House for 10 Children," 1.

50. Asch and Musgrove, *Chocolate City*, 192–93; Smith, *Captive Capital*, 65–66; Anna Mae Patterson, in discussion with the author, May 2021.

Though the Community's first few members were all white, early on they chose the Lincoln Civic Association rather than the citizens' associations in the parish area. The civic association's several dozen members represented the full breadth of the neighborhood not only racially but culturally and economically, with both property owners and tenants. Together they worked for the civil rights of all people in the area. Grace, who was part of the established Black middle class in the neighborhood, was part of the leadership. In the Community's first few years, several young white Community members who were new to the city became leaders as well. Dora, for example, was liaison to other civic associations—and a couple of Community members served as president. Anna Mae, a white woman not yet thirty, joined the association in early 1966 and was president in a matter of months.[51]

At that time, their neighborhood faced an existential threat: the State Department wanted a fifty-acre area near Dupont Circle for a complex with embassies and related offices, and housing for diplomats.[52] To build the chanceries, they would "tear down all the houses along 22nd Street, N Street, 21st Street, Newport Place," where Community members lived and worshiped, Anna Mae said. Civic association leaders imagined "how dead it would be if it was only an embassy complex where people went home after hours and there was nobody on the streets at night. There would be no stores. There would be no people living there."[53] That's what happened in the nearby Foggy Bottom neighborhood when the federal government removed 300 families to build new War and Navy Department headquarters. The chancery plan would displace an estimated five hundred low-income families.[54] Many of the Black families who had lived there for generations "would have found it very difficult to afford housing," Anna Mae said. The Lincoln Civic Association filed a comment drawing on social reformers' work on the value of vibrant neighborhoods.[55] "Each of us adds to the area," Anna Mae wrote. "We thrive on the vitality of urban variety—its business, its government, its culture, its religion, its total community." Because each

51. Dobbins, "Just a Reminder," 13; Schramm, Summary report for 1966, in Community of Christ Papers; Patterson, in discussion with the author, May 2021; Fautz, "Lincoln Civic Association," 3; "Community Notes" (December 1967).

52. "Lincoln Civic Association Urges 'People,'" 5; Milius, "U.S. Is Revising Chanceries Plan"; Grigg, "House Unit Hears Foes of Chancery Enclave."

53. Patterson, in discussion with the author, May 2021.

54. Asch and Musgrove, *Chocolate City*, 257; Carper, "Adams-Morgan Chancery Sites Voted."

55. Patterson, in discussion with the author, May 2021.

individual is valuable, the embassy-complex plan would cause community disintegration and deny personhood to the residents.[56]

Civic association members testified before a Senate foreign relations subcommittee, raising the issue of DC's lack of affordable housing. They brought enough people to pack the hearing room, astonishing the legislators.[57] John informed the senators and staff that they noticed that the chancery plan "draws boundaries for the area that are almost surgically precise in the manner in which they skirt nearby areas that are more wealthy, more upper-class, more white."[58] The plan failed to move out of committees. Newspapers named only citizens associations among the opponents, yet the civic association showed the effects on the whole neighborhood at a time when Johnson's presidential administration was promoting policies to end poverty.[59] Anna Mae also wondered if the Johnson administration found its funds limited because of the Vietnam War. "Johnson wasn't able to have both guns and butter," she said.[60]

Many social needs went unmet as the government expended both money and young men in Southeast Asia. Calling out that harm for all people in the United States, Martin Luther King Jr. launched the Poor People's Campaign in 1967. Some of the campaign staff had an office in a church in DC. Community of Christ members offered themselves as people who lived in the city and supported the goals and values of the campaign. Some had seen that white people seeking to be allies in civil rights often told Black organizers how they should be doing their work. They tried to take a different approach. "We were just cogs in the wheel," said Judith Anderson Glass, who moved to DC and joined the Community in 1966. In the spring and summer of 1968, the campaign staff put them to work at the office, stuffing envelopes, making copies with a mimeograph machine, and calling churches to ask if they would provide a place to sleep for some of the people who had gathered on the National Mall for a nonviolent protest, creating a camp in front of the US Capitol called Resurrection City.[61] Frequent rain storms turned its grassy stretches into mud. Two men who were arrested during a demonstration at the Capitol then stayed with the Anderson family

56. Patterson, "'X' and 'Y' of Christian Mission," 2.

57. Patterson, in discussion with the author, May 2021; Patterson, "'X' and 'Y' of Christian Mission," 5.

58. "Excerpts from the Statement," 4.

59. Carper, "Adams-Morgan Chancery Sites Voted"; Milius, "U.S. Is Revising Chanceries Plan"; Grigg, "House Unit Hears Foes"; Patterson, in discussion with the author, May 2021.

60. Patterson, in discussion with the author, May 2021.

61. Judith Anderson Glass, in discussion with the author, May 2021.

for a couple of nights after release. The men, a white Louisiana sharecropper and a Black man from New York City, talked with the Andersons about theology, the Bible, and "the necessity of the loose organization which so frustrated the WASPS and those who have taken on their ways."[62]

King led the planning for Resurrection City, but he did not get there with them. On April 3, 1968, he preached to sanitation workers in Memphis about witnessing God's work and human response in the middle of the twentieth century. "The masses of people are rising up," he proclaimed. "The cry is always the same: 'We want to be free.'"[63]

An assassin murdered King the following evening. That night knotted itself into the memories of people across DC. "We had hoped the campaign would be a real test of militant nonviolence," David and John wrote about the Poor People's Campaign. "Dr. King's death shattered us as it did so many other Americans and seemed to smash the last vestiges of hope for peaceful change in this country." Community members gathered first in Mary and John's home, then joined those who filled to overflowing a eucharistic service at St. Stephen and the Incarnation Episcopal Church[64] on 16th Street, two blocks from one of the main riot corridors. Paul Moore, at that time the suffragan bishop for the Episcopal diocese, wrote, "The church was so full that people coming in could hardly find a place to stand, yet when the prayers began a reverent silence enveloped the congregation, and we could plainly hear the wail of sirens, the sound of gunshots, and the fearsome sound of men running as fast as they could, soles beating on the pavement."[65] In neighborhoods across the city, anger and grief poured out, the flames and jagged glass of broken windows an outward and visible sign of inner and spiritual desolation.

The blocks around Community members' homes and worship space in Dupont Circle were among the places most affected. The people there held a complicated mix of emotions after having lived such a large-scale uprising.[66] Looking around at the state of society, with its racial and class divisions, "there's a whole lot to rebel about," Margaret Elsie said. At some point in the following weeks, John preached a sermon that would stand out in Margaret Elsie's mind for decades. "Sometimes you have to pick up a brick and throw it," she heard him say. "I interpreted that as sometimes you

62. Anderson, "Phoenix Shall Arise," 9.

63. Washington, *Testament of Hope*, 280.

64. Schramm and Anderson, *Dance in Steps of Change*, 41–43, 77.

65. "Brief History of the Parish," para. 4. A suffragan bishop assists the diocesan bishop.

66. Asch and Musgrove, *Chocolate City*, 357–58.

see something, and you have to respond dramatically."[67] She didn't interpret it as a call for violence or revolution. "Are you with us, throw the brick" was repeated in the Community as a call to make a decision and not feign neutrality.[68]

❧

As Christians took responsibility for the world they lived in, reading and dialogue would enhance their engagement. Toward that end, the Community started self-publishing a magazine, *Stance*, in March 1966. David Anderson wrote in the first editorial, "In a community that includes poverty and prosperity we find ourselves concerned with both the 'culturally deprived' and the 'culturally alive,' with those who worry about where their next meal is going to come from and with those who wonder where they'll find meaning after the penthouse cocktail party breaks up, and with all those burdened and broken, who, like ourselves, fall in between those extremes."[69]

The stapled-together 8.5 x 11-inch sheets of paper copied on the mimeograph machine in the Schramms's basement looked humble, but they held some serious articles. Writers included scholars from seminaries and universities, political activists, and journalists. Charles, the Center for Applied Linguistics founder, who knew twenty-one languages, submitted works of original scholarship and gained attention outside of the Community.[70] In Charles's translation of Ps 25 one Advent, he put the psalm in contemporary language. Verse 17 in his version reads, "Ease the pain in my heart, /And take me out of my problems."[71] In another article, he wrote about lessons gleaned from studying Colossians. The Community was in an opposite situation to the church that the epistle addressed, Charles wrote. Instead of Christians being a minority in society, in the 1960s United States, Christian symbolism was everywhere, yet "the number of men and women for whom the Christian message has any real vitality is very small."[72]

Initially a way for "the scattered friends of the Community" to receive updates on what was going on with the gathered and "with our thinking as well," *Stance* reached a broader audience, attracting several hundred

---

67. Margaret Elsie Pearson, in discussion with the author, April 2021.

68. Schramm, "Throwing the Brick," 5.

69. Anderson, "Stance: An Introduction," 3.

70. Anderson, "Editorial Adieu," 3.

71. Ferguson, "Advent Psalm," 4.

72. Ferguson, "Paul's Letter to the Community," 1, 6.

subscribers.[73] There were readers across the United States and in Canada, India, Italy, Sweden, and Uganda. A few colleges offered it in their libraries. It enjoyed some popularity in larger Christian circles concerned with social justice, among intentional communities and other groups living and working together.[74]

Its commentaries and editorials covered international and national politics as well as local issues such as advocating for a subway for the working class rather than freeways that destroyed neighborhoods.[75] Book reviews were plentiful on a variety of topics, such as decolonization, Indigenous people's liberation, and white supremacy. In 1969, Community lay leader Lydia Mosher reviewed a book of sermons by Albert Cleage Jr. about Christianity and the Black Power movement. Lydia grew up in Detroit near the Shrine of the Black Madonna, Cleage's church.[76] In *The Black Messiah*, Cleage declared that Jesus was Black and came to unite "all these efforts, all these ideas, all these conflicting opinions," and build a nation for which individuals are willing to sacrifice themselves.[77] In her review, Lydia reexamined her identities as she considered Cleage's rhetoric. She wrote in *Stance*, "I'm a Christian. I'm Black and I'm proud. I am a teacher, wife and mother. I am an individual."[78]

Stance provided a space for the people of the Community to express themselves in playful ways also. One of the first four members of the Community is described in the October 1968 issue in this way: "Kathleen Keating, having conquered both housewifery and mothering, is now reaching new peaks of grooviness as a student at Federal City College." Updates about jobs and lives also took whimsical or earnest form: "Peter Mosher's new assignment lets him sit around the Circle all these beautiful afternoons rapping with the winos and the hippies."[79] Surely not written by Dora herself, a bio for her suggests that she "sometimes calls herself a crab but that's really because she is afraid that people don't see the real depths of her warmth and compassion. She's probably the sexiest radical in the Community."[80]

When Bruce Johnson met Dora, he was smitten. It was glamorous to him that she came from another country and spoke five languages. They

73. Anderson, "Stance: An Introduction," 3.
74. "FYI," 3; Glass, in discussion with the author, May 2021.
75. Anderson, "Tragedy and Absurdity," 3.
76. Lydia Mosher, in discussion with the author, February 2023.
77. Cleage, *Black Messiah*, 25.
78. Mosher, "Black Power Christianity," 14, 17.
79. "Contributors" (October 1968), 21.
80. "Contributors" (February 1969), 8.

also shared a commitment to civil rights and racial integration. Bruce attended Wheaton College on a full scholarship and admired Billy Graham, the evangelist closely associated with the Christian school in Illinois. Graham began desegregating his events in the US South in 1953–54 and was ahead of many white southern Christian leaders in criticizing religious justifications for Jim Crow.[81]

Dora and Bruce married in 1966. Dora's brother, Philip, also became involved in the Community and on the editorial staff of *Stance*. When their cousin Anie came from New York to visit, she not only shared meals with Dora and other Community members, she also attended worship. Anie, a minister's daughter and granddaughter, had "lost a little faith in the organized church. It was very refreshing for me to go to church—my impressions of the Community of Christ were very positive," Anie said. "Dora was the center of it all."[82]

Rather than being nurtured into a leadership role, Dora's natural leadership came out from the start. Many Community members looked to her as her younger cousins had while hiking in the mountains in Lebanon. From early on Dora was an evangelist also—though the Community was squeamish about the *e* word. But the fact was, she invited a lot of people. There were seven other adults in addition to the Schramms when Dora joined in 1966. She brought friends, coworkers, and, later, renters from the parade of people who stayed in a room on the top floor of Dora and Bruce's home for a few months or a few years.[83] "Dora was the one who glued the whole community together," Anna Mae said, "by force of her intellect and her faith and her personality."[84]

Dora argued that it wasn't enough for activist-minded Christians like those in the Community to point out injustices and intolerance by those around them, and especially people in power, Dora said. Jesus calls his disciples to preach the gospel. "We, too, must preach that message and not be ashamed," she said. The message was not only a confrontation with injustice but also "hope of the new order that has come." She held that tension herself, of being part of the old order and trying to change it while acknowledging

81. Moyer, in discussion with the author, September 2021; Miller, *Billy Graham*, 18–19, 28–29, 62.

82. Khachadourian, in discussion with the author, March 2021.

83. D'au Vin, "NW Group Shows Big Deeds," D8; Oakley Pearson, in discussion with the author, April 2021; David Anderson, in discussion with the author, March 2021; Dorothy Pedtke, in discussion with Laci Barrow, Christina Nichols, and Martin Johnson, September 2016.

84. Patterson, in discussion with the author, June 2021.

failure. Dora said to others in the Community, "We are very uncomfortable with the fact that we live lives of sin and grace."

Dora struggled with not always feeling that her faith and life were integrated. One example was her strong convictions against violence, born of having lived through war with greater proximity and intensity than many—"my entire childhood and teenage years were spent in an environment of war," she wrote.[85] When she took the oath to become a US citizen, she refused to swear that she would use a weapon in the nation's defense if necessary.[86] Yet while she proclaimed nonviolence, "every day I submit to the violence of hierarchies and the damage it does to all," regardless of one's status.[87]

She said this in a shared word—the Community's term for its regular (but not weekly) testimony-like practice. A person who was moved to do so would reflect on their hopes or fears, or thoughts the homily stirred in them. "We spend our lives trying to create an identity for ourselves. We push and pull," Dora lamented. "We play by the rules, or we break them. We look for a mission, or we roll with whatever comes our way. At the base of it all, we desperately want to be justified. That which we are doing has to be right or else there's no point in continuing." Seeking to be faithful to each of their callings was the work of a lifetime.[88] Community members took the time to help each person discover what that calling was and what gifts they had to use in living it out.[89]

85. Dora Johnson, untitled selection in *Thoughts on the Lenten Season 2002*, March 21

86. Klonowski, "Community Sketches," 11.

87. Johnson, shared word in the Community of Christ, 7.

88. Johnson, shared word in the Community of Christ, 9.

89. Nyla Rasmussen, in discussion with the author, June 2020.

3

"What Would You Rather Do More Than Anything Else in the World?"

VALBORG ANDERSON SOLD THE family home in Minneapolis and headed to the airport with her cat, Missy. At fifty-six years old, she left the state where she had lived her whole life. She traveled south and east more than a thousand miles to DC, to join a Christian community she visited only months before, on Easter Sunday.[1]

She was a Lutheran all her life, active in churches that belonged to the Missouri Synod—a more conservative branch of the Lutheran family tree. Valborg and her husband, Bill, took part in integrating the congregation where they were members in their final years in Minneapolis. They invited one of their Black friends to attend worship, and some church members left because of that.[2]

Valborg also became convinced that the Vietnam War was terribly wrong. She sometimes said she moved to DC to be able to protest the war in front of the White House. And demonstrate she did, a little white-haired dynamo running around in tennis shoes to various marches and mobilizations.[3]

Church was the center of her social life in Minnesota, but more with others in the church and less with the neighborhood around its building. She saw the Community of Christ engaging all of its neighbors as Mary and

1. Judith Anderson Glass, in discussion with the author, May 2021; Anderson, "Dateline: December 8," 2.

2. Glass, in discussion with the author, May 2021.

3. Schramm and Anderson, *Dance in Steps of Change*, 74; Wendy Ward, in discussion with author, December 2021; Schramm, "Gifts of Grace."

John Schramm shaped ministry and mission around the idea of each person discovering their gift. That appealed to Valborg. Whether it was a hunch or a spiritual hunger, something was drawing her toward this community, this approach to connecting political convictions with a sense of calling.[4]

૨ล

It was during the season of Advent, on the kind of day when "frosty ferns and foliage etched the windows, filtering the light," when Valborg Delia Christiansen came into the world in 1909.[5] Her father had the occupation then called druggist in a town along a reservation's edge in rural Minnesota. As winters were cold, summer evenings were hot and humid, filled with sounds of loons in the marsh, crickets and katydids, and occasionally a train whistle.[6]

In church, she found that the Eucharist was central to her faith. "I was 12 years old before I was permitted to kneel at the altar," she wrote, "but that is when the mystery, the majesty, the joy of my Christian belief was revealed. Those hour-long, sometimes tedious sermons could be endured because I knew that my rather rebellious heart would be forgiven, and I needed that assurance frequently!" She was "gladdened and strengthened," as the catechism said.[7]

Valborg's love of language expanded to Latin, Spanish, and Norwegian when she attended St. Olaf College. Her father died near the end of her first year. No longer able to afford tuition, she found a job as a doctor's assistant to help out at home. She still felt drawn to words, but was too tired in the evenings to create plots for fiction, so she began to write poetry. Amid the Great Depression in the 1930s, Valborg and her mother moved to Minneapolis. Valborg had a relationship with a man that resulted in the birth of her oldest son, Charlie. After she met and married Bill Anderson, she gave birth to David in 1941 and then Judith in 1942.[8]

The Andersons had a typical postwar American experience for a family descended from European immigrants. In the early 1940s, they had a fourplex house in a low-income neighborhood with Native American,

---

4. Glass, in discussion with the author, May 2021; Schramm, *Gifts of Grace*, 67; Schramm, "Gifts of Grace."

5. Anderson, *Thoughts, Faith, and Friends*, 13.

6. Anderson, *Thoughts, Faith, and Friends*, 81; David Anderson, in discussion with the author, March 2021.

7. Anderson, "Strictly Personal," 18.

8. Anderson, in discussion with the author, March 2021; Glass, in discussion with the author, May 2021.

Black, and working-class white families. There were three rooms for five people. After Valborg gave birth to her fourth child, named William after his father, they moved twice, each house a little larger and a little closer to the suburbs. The economic boom shifted their family into the middle class. By the 1960s, they lived in a majority white neighborhood.[9]

But their improved social status didn't protect them from suffering. As their youngest child grew, it was clear something was wrong. William never learned to walk and was diagnosed with cerebral palsy. Almost a century earlier, the condition was identified and defined—as motor-control-related muscle disorders that caused unusual development in the womb or injury during birth. Yet research into treatment options was only beginning in earnest when William was born. He lived just beyond his toddler years.

Amid such grief, literature and jazz buoyed Valborg. The radio in her kitchen was on all day and into the night. In the evenings while Bill watched their black-and-white television, she ironed his shirts and listened to Dave Brubeck, the Modern Jazz Quartet, and whatever else came on. When she found time to read, her favorite writers were Pearl S. Buck, F. Scott Fitzgerald, Ernest Hemingway, and Sinclair Lewis.[10]

In 1966, things weren't going well for Valborg and Bill financially. It wasn't the first time Bill got laid off, this time after being a foreman in a manufacturing company. The job had offered no pension in any case. Bill and Valborg figured they were still young enough to get work in DC. David already lived in DC. Judith moved there, then Bill, and finally Valborg. Soon after they had all reunited, buying a house across the street from the Schramms, Bill had a stroke. Then he fell and broke his hip. He used a walker after that, moving around Dupont Circle to Community ministries and other activities.[11]

Valborg sought a role for herself in this new place and a new community. She talked to Mary, thinking in terms of finding out "what she should be doing." Mary changed the question, asking, "Val, what really would you like to do more than anything else in the world?" Valborg thought about it for a few more months and then went across the street to the Schramms's home and said, "This sounds so strange, but I just love to visit with people over a cup of coffee. I love hospitality."[12]

---

9. David Anderson, in discussion with the author, March 2021; Glass, in discussion with the author, May 2021.

10. Anderson, "Some Call It a Day."

11. Glass, in discussion with the author, May 2021; Anderson, in discussion with the author, March 2021.

12. Schramm, "Gifts of Grace."

The Community bought her a thirty-cup coffee maker. She would plug it in each morning and every day had an open house. At first it was mainly Community people stopping by before or after work. Then people from the neighborhood learned that she had a pot of coffee on and an open door, and they came all day long. Mary thought that anyone seeing all the people going up and down the steps might have thought the house was a place to buy drugs. Instead, it was a place where people could go to sober up. Val became a one-woman social service agency, making referrals if people wanted help. But mostly she and Bill listened. She might not get done much of what she intended to do on any given day, but people were primary. "Nothing came before that listening," Mary said. "That was her ministry."[13]

She extended hospitality also to people who came to DC for demonstrations against the Vietnam War and for various social justice causes. The family built up a reputation for offering whatever space they could spare, including the couch and floor, to protesters, and their attic and extra bedroom for young people who came to the city for low-paying nonprofit work and church-related service. The Andersons also hosted Bible study for many years. Their home was cluttered in a welcoming way, with a jar of licorice by the door. They had posters and artwork on the walls, shelves of interesting books and pottery—much of it acquired from the Sign of Jonah, the Community bookstore where Bill was the bookkeeper. There were also stacks of books and articles from magazines and newspapers that Valborg clipped and kept, rarely throwing anything away.[14] Their table, inherited "yet not old enough to be antique," was a place where children did their homework and adults had heated discussions, rolled out pies, kneaded dough, and passed around bread and wine along with meals "for one or fourteen."[15]

The table also became the location for writing and editing articles for *Stance*. Valborg was a tough but kind editor, shaping the theological tone of the magazine. In summer 1968, Valborg took charge of typing up the articles to put on stencils to run through the mimeograph machine in the Schramms' basement. Then she took the copies of the magazine back across the street for collating, stapling, and labeling. Many Community members thought she was chain smoking during this operation or at Bible study. But the truth was she'd light a cigarette, take a few puffs, and then place it in an ashtray and forget about it while she was occupied. By the time she'd

13. Schramm, "Gifts of Grace."

14. Glass, in discussion with the author, May 2021; Margaret Ann Hoven, email message to author, August 16, 2021; Linda Wells, in discussion with the author, November 2021.

15. Anderson, *Thoughts, Faith, and Friends*, 55.

remember it, it would've burned out. So she'd light another and go back to the work she was doing, beginning the circle again.[16]

Stance became an outlet for her poetry as well. Poetry was a form of praying for her.[17] She lifted up life in community and the necessity of humor in "A Sixty-Six-Second Sermon on the Prodigious Proliferation of Ponderous Pronouncements":

> . . . if you can love me
> (with my imperfections), and I can love you
> (with your dubious directions), we will have,
> I reckon, reciprocity.
>
> Shall we laugh? . . . together? . . . at us?[18]

She was not afraid to turn a critical eye to herself and humanity, lamenting pollution:

> From my kitchen window I can see
> the Spirit's tongues of flame,
> the yellow-crimson maple tree
> glowing in the slanted sun:
> A Pentecost.
> And, from that same window,
> that same dying sun bathes
> a rat poised on alley-trash
> exulting in the wastes of man:
> a Confession.[19]

ʅ●

The interweaving of faith, political engagement, and life together with other Christians began with honoring each person's unique contribution to make in the world. This was not merely navel-gazing. Being concerned with the whole person, and not merely their physical needs, meant looking beyond the usual social service programs (as important as they are). Whether it was working with the Poor People's Campaign or with the local civic association opposing the embassy complex plan, they started with each person's value.

---

16. Glass, in discussion with the author, May 2021; Anderson, "Some Call It a Day."

17. David Anderson, in discussion with Laci Barrow, Christina Nichols, and Martin Johnson, September 2016.

18. Anderson, *Thoughts, Faith, and Friends*, 64–65. Ellipses in original.

19. Anderson, *Thoughts, Faith, and Friends*, 11.

One was never too young for this message, either. In the summer program the Community initiated, members such as Lydia led activities for children from the local public schools on the theme of giving and receiving gifts. In that environment, the children learned that each of them had God-given gifts to share with everyone around them.[20]

Mary, like others at the Community and beyond, was influenced by Gordon Cosby and Elizabeth O'Connor of Church of the Saviour. Churches were often no different from society in trying to fit people into a mold rather than helping them become who they can be.[21] Mary especially appreciated O'Connor's interpretation of the Parable of the Talents. "Our gifts are a loan and we are responsible for spending them in the world and we will be held accountable," Mary summed it up. It is difficult to find out God's will for your life. "I don't care whether you're eight or eighty," Mary said, "you are responsible for finding out the things that God would have you do." A part of that discovery of one's gifts is learning that "our worth is not the same as our usefulness."[22]

Mary thought about the old debate of faithfulness versus effectiveness. She wanted to be effective, but it's not up to any of us to determine what the final outcome will be. Mary imagined that at the end of the day, God takes all she did and blows on it like wheat and chaff. When the chaff is gone, "as often as not, there's nothing much left there." But from our ministries, God takes what God can use for the kingdom. Though we fail sometimes, God picks us up, dusts us off, and sends us out the next day to try again. In the midst of this daily cycle of seeking God's will for our lives, Mary and John encouraged everyone to pay attention to what they enjoy. "I don't think God gave you a gift or an ability to make you miserable," Mary said. "God made us to be fulfilled by the gifts that God gave us."[23]

Evoking people's gifts was not only about spiritual growth for its members in the Community, it was one of the central purposes of church. "In too many cases the church has a program and asks you to keep that program going by enlisting you on a committee," John said. People are more passionate when they know their gift, their calling. Letting the common life be shaped in turn by people's gifts and passions meant a thriving church. That's what John drew from what he read at the time on the health of congregations. If the people who would participate in a given program have a direct role

20. Anderson, "Summer Program," 9–10.

21. Schramm, *Gifts of Grace*, 12, 20, 34; O'Connor, *Journey Inward, Journey Outward*, 32–33.

22. Schramm, "Gifts of Grace."

23. Schramm, "Gifts of Grace."

in creating that program—versus electing people to serve on a committee that then recruits volunteers—the more they feel they own the program. That sense of engagement and evoking people's gifts was only possible, they believed, because the Community stayed relatively small. John and Mary agreed with Gordon Cosby that it's difficult to pastor more than ninety people if you really want to know each person well enough to help them develop their unique ministry and share in the decision-making of the community.[24]

This vision shaped not only what the Community did but also what it didn't do. "Nothing was sacred" in terms of programming they had to have. "There was a period of time when no one really wanted to teach Sunday school," John recalled, "and therefore we had no Sunday school for a period of months." They told themselves, "If nobody wants to do it, they're not going to do the kids one bit of good."[25]

At first, this notion of the church's common life flowing from its people's gifts wasn't making sense to Bob Keating, one of the four adults who began the Community. One afternoon after Sunday worship, John told him that once he had figured out what he'd rather do more than anything else with his free time, "the other three of us will try to find a place for you to do that." A few days later, Bob came back to the group: "I've got it. More than anything else in the world, when I come home from work, I would like to build model airplanes."[26] Mary recalled, "The rest of us could hardly keep from laughing." But Bob claimed the gift.[27]

John continued visiting every park, school, business, restaurant, and bar in the square-mile parish. He met people and asked about local needs. He was trying to connect with families in the area, and it wasn't going all that well.[28] At a playground, John approached the director—an employee of the recreation department—to thank him for his work. The director said, "You're the first one in five years who ever came up to say, 'Thank you.'" John was delighted by how touched the director was by his gratitude. "But then I couldn't resist, you know, the big pastor image," asking if there was anything this new community could do to assist the playground director. The man replied: "There's only one thing. I got twelve kids trying to get ready for a model airplane contest. I don't have any people to help. Would you have one of your members?"[29]

24. Schramm and Hayden, "Community of Christ."

25. Schramm and Hayden, "Community of Christ."

26. Schramm and Hayden, "Community of Christ."

27. Schramm, *Gifts of Grace*, 65.

28. Schramm, *Gifts of Grace*, 65; Schramm, "Community of Christ."

29. Schramm and Hayden, "Community of Christ."

Different from many congregations as ministries begin, the Community was less a parent than a doula. It provided spiritual and emotional support to members to bring their ministries to birth. They did this from the gifts they identified within themselves and needs they witnessed in the world. As with Ruth Schumm and Home Buyers, the focus was on each person "individually finding our gifts and where we felt called," Anna Mae said, rather than seeking to control or own those ministries. "That was actually one of the strengths."[30] Allene, one of the earliest people in the Community, went so far as to say that the "byword of the Community is not what we do as a church, it's what we do individually."[31]

The Community nurtured dreams and ideas, but it didn't expect everyone to be committed to any of them. Mary felt that pastors make a mistake when they think they have to wait until everyone is on board with a particular effort. "If just five or ten people feel strongly about where the church ought to be serving," she said, "it really doesn't mean that everybody feels that way or feels called to that ministry. But those that do in a parish ought to just take the ball and run with it and not worry about everybody else." This connected with the Community's outward focus and not on building up the institution. "You didn't worry about preserving yourself if you didn't have much to preserve," Mary said. "It was a very freeing thing."[32]

With that freedom came a tension perhaps best identified in the sociological classic *Habits of the Heart: Individualism and Commitment in American Life.* US society cultivated over centuries a notion of freedom that ramped up after WWII. That "freedom of each person to live where he wants, do what he wants, believe what he wants," the authors note, "makes community ties so fragile."[33] There was a tradeoff in the Community's approach. On the one hand, noted member Haven Whiteside, the Community didn't organize central activities beyond worship. On the other hand, the Community's approach allowed members to see their work as an expression of their Christian life. This was in contrast to viewing Christian activities as good works tacked on to the rest of their life, often sequestered into one evening or weekend afternoon. For Haven, "really my work and my charity are one and the same."[34]

---

30. Anna Mae Patterson, in discussion with the author, May 2021.

31. Paka, "Churchless Congregations Growing," C21.

32. Q-and-A session during Schramm and Hayden, "Community of Christ."

33. Bellah et al., *Habits of the Heart*, 24.

34. Whiteside, "Search for a Responsible Future," 17.

Someone with a vision or dream shared their idea with the Community at large. "If anybody was interested," they'd gather for a few evenings, "however long it took to kind of flesh out the idea," John said. Putting forth a vision involved a certain amount of risk. "None of us risk easily," John noted. "My hope is that the church, that other Christians help me be free to risk more, not deter me from risking more." If the group caught on to the vision that flowed from someone identifying their gifts, they would help make it a reality.[35]

Anna Mae's dream was to start a plant shop. More than that, she wanted to bring beauty into people's home environments. One time taking the train from New York City back to DC, she felt acutely the lack of "trees and shrubs and flowers and green." Seventeen people formed a group to talk about the idea and visualize how it might come into being. They chose the name Third Day, drawing from the biblical creation story. That is when God calls forth vegetation from the land (Gen 1:11). The Third Day also represented the mystery of new life, being the day Jesus rose from the dead.[36]

The group, with a majority of members from the Community, decided to back the idea, including by buying $1,000 in shares of the business, which paid taxes, and electing the board of directors. In that way the Community became the sole shareholder in the Third Day. For the rest of the funding, one of the financial minds in the group suggested selling unsecured loan certificates for $100 a piece, promising 6 percent interest after five years—if the business succeeded. They met their goal of raising $5,000. Community members continued nurturing the plant shop by volunteering alongside the staff, most of whom were not part of the Community. Anna Mae was the manager and Oakley Pearson was the first employee. Oakley had been a Peace Corps volunteer in a small town in Colombia, and he had learned about plants that live in the tropics, which is what most common houseplants are.[37]

At the time, it was difficult to buy indoor plants in an inner-city neighborhood such as Dupont Circle. To find a source for wholesale plants, Anna Mae went to every nursery in DC and the suburbs for perhaps thirty miles. Most staff "either told us that it was a stupid, impossible idea to have a shop that only sold indoor plants" or wouldn't share sources for inventory. Then she tried a greenhouse run by a pair of brothers in Maryland selling houseplants as well as annuals and perennials. They helped enthusiastically with getting the Third Day started.[38]

35. Schramm and Hayden, "Community of Christ."

36. Patterson, in discussion with the author, June 2021.

37. Third Day Policy Statement, in Community of Christ Papers; Patterson, in discussion with the author, June 2021; Margaret Elsie and Oakley Pearson, in discussion with the author, April 2021.

38. Patterson, in discussion with the author, June 2021.

Looking for a space in Dupont Circle, Anna Mae and others found one with an affordable price, large windows for light—and a reputation for being cursed. Many different businesses had been there before and failed. But the location at the corner of 22nd and P Streets, just across from the edge of Rock Creek Park, was otherwise excellent. On a warm day, one might step in from the verdant outside and have the sense of taking all that green home. The shop opened in January 1972, announcing itself as "an affirmation of life through green growing things." In addition to its inventory, "it will also carry a hope, a dream—that the gentle mystery of greenness and growth will bring renewed spirit to the city and those who live there."[39] On their first day, "people just flooded the shop," Anna Mae recalled. "It was so overwhelming that first week that we ran out of plant material." They called the brothers at the greenhouse "and said 'Help!' and they promptly brought us in a whole bunch of other plants."[40]

They created a business model based on helping people succeed in growing plants that flourished and that helped them to flourish in turn. They created cards for each variety of plant with its needs. Customers were allowed to purchase only two plants at a time to make sure they could care for them before they got more. They sold ceramic pots handcrafted by local artists and had a plant hospital to diagnose pests or problems such as under- or overwatering. They even offered plant-sitting services when customers went out of town. The Third Day also had a children's corner. Children could buy plants for the cost that the store paid, with no markup. Anna Mae had the idea after hearing that John and Mary's daughter Karen was brought to tears when a florist ignored her at the counter as she stood clutching her money trying to buy a Mother's Day gift. Anna Mae insisted on vacation time for the staff, and the shop closed the week between Christmas Day and New Year's. During one of those breaks, Third Day staff and volunteers visited nursing-home residents and left for each a gift of a small cactus garden, wax begonia, or spider plant.[41]

When the owner of the initial space sold the building to turn it into condominiums, the Third Day found a larger space and succeeded there as well, paying back its loans after the five-year mark. Meanwhile, they inspired imitators, with perhaps three dozen plant shops sprouting in other locations. After their initial struggle to find sources, they created a list and shared it with anyone who asked. It was a way of blurring the lines between

39. Braaten, "Blooming Idea."

40. Patterson, in discussion with the author, June 2021.

41. Patterson, in discussion with the author, May and June 2021; Margaret Elsie and Oakley Pearson, in discussion with the author, April 2021; Ward, "Plants for the Elderly," 14.

business and nonprofit. They sought to have practices that put people first.[42] "If I had my druthers, I'd give all the plants away," Anna Mae told a reporter from the *Washington Star*.[43]

While the Third Day had a mission, it didn't describe itself as Christian, since many of the staff were not. Yet they all shared two basic values of "reverence for life" and "radical self-expenditure: personally, by a willingness to give of oneself; corporately, by basing decisions on values rather than self-preservation."[44] Staff members who were Christian didn't engage in evangelism. "If you serve people with something that is important for their flourishing, their well-being, that is a statement of the love of God and Christian witness," Anna Mae said. That approach leaves people free to respond with questions or "to want to become more connected."[45] Inside the shop, they did not have a rack with the Community's brochure or a card with worship times. Yet its connection wasn't a secret—local news coverage named the Community of Christ as owners of the Third Day, as well as the Sign of Jonah.[46]

Two buildings away, the Sign of Jonah was a business that was more openly a ministry of the Community. The Sign of Jonah opened in July 1967 on the 2100 block of P Street NW. In exploring her gifts, Mary discovered that she had some of the gifts needed for starting a store: she loved decorating the space, choosing what to sell, and educating customers.[47] Like the Third Day, its name was inspired by Scripture: as Jonah spent three days in the belly of a sea creature, so Jesus would be in "the heart of the earth" for three days (Matt 12:38–42). Christians are sealed with the sign of Jonah when living by the power of the resurrection. In an introduction for the shop, Mary and others summed up its philosophy in an adaptation of Jesus's words: "This generation asks for a sign; and there will be no sign given to them except the sign of Jonah. Resurrection! Life! Creativity!" The artwork in the shop proclaimed these themes.[48]

Both the Sign of Jonah and the Third Day were inspired by the Community's theology of Christians being fully engaged in the world. Margaret Elsie, who was involved in both commercial ventures, wrote in *Stance* after

42. Patterson, in discussion with the author, June 2021; Third Day Policy Statement, in Community of Christ Papers.

43. Braaten, "A Blooming Idea."

44. Anderson, "Time to Look," 7–8, 12.

45. Patterson, in discussion with the author, June 2021.

46. Shelton, "Selling the Green," F1; Braaten, "Blooming Idea."

47. Schramm, "Gifts of Grace."

48. "Sign of Jonah: An Introduction," 5.

the Sign of Jonah's first five years (and Third Day's first six months) that they sought to respond in a human way to everyone who came to them, not only seeking a sale. They offered free coffee and staff were open to conversations, touching on life and love and sometimes faith (but not steered by staff in that direction). Showcasing the work of local artists and craftspeople, they supported their vocations as well as bolstering their income.[49] The Sign of Jonah didn't require any of its stock to be religious, implicitly or explicitly. "We're somewhere between the old, overt religion and the new secularization—(sometimes it's a less than happy compromise from either point of view)" Margaret Elsie wrote in *Stance*.[50] Some customers were taken aback when they discovered the Christian aspect of the business: a person exclaimed one day, "Good grief! Do you sell religion here?" But another customer told them, "This shop is an oasis in the desert of trash."[51]

In some ways, the store stood in as the Community's building in outreach to newcomers, serving the same purpose as a sign in front or a banner hanging off of a steeple. Except it was also a gentler way in for people who weren't sure that they wanted to be part of a church. Wendy Ward lived with several other Lutheran college graduates, "in this really dilapidated basement apartment off of Dupont Circle, doing that college-graduate-out-on-our-own-for-the-first-time thing." She was disenchanted with the traditional church. Walking around Dupont Circle, she found the Sign of Jonah and with it an "opportunity came to be part of a community, people who were socially active, involved in the peace movement, doing things, doing worship in an alternative way," she said. She thought, "That sounds exciting."[52]

The Sign of Jonah was also a beacon for John Stewart, who was twenty-two when he moved into the city in 1968 after growing up in a Virginia suburb. He had been involved in a coffeehouse called the Iguana, hosted by a Lutheran Church not far away, called Luther Place. The coffeehouse hosted open-mic performances of the kind of music that John, who played guitar and flute, enjoyed. He would also attend the contemporary worship service at Luther Place—another effort to reach young people and others less interested in more-traditional worship services. But at some point those initiatives started to lose steam.[53]

People at Luther Place told John Stewart about the Sign of Jonah, and he decided to visit. There he met Mary Schramm and Bill Anderson, who

---

49. Schramm, "More from the Store," 8.
50. Anderson, "Whither the Sign of Jonah?," 1.
51. "Conversations at the Sign of Jonah," 5
52. Wendy Ward, in discussion with the author, December 2021.
53. John Stewart, in discussion with the author, January 2021.

kept the books. Bill and his family hosted Sunday evening services in their home and John decided to give it a try. Two tries, in fact. His first day in the Community, he attended both the morning service in the basement at 2107 N Street, and the evening service at the Andersons. Later in 1970, after John and Bobbie Stewart married, she became a regular also. They had met at the Iguana coffeehouse, where Bobbie was occasionally mistaken for Joni Mitchell by looks alone. (She didn't sing.) Bobbie grew up Lutheran in Tennessee, but at that point she felt uncomfortable in a traditional church building. The Community's services in row houses gave her a way to be part of Christian worship.[54]

❦

While the Community didn't exert control over the various ministries it supported that were started by its members, that didn't mean they all remained the wheelhouse of the person who initially envisioned them. With the Third Day plant shop, when Anna Mae left DC for several months, others managed the shop without her. Margaret Elsie was bookkeeper, and along with Oakley and others the staff of twelve or thirteen part-time people became invested in the shop. When Anna Mae returned, "it was no longer just her dream; it was more," Margaret Elsie said.[55]

The staff began cooperative management, making all decisions by consensus. This included the philosophical—how they felt about profit—and serious questions about worker benefits and cost-sharing for health insurance. There were also arguments about the optimal place in the shop to store the paper bags. They met for hours until everyone could agree to accept a given approach to something. Still, their rotation of daily, weekly, monthly, and quarterly tasks "was incredibly efficient," Margaret Elsie said. "It was a very intentional process," Oakley said, "growing out of the intentionality of the Community." The real-life example helped them envision "how that kind of collaboration and organization could be really effective and so much more fair than the standard model," Margaret Elsie said.[56]

54. John and Bobbie Stewart, in discussion with the author, January 2021.

55. Margaret Elsie and Oakley Pearson, in discussion with the author, April 2021.

56. Margaret Elsie and Oakley Pearson, in discussion with the author, April 2021.

4

"We Should Be Doing Something Ecumenical"

ECUMENICAL WAS NOT A word most people knew when they came to the Community. They joked about how hard it was to even learn to pronounce it. And it usually described abstract dialogues among bishops and theologians, not life together in Christian communities. But as new people joined the Community—about a dozen people each year in the early years—they learned about ecumenism by living it out. They came from nine Christian denominations, bringing the gifts of each, along with plenty of hurt from childhood churches. They saw the blind spots as well as the distinct contributions of each tradition, and they showed little chauvinism.[1]

The Community had a subset of members who belonged to a denomination, the American Lutheran Church. A few were active in it—attending annual gatherings, for example—and kept others informed on churchwide events. The Community covenant clarified that full fellowship was open to members of any denomination and welcomed other subsets of the larger body who wanted to affiliate with another denomination.[2] The Community was standing in contrast to nondenominational churches, David wrote in *Stance*: "We all want purity of doctrine from the other guy. Too often the liberal response to the reactionary purists is to say, all right, we won't have any doctrine at all."[3] Being ecumenical allowed the

1. Community of Christ Papers, Swarthmore College Peace Collection; Rachel Medema Haxtema, in discussion with the author, October 2021.

2. Anderson, "Looking toward Denver," 2; Covenant of the Community of Christ, 1 January 1971, in Community of Christ Papers.

3. Anderson, "Remembering the Reformation," 3.

Community to celebrate its differences in theological background rather than mixing them into a slurry.

At the same time, the Community's ecumenism was not interested in maintaining denominational identities while merely collaborating where possible. To another member, Bettie Currie, being ecumenical was believing that unity is a gift of God already received, "though Christians often display it poorly." An ecumenical congregation recognizes that "no denomination has full knowledge of God" or God's will, but shares the gifts of each tradition to move toward a greater understanding of God and a shared mission.[4]

The Eucharist was at the center of the Community's life and relationships. After the celebrant consecrated the elements at the altar, the bread and wine passed from one person to the next in a circle as was the practice in worship. The last person in the circle offered the bread and cup to the celebrant.[5] This method of sharing Communion from person to person impressed Linda Wells, a young woman renting from Ruth Schumm, also the Community's landlady, who suggested she visit. "I loved it from the first minute," Linda said. She grew up in a nondenominational church where Communion was monthly at most. Congregants passed a plate with pre-torn pieces of bread down the pew and each received "a little bitty cup with a little bit of grape juice in it."[6] There was "little or no instruction as to its meaning." The Community talked about the Eucharist "and each week we served one another—a live interaction."[7] In its theology of the Eucharist, individuals from their various backgrounds retained their beliefs. Some of them wondered at times if what they were doing was wrong. They lacked permission from any church hierarchy and didn't seek a notable theologian to provide a justification.[8]

The question of Communion became more complex when Catholics joined the Community, beginning in its first year. When Lutherans such as Margaret Elsie were growing up in the 1940s and 1950s, "Catholics were others," she recalled. "I don't feel like I had any prejudice against them or anything, it's just that they were not part of my immediate sphere of activity and friendship."[9] Many Catholics her age would have said the same. During the previous century, instances of anti-Catholic violence—interwoven with anti-immigrant prejudice—flared in various times and places in the

4. Currie, "What Does It Mean," 5–6.

5. Schramm, "Community of Christ," 18.

6. Linda Wells, in discussion with the author, November 2021.

7. Linda Wells, email message to author, March 20, 2023.

8. Anderson, "In Closing," 23; Lokken, Review of *Lutherans and Catholics*, 19–20.

9. Margaret Elsie Pearson, in discussion with the author, April 2021.

United States. As a result, one historian notes, "Catholics had for generations been taught to cleave to their own—to send their children to Catholic schools, support local Catholic institutions, and center their social lives on the parish."[10]

Attitudes were changing by the mid-1960s. Openness was a primary idea when the Vatican invited more than 2,200 global leaders in the church to the first session of the Second Vatican Council in October 1962: openness to other faiths, openness to ecumenism, openness to shaping and being shaped by the larger society. (The First Vatican Council, in 1870, had made the teaching of papal infallibility "an article of faith" rather than "merely a theological opinion,"[11] as it was prior to that and remained in the minds of some.) By the closing session in December 1965, there was "a permanent end to Catholic isolation from the larger Christian community."[12]

Vatican II also sought to bridge the separation between priests and the people and reshape Catholic Mass. In decades prior, it was common for the faithful to pray the rosary in the pews while a priest recited the Latin with his back turned to the congregation. With the liturgy reformed after the second session in 1963, the emphasis shifted to have Mass be a shared work of the priest and congregation. The bishops and other leaders at the sessions entered into a conversation already taking place. French and German monks began the Liturgical Movement in the early twentieth century, seeking to reclaim liturgy as an act of public service in the religious realm, "the work of the people"—the meaning of the word in its New Testament roots. The Liturgical Movement invited the faithful to pose the question, "Why go to church?"[13] While Catholics had varying responses to Vatican II across economic classes and generations, younger and highly educated Catholics especially embraced the liturgical changes.[14]

Vatican II's statement on the purpose of liturgy dovetailed with the Community of Christ's understanding of religious services inspiring and sustaining mission and discipleship. That's what drew in Dorothy Pedtke, a twenty-seven-year-old graduate student at Georgetown University. She had grown up around the campus of the University of Notre Dame, "where there's every kind of Catholic." When she was a preteen, she attended a summer program held by the UND liturgy department. She met Catholics from the Grail, an international women's movement that built a reputation

10. Tentler, *American Catholics*, 82–83, 97–98, 305.

11. Tentler, *American Catholics*, 135.

12. McDannell, *Spirit of Vatican II*, 67.

13. McDannell, *Spirit of Vatican II*, 40–41.

14. Tentler, *American Catholics*, 228–29.

during the 1940s and 1950s of being committed to liturgical renewal. Arriving in DC in the mid-1960s, Dorothy worked at the Center for Applied Linguistics. Dora invited her to visit the Community, and she did. Dorothy was "seriously Catholic, but interested in the social service part of what the Community was doing, the inner-city ministry." She happily attended Lutheran liturgies as well as "theology and scripture studies, and the Community did plenty of that." Dorothy saw that "John was very interested in building ecumenical community," and not only among an assortment of Protestants.[15]

Vatican II's 1964 Decree on Ecumenism, *Unitatis redintegratio*, not only permits but exhorts "all Catholic faithful to recognize the signs of the times and to take an active and intelligent part in the work of ecumenism." This fosters humility: "Christ summons the Church, as she goes her pilgrim way, to that continual reformation of which she always has need, insofar as she is an institution of men here on earth." Yet denominations do not yet possess the unity that would allow a shared Eucharist, the Vatican II leaders declared. They did not permit celebrating the Eucharist together as a way to pursue that unity.[16]

Being "a mixed Protestant and Catholic community" was unusual in the mid-1960s when the Community started, from what Anna Mae observed.[17] Some of the Catholics participating in Community life had no problem with intercommunion, but others were hesitant to receive the Eucharist from anyone other than a Catholic priest. Dorothy said, "It was a very sensitive time for the Community."[18] John sought to arrange for a eucharistic service led by a priest that would still be under the umbrella of the Community's various Sunday and weekday evening services. "I asked some of the activist priests in town and none of them were willing," he recalled.[19] Some may have feared discipline, or they may have declined to seek permission through whatever process it may have been granted.

Across town from Dupont Circle, in St. Anselm's Abbey in Northeast DC, a monk named Dunstan Hayden was struggling with what the changes in the church meant for his life as a Benedictine and priest. Dunstan grew up in a

15. Pedtke in discussion with Chris Nichols and Martin Johnson, September 2016.
16. Flannery, *Vatican Council II*, 452–70.
17. Patterson, in discussion with the author, May 2021.
18. Pedtke, in discussion with Chris Nichols and Martin Johnson, September 2016.
19. Schramm, in discussion with the author, May 2020.

suburban Catholic subculture in Chevy Chase, Maryland. His parish "was like every other Catholic church, except the pastor was very smart and he would make statements like, 'Now, we don't want to bother with things like bake sales. That's beneath us.' He realized there are an awful lot of doctors and lawyers and middle-class people in his congregation. So he played on that. The church was financially very sound."[20]

When Dunstan was a child, his school showed them movies about missionaries in the South Pacific. For him, it had the opposite of the intended effect: "All I could think of was, 'God, please don't send me to the South Pacific. I don't want to be a missionary on the islands of the South Pacific.'" What he did admire, by the time he got to the high school connected to St. Anselm's Abbey, was that "quite a number of the monks taught at Catholic University. So it was a combination of scholarship and religious life. And I wanted to be a scholar."[21]

He had "a conviction of being called." His older brother Hillary had already entered vowed religious life at St. Anselm's. First, though, Dunstan attended the University of Chicago and earned a bachelor's degree in "the great books." Like other students at the time, he was given the option of testing out of many of the courses. He passed enough of the preliminary exams that he earned his degree in two years. Graduating at twenty years old, "I immediately went into the monastery," he said. His life experience "was extremely limited."[22]

By 1966, in the months after the last session of Vatican II, at the monastery one of the few signs of the momentous shift was that the choir director had quit because he couldn't bear to give up Gregorian chant. The council documents had lifted up liturgy in vernacular languages rather than exclusively Latin, so the monastery began adapting its prayer and music to English. Dunstan took on this task, and began composing some simple music. He also became headmaster of the school. Amid those activities, "I received what I thought was an inspiration from the Holy Spirit, namely that our monastery ought to be active in the ecumenical movement." Dunstan said to himself, "This is an important offshoot of the Second Vatican Council, and somebody should be doing something. So it's my business to push for it." He went to the superior and said, "Father Abbot, we should be doing something ecumenical." He was assigned an ecumenical committee to chair. He called up some friends and said, "Give me the names of some

---

20. Dunstan Hayden, in discussion with the author, May 2020.

21. Hayden, in discussion with the author, May 2020.

22. Hayden, in discussion with the author, May 2020.

non-Catholic ministers." Coincidentally, they were all Lutheran. One of them was John Schramm.[23]

Dunstan invited the group of a half-dozen Lutheran pastors to come to vespers at the abbey and stay for dinner. "And then we went downstairs and we had coffee and I gave a little talk about monasticism."[24] John invited Dunstan to share that talk again with the Community, which he did. John also took the abbey up on its offer of a room for a weekly retreat for silence and study. "I went to the canonical hour services," John said. "Dunstan was one of the priests who came in with a cup of coffee and we got to visit every week." As John and Dunstan's friendship grew, Dunstan began attending the Community's retreats and worship.[25]

John asked Dunstan about having Mass for Catholics in the Community. Dunstan received permission from his abbot and invited them to come to St. Anselm's abbey and school on Sunday mornings. "In 1969 I finally decided, given the impetus of Vatican II and the different perspective for seeing things, that it really didn't make sense to pretend that we were all on opposite sides," Dunstan said. Dunstan didn't feel it was transgressive to have intercommunion. Yet it took some time for Dunstan "to begin to be identified with this ecumenical group and not feeling guilty about it." Having reached that conclusion, he made Communion open to "anyone who came to the service at the abbey, Catholic or not."[26] One Sunday at Community worship, Dunstan stood up from his folding chair in the basement and announced, "From now on, I'm taking Communion."[27] The group applauded, and other Catholics such as Dorothy then felt free to take Communion also.[28]

Dorothy noticed that the Community didn't talk much about the differences in eucharistic theology present among those gathered for worship. She remarked on it to Dora. Dora agreed that there was no discussion or argument over whether to have the Eucharist weekly, even as their beliefs about what it meant diverged. Dora pondered this: "When we gather, however, the experience of sharing this most precious of meals seems to take over, and we set aside our differences. Did Christ intend for this to happen?"[29]

23. Hayden, in discussion with the author, May 2020.
24. Hayden, in discussion with the author, May 2020.
25. John Schramm, in discussion with the author, May 2020.
26. Dunstan Hayden, in discussion with the author, May 2017.
27. Hayden, in discussion with Laci Barrow and Martin Johnson, September 2016.
28. Pedtke, in discussion with Chris Nichols and Martin Johnson, September 2016.
29. Dora Johnson, untitled selection in *Lenten Booklet 1989*, March 23.

ॐ

Anna Mae wanted to go to graduate school, and she needed to pass the test that most of them require. "I was, for the umpteenth time," she said, "trying to take the graduate record exams. And I'm very capable in every area except math." This despite her mother being a math teacher. Dunstan also taught mathematics, so she asked if he'd help her study. Anna Mae also started attending the eucharistic services Dunstan led.[30]

Somewhere in the mix of liturgy and mathematics, they fell in love. In 1969, Dunstan gave himself twelve months to decide whether he would leave the monastery or not. "He's a man of great integrity," Anna Mae said. "That was a very challenging year for him and for all of his fellow monks at the monastery, some of whom he talked with."[31] When Dunstan entered monastic life, "I thought I understood the institution to which I was being called. I found out it wasn't quite what I thought, and I found out that I wasn't quite the person I thought I was."[32]

Divisions deepened in the monastery. The Catholic Church after Vatican II was "going backward instead of forward," Dunstan said. "The monastery never came to terms with Vatican II because the abbot couldn't face it. So his solution was to straddle the fence, which didn't work." The monks were split between those who embraced the changes and those who did not.[33]

Dunstan had a soup in his head. The ingredients weren't easily separated. "It was a combination of finding the monastery an impossible place to live and being in love with a woman," he said. A man in his thirties, he realized his professional life stood in stark contrast to his personal one. He had a doctorate and had published books in mathematics. "I was a good teacher; I gave lectures all over the country and at teachers' conventions," he said. "Professionally, great success. Personally, a disaster. I realized I needed serious psychiatric help and it was impossible to get as a member of the monastery because the abbot didn't approve of such things." The abbot was an Englishman and "his version of how you dealt with the problem was you muddle on through."[34]

Dunstan had to choose a path. He had been at St. Anselm's for eighteen years—almost his entire adult life. "I decided I couldn't stay in the

30. Patterson, in discussion with the author, May 2021.

31. Patterson, in discussion with the author, May 2021.

32. Hayden, in discussion with the author, May 2020.

33. Hayden, in discussion with the author, May 2017.

34. Dunstan Hayden, in discussion with the author, May 2021. The vivid image of a soup in one's head comes from Hayden. The author merely changed the grammar.

monastery any longer," he said.[35] After leaving, "I was able to find a good psychiatrist. He was a great help to me, but also a great help were John and Mary Schramm and the early members of the Community of Christ. They gave me a picture of a better way to live."[36]

Only after Dunstan left vowed religious life did he and Anna Mae talk about getting married. At that point in his life, Dunstan was closer to his brother monks than his biological family. Anna Mae hadn't met his parents or other members of his "good Irish Roman Catholic family," most of whom were opposed to the marriage. One of his older sisters, who was "a much more independent kind of person," Dunstan said, "had no problem with it. The others realized what was happening and they couldn't do anything about it."[37]

Less than two weeks after Dunstan and Anna Mae became engaged, Dunstan's father died of a heart attack. Anna Mae, John, and Mary attended the wake. Family and friends had gathered at a large hall with chairs all around at the base of the walls. Dunstan's mother was at the far end. When Mary Mercedes Hayden saw Anna Mae enter, she rose from her chair and walked toward her, meeting her in the middle. She embraced Anna Mae and said, "I'm so sorry that this is the way we had to meet for the first time." Anna Mae was deeply moved. "What a gracious gesture on the part of a woman who had just lost her husband and whose son was leaving the monastery and the priesthood."[38]

A few months later, John married Dunstan and Anna Mae at the house outside the city where Community members often went for retreats. Dunstan's mother attended their wedding along with two of his siblings and one brother-in-law. Others stayed away, including Dunstan's older brother Hillary, who remained a monk at St. Anselm's Abbey.[39]

ɜ☙

The Community not only practiced ecumenism among Christians, it attracted spiritual seekers and people of other faiths. A few Jewish and Sikh people took part in some aspect of the common life. Mrs. Soon, a Buddhist woman who lived nearby, came to services once in a while. She didn't take

35. Hayden, in discussion with the author, May 2017.

36. Hayden, in discussion with the Community of Christ, September 2021.

37. Hayden, in discussion with the author, May 2021.

38. Patterson, in discussion with the author, May 2021; Hayden, in discussion with the author, May 2021.

39. Patterson, in discussion with the author, May 2021.

part in the Eucharist, but she liked the energy in the room. The Community did not attempt to create a joint set of beliefs. "Jesus is Lord" was the only creed. Even if individuals couldn't agree with that statement, they could be part of the group, and they all got along well.[40]

The Community wanted to honor the Jewish roots of Christianity. One way it sought to do that was to hold a seder during Holy Week, an idea some churches across the theological spectrum picked up. (Many think of the Last Supper of Jesus and his disciples as a seder, though seders were a later development of rabbinic Judaism.) Some trace the practice to the post-World War II era. The war was the first time many Jews and Christians developed relationships with each other as they fought side by side. In response to the horrors of the Third Reich, some Christians lifted up Jesus' Jewishness and the gifts of Judaism inherited by Christianity.[41]

On Maundy Thursday, the Community had a version of a seder with a liturgy it put together for the occasion. Participants read: "Christians and Jews celebrate their own feasts in their own ways and we can see in these celebrations the common bond of the symbolism of the Exodus. Jesus was a Jew and today we wish to draw upon the traditional Jewish Seder and the words of the New Testament to help us more fully appreciate Jesus' observance of His Jewish heritage, whose laws He kept." Rather than going through the Haggadah, they described what the Jewish liturgy includes for the Passover meal. They then included foot washing and Communion as is traditional for a Maundy Thursday service. The centerpiece of the table, one early Community liturgy specifies, was to be "a white frosted cake, molded in the shape of a lamb, or an angel food cake whose circular shape symbolizes eternal life."[42]

With such a wide variety among its people and kinds of gatherings, John Schramm sought a form for the Community that he hoped would bring greater unity. John proposed creating more opportunity for "smaller cellular units" focused on a particular mission, which would meet weekly and include worship—similar in structure to the Church of the Saviour. These groups would be in addition to a Sunday morning service. The question was, John wrote, whether it was essential to Christian community "for everyone to be together in the same room at the same time on Sunday morning for a worship service." If that wasn't a necessary feature of life together,

40. Schramm, in discussion with the author, May 2020; John Stewart, in discussion with the author, January 2021.

41. Perriello, "Exploring Christian and Jewish Connections," para. 4; McDannell, *Spirit of Vatican II*, 30.

42. "Maundy Thursday Passover Meal," 11 April 1974, in Community of Christ Papers.

they could create a practical option for multiple worship services that might yield growth in membership.[43]

The following issue of *Stance* offered several responses to the proposal. Dora had hesitations. She wondered if the proposal was turning to a religious rationalization rather than a practical conversation about finding a larger space so they could all continue to worship together.[44] Bob and Kathleen Keating, the couple who joined John and Mary in leaving the suburbs and moving into the city, each wrote an article in favor of the proposal in the following issue. They had moved to the adjacent neighborhood of Adams Morgan and saw an opportunity to host a house church. They saw such gatherings as an opportunity to "share most intimately the joy and frustrations" of their mission and witness, Kathleen wrote in *Stance*.[45]

A dissent in the same issue came from Don Bibeau, who came to the Community in 1966. An Indigenous Minnesotan who had studied at St. Olaf College, a Lutheran school,[46] Don was among the people who were "part of the Community and its various missions" yet were "quarreling with scripture, . . . who think that what the Church really needs is a wrecking crew." For such people, it removed "a large stumbling block" when they heard John say that "it is not a matter of the individual affirming Christ as Lord, but that the individual chooses to associate with a group or Community which does affirm that Christ is Lord." He agreed with the goal of welcoming new people, but "in order to do so I think the Community should strive to make the way as wide as possible, and definitely not anything straight or narrow." For Don, welcoming such people was a question of loving diversity among its participants.[47]

The Community adopted the small-groups plan proposed by John during 1967. Don observed a loss of "free spirits" who floated through the Community. "Not too many seem to come around anymore—not even to our parties!"[48] Don himself continued on the staff of *Stance*, becoming editor for a year in 1967–68. Not long after, he moved to Leech Lake Chippewa Reservation, working for the Lutherans and the ecumenical body the Minnesota Council of Churches. He continued to reflect on his time with the Community and in DC and his experience as an Indigenous person. Writing in *Stance*, he drew a parallel from the abandonment of the urban areas

43. Schramm, "Restructuring the Community," 5.

44. Johnson, "Some Hesitations," 3.

45. Keating, "Community Is—," 6.

46. Bibeau, "Learn Baby, Learn!" 2.

47. Bibeau, "Dissent," 1, 4.

48. Bibeau, "Dangling Conversations," 2.

called ghettos to areas on the reservations stretching for miles suffering from "the full-blown poverty cycle." The churches did little. The Catholics simply had Mass and the Lutherans were no different from an Elks or Eagles Club, "except in the clubs you can get more to drink." In contrast, in their lifestyle the Chippewa people "seem to practice Christianity without necessarily professing it. Not the theological or dogmatic variety of organized white religion, but the simple parabolic teachings of Christ." The dramatic contrasts included relationship to the land: it was "not merely real estate!"[49]

≈≈

Two years later, the Community was going through another of its periods of intense self-examination, seeking to figure out what form best served its goal of creative response to the world. There was also a practical concern: the Community was too large to fit into its rented worship space all at the same time. Valborg devoted a special issue of *Stance* to the topic, airing their dirty laundry, as they put it, and inviting readers from across the country and beyond to join in the conversation. She solicited writing from fourteen people with points of view as far apart as she could find.[50] People debated decision-making styles and the role of small groups and priors, who were lay leaders, one for each of the six worship groups.[51] The people present since the beginning lamented the inability to have the same depth of relationships with each other at their larger size. Whether continuing to divide into small groups while increasing communication among them, or some other solution, Mary wrote, "we must continue to struggle to be more than just another small church."[52]

Another person who weighed in was Rosemary Radford Ruether, a theologian who by that point already had a prominent voice on the left. She spent much of her childhood in DC's enclave of Georgetown.[53] In parochial school, she wrote, "I was earnestly taught by many a Catholic nun that I was 'the luckiest child in the world,' because I had been blest to have been born a Roman Catholic in America."[54] Yet she had a free-thinking mother and relatives from multiple faith traditions. In early adulthood, she joined

49. Bibeau, "Meeting of White and Red," 7.

50. Staff of *Stance*, "Editorial Introduction," 3–4; Schramm and Anderson, *Dance in Steps of Change*, 75.

51. McArdle, "Cutting the Umbilical Cord," 7.

52. Schramm, "Death Wish/Wish Dream," 7.

53. Ruether, *My Quests for Hope*, 13–15.

54. Ruether, "Piety of Political Repression," 11–12, 17.

the civil rights movement and activism against the war in Vietnam, and returned to DC to teach at the school of religion at Howard University, a historically Black school.[55]

As she attended various gatherings with Christians and other people of faith, people at times questioned why Rosemary remained Catholic or even berated her for it. She wrote: "Such people seem to have a stereotyped view of Catholicism, which they find incompatible with who I am. When I explain that this is a very complex community of a billion people, much of which is very compatible with who I am, this seems hard for them to understand." With some Protestants "who appeared to understand ecumenical mutuality," she discovered that they believed their churches to be superior, as though there were a competition among denominations. They acted "as if renewal was a sectarian possession, rather than a life process belonging to us all in our particular historical contexts."[56]

One such negative experience was with an Episcopal priest who assumed Rosemary wanted to join the vanguard of women seeking ordination but first demanded she "get with it" and become an Episcopalian. Rosemary stopped attending services in the congregation he pastored. "Our family joined the Community of Christ, an ecumenical church of Lutherans and Catholics," which was pursuing social justice, she wrote. "In this church Catholics and Lutherans were coleaders and members: one group was not the guest of the other."[57]

Having arrived in spring 1969, Rosemary shared her observations two months later in the special "community issue" of *Stance* in an essay titled "The Myth of the Community of Christ." Monthly Community meetings were as good a forum for communication as any she had attended, with a high level of participation as they "raised and bandied about" general issues, clarified statements in discussion, and made concrete decisions. Yet she observed frustration at the meetings, and she attributed it to unrealistic expectations for group interactions. She wrote, "Their minds fixed on the absent ideal, the perfectly adequate present was overlooked."[58]

Though she is known primarily as a feminist in many circles, Rosemary was breaking fresh ground in many areas related to liberation theology, said Larry Rasmussen, a Christian ethicist who joined the faculty at Wesley Seminary in 1972. They were at a meeting together and Rosemary

55. Ruether, *Women and Redemption*, 221; Ruether, *My Quests for Hope*, chap. 1, chap. 2. The name later changed to the Howard University School of Divinity.

56. Ruether, *My Quests for Hope*, chap. 2.

57. Ruether, *My Quests for Hope*, chap. 2.

58. Ruether, "Myth of the Community of Christ," 11.

told him that she and her family were part of the Community. She knew that Larry and his wife, Nyla, were Lutheran. There was a Lutheran group within the Community, but it was not the primary tradition, she told Larry, because there were Roman Catholics and other denominations as well.[59]

People in the Community observed that Rosemary didn't strive to fit into traditional gender roles. While they were volunteering with a Community group in the meal ministry at St. Stephen and the Incarnation Episcopal Church, it appeared to John Stewart that Rosemary didn't spend much time in any kitchen.[60] Rosemary and her husband, Herman Ruether, who was a political scientist who was called Herc, and their three children took their turn among the families hosting Community gatherings at their home. Mike Schramm became friends with Rosemary and Herc's son, David. In Mike's observation, "Rosemary was definitely the head of the household." The Schramm children were impressed by her, even as they were unaware of her being "one of the foremost feminist theologians," Karen said. "We just knew her as Rosemary." In group discussion in the living rooms of Community members or her own home, she would sit with her legs apart, smoking a cigarette.[61]

The adults found her formidable also. "She was a powerhouse in terms of her intellect and her personality," Margaret Thomas said.[62] Her presence when leading worship at her home was impressive. As was her analytical ability in Community meetings. "She held her opinions very fiercely," David Anderson said.[63]

One of those opinions related to direct political engagement versus artistic expression around social justice issues. Some core people in the Community saw the latter as one of the hallmarks of their life together. Rosemary advocated that the Community be more involved in grassroots activism.[64] As Rosemary engaged with various leftist groups, she believed it was pressing to cut through the fearmongering of international anticommunism and spread broadly the message of how ordinary people were not served by US policies. She urged Community members to work in advocacy and electoral politics—all rooted in a community. She wrote in *Stance*: "These are indeed

59. Larry Rasmussen, in discussion with the author, May 2022; Larry and Nyla Rasmussen, in discussion with the author, June 2020.

60. John Stewart, in discussion with the author, April 2022.

61. Karen Martin-Schramm, Kathy Schramm Falk, and Mark and Mike Schramm, in discussion with the author, March 2021.

62. Margaret Thomas, in discussion with the author, October 2021.

63. David Anderson, in discussion with the author, March 2021.

64. John Stewart, in discussion with the author, April 2022; Korinne Thompson, in discussion with the author, February 2022.

times to puzzle the best of us. We are never quite sure how our best instincts may be subtly blending with our worst. Perhaps our best hope is to have a critical community around us that can both vehemently argue with and vehemently love each other. That is the kind of community the Community of Christ has to be now more than ever."[65]

Even as she challenged the Community early on to appreciate what they had rather than pining for an ideal, Rosemary later joined those longing for a quality they felt was missing. In summer 1971, she wrote in *Stance* about a theme in her work at the time: the way that competition erodes community. Women have been socialized with a cooperative spirit, to be buoyed by successes of their family members, in contrast to the competitive spirit, seeing life as a zero-sum game. Related to this, Rosemary commented that she felt she couldn't share her successes in the Community. She perceived "a kind of uncomprehending or 'blank' silence" when she talked about aspects of her life and work, such as traveling to several cities in one week or speaking at Harvard.[66] Valborg, who was editor of *Stance* at the time, responded on the same page, gently suggesting that maybe the feelings of being "too much" came from within Rosemary. Rosemary may have misinterpreted the group's awe. Valborg respected Rosemary's church reform activism and accomplishments. Her only possible response was, "Yup, that's our Rosemary! She's our family!"[67]

Rosemary called herself a "somewhat uneven member" until January 1972, when she differentiated herself in "a theological reference group" along with Herc and another couple in the Community from a Catholic background, Allene and Ron Grognet. She wrote to the Community at large, "This is not exactly a 'Dear John' letter (ha!ha!), but it may be something close to it." She found the Community's social action involvements to be "too quietistic and tangential to what is really going on." Rosemary didn't have time to push the Community in the direction she had gone, since "in this group we move beyond what most of the Community are ready to handle theologically."[68] Attached to the letter signed only by Rosemary, their group shared with the Community a document all four of them signed, "A Call for a Group to Explore a New Human Perspective." They hoped to gather an interfaith group to "examine the religious traditions to see what resources can be salvaged from them." They eschewed the doctrine

65. Ruether, "Going Away," 14, 17.

66. Ruether, "From Competition to Community," 7.

67. Anderson, "Dear Rosemary," 10.

68. Rosemary Ruether to the Community of Christ, 10 January 1972, in Community of Christ Papers.

of Jesus as past or future Christ, believing that "none of the marks of defini-
tive messianic fulfillment actually came about with the work of the historical Jesus," they wrote. For Christian theology to separate the Messiah from
the Messianic Age had implications for social change movements, as the
Christian doctrine can be transposed to revolutionary groups with their
own expectation of fulfilled messianism after the revolutionary leaders are
in power.[69] Rosemary expressed hope for continued dialogue and connection between their group and the Community. That might be in conversation at congregation-wide meetings or sharing "a celebration, such as a
Seder at Passover time."[70] She continued to write for *Stance*, including on
international Catholic events.

It was one of several times Rosemary went beyond the position she
had held and the communities she was part of, which is perhaps necessary
for breaking new ground, noted her colleague and Community member
Larry Rasmussen. He saw the issue as one of the Community's focus on
individuals' gifts and callings rather than the identifying larger issues most
pressing at that moment. That gifts-driven model is different from saying,
"Here are the main issues and how we're going to organize around them."
The Community was relatively radical as compared to other groups that
were mostly white and middle class, Larry said, but it wasn't radical enough
for Rosemary "or anybody who was really cause-oriented."[71]

For Community leaders, the fundamentals of Christian faith were the
basis for social justice. Its commitments came out of its understanding of
what the church is called to be in the world. For example, Larry said, there
were strong feminists, but people didn't say, "This is a feminist community
that I'm joining." It was "the Community of Christ that I'm joining and it's
concerned about racial justice and gender justice and economic justice."
Rosemary did not hold the same core views on Christianity. Though "the
only confessional statement that people had in the Community was the
early Christian one, Jesus is Lord," Larry said, "if you've got an argument
with a Christology that isn't spacious enough, then you've probably got an
argument even with that."[72]

Beyond the basic confessional statement, the other unifying element
in the Community continued to be the Eucharist. That role became even
stronger after Catholics began communing with the whole group. The

69. Ruether et al., "Call for a Group."

70. Ruether to the Community of Christ, 10 January 1972, in Community of Christ
Papers.

71. Larry Rasmussen, in discussion with the author, May 2022.

72. Larry Rasmussen, in discussion with the author, May 2022.

Community changed its covenant. Instead of simply stating that all baptized Christians were welcome to receive Communion, it wrote that the Eucharist "both expresses and increases our oneness."[73] Lois McArdle, one of the Catholics, wrote in 1969 in *Stance*, "The more I muse on what draws the Community together, the more I return to a common attitude toward the Eucharist as the necessary magnet." Everything else was secondary, including social justice, she wrote.[74] One of the first Community business meetings that Larry attended was in 1972, while the Community was still in the basement space in Dupont Circle. John Schramm had a small table next to him with bread and wine. About halfway through the meeting, amid animated discussion, John paused. He consecrated the elements, and the bread and wine passed from one person to the next in the circle. The business meeting then continued. Larry was impressed by the tenor of the discussion in the meeting.[75] "If Dora Johnson didn't agree with Dunstan or David on something, she let them know," Larry said. "But disagreement is possible because you have something like almost spontaneously celebrating Communion."[76]

❧

Walt Scarvie, a musician-theologian with warm twinkling eyes recognized by his worn gold-colored houndstooth coat, joined the Community in 1967, bringing a wealth of gifts for liturgy. He had a strong Lutheran background and worked as Lutheran campus pastor to the universities in DC, spending most of his time at American and George Washington. Walt's understanding of the Lutheran tradition was that it was not in the business of building up Lutheran institutions, he wrote. Instead, they had a responsibility to redo the church for the sake of the gospel. This meant that no one can be theologically pure, and no structure or ceremony is perfect. Instead, he wrote, the form of church life and its liturgy come from human creativity.[77]

Walt noted that all liturgical language is borrowed, whether metaphors from ancient scriptures or fresh idioms from our daily lives. To have multiple people grapple with expressing their perception of God enriches

73. Covenant of the Community of Christ, January 1971, in Community of Christ Papers.

74. McArdle, "Cutting the Umbilical Cord," 7.

75. Larry Rasmussen, in discussion with the author, June 2020.

76. Larry Rasmussen, in discussion with the author, May 2022.

77. Korinne Thompson, untitled selection in *Lenten Booklet 2012*, March 7; Scarvie, "Adiaphoristic Principle," 3.

the individual and the community. Christian worship has three necessary elements: proclaiming the word, celebrating Communion, and gathering in the name of Jesus. These form the hinges on which the door of innovation can swing, Walt wrote.[78]

Creating liturgy was both an individual and a group process. Several people who wrote liturgy contributed them unsigned. They drew on the experiences of the gathered and in the act of worshiping with them the liturgies became a collective creation. For example, the Community's Ash Wednesday liturgy in 1969 and 1970 includes "A Litany for Right Now." Like the element of anamnesis in the ritual of the Eucharist, they remembered and brought into the present a moment, in this case the passion of DC in April 1968. "For the still charred streets of our city, the ashen and angry rubble of 7th and 14th streets," the Community spoke in worship, with the response "We ask your help, Lord." In 1970, they added physical objects to the litany, such as a piece from a burned building.[79]

Even their most self-consciously innovative liturgies built on the form that is common to Lutheran, Catholic, and Episcopal liturgy (and other traditions to varying extents). In one service, the Community heard Job 1:6–12 and then an ad lib reading from the day's newspaper. They then recited a confession written for the occasion. "O God our Father, we confess our feeling of powerlessness. We feel like Job, like pawns being moved about in some game we don't understand," the Community wrote. "We confess that we have often copped out. . . .We have excused ourselves by blaming 'the system,' the structures that move us that we can't control." In their Easter Vigil liturgy in 1969 they asked for help to know God as one who is beaten in police precincts, "who hangs on street corners, who tastes the grace of cheap wine and the sting of the needle, . . . who pays too much rent for a apartment because he speaks Spanish," who is sold out by political leaders of all stripes, and yet who is organizing people to transform the world.[80]

As Christians more broadly continued to read, write, and have debates about ecumenism when attempting to have worship together, perhaps at a conference or a meeting for dialogue, the Community shaped its services as a group. "Many people, I think, would say that as an ecumenical community, we were loosey goosey, but that's really not true," Anna Mae said. For people such as Anna Mae, who had always taken an interest in reading

78. Scarvie, "I Hear You Saying," 9–10, 16; Scarvie, "What Language Shall We Borrow?"; Scarvie, "Crisis of Belief and Liturgical Integrity," 21–24.

79. Ash Wednesday Liturgy 1969 and Ash Wednesday Liturgy 1970, in Community of Christ Papers.

80. Untitled liturgy, 26 February 1969, in Community of Christ Papers; "Of Darkness and Light," Easter Vigil liturgy, 1969, in Community of Christ Papers.

and studying liturgy, the Community made her a full participant in writing it.[81] In one, she wrote the prayer of confession, naming their struggles with broader issues of racism and classism, as well as ones specific to the Community: "We long for communion within and among us, and usually refuse those gifts of community offered us each day," Anna Mae wrote, "we confess we don't know the language of our faith. We do not speak easily in the words of the scriptures. We have not accepted the discipline of keeping alive the psalms . . . and the gospel of Jesus." Despite this, God called them to recognize the divine's presence in their lives.[82]

Anna Mae's liturgy includes a litany often recited in the Community, which gave them the phrase "dance in steps of change" that had a lasting place in the Community's life. Those gathered in worship praised God for human history, "for joy and pain that dance in steps of change." Echoes from Scripture and the life of the church resound in the litany alongside contemporary concerns of conflict in the world and in the church: "In spite of the schisms you have willed us one, we find your body in our corporate life. Be praised!"[83]

The litany's author was Mary Catherine Bateson, who spent half of the summer of 1966 living with the Schramms and worshiping among the gathered. A cultural anthropologist who was married to an Armenian American, she and Dora became friends while she worked on a handbook of the Arabic language published by the Center for Applied Linguistics. Mary Catherine was born in 1939 to anthropologists Margaret Mead and Gregory Bateson. Mary Catherine's mother raised her in a joint household with another family in New York City, which she lauded as teaching about community. "My mother created a village, and it was wonderful," Mary Catherine later said. "We didn't have sofas, we had beds with backs on them so my mother could always offer someone who needed it a place to sleep. So people came and went."[84]

Mary Catherine found like-minded people in the Community during a period of growth in her life. During her summer in DC, she reflected on a formative moment in her thinking about community. She was hiking in the Sinai desert with other American teenagers and members of an Israeli youth

81. Patterson, in discussion with the author, May 2021.

82. Anna Mae Patterson, "Liturgy of Prayer and Rejoicing," 10 November 1974, in Community of Christ Papers.

83. Mary Catherine Bateson, litany in "Liturgy of Prayer and Rejoicing," in Community of Christ Papers.

84. Patterson, in discussion with the author, May 2021; "Contributors" (August 1966), 3; Green, "Mary Catherine Bateson"; Green, "Anthropologist's Take on Homemaking."

movement. She was struck by the contrast between the movement's spirit of mutual aid and the message she had grown up with in the United States that asking for help was burdening others. One afternoon she grew dizzy. Several of the Israeli teenagers put her arms on their shoulders and helped her along. At first, she was angry at them, embarrassed. But the next day, able to walk again, she helped another teenager from New York, carrying her pack for her and having her lean on her shoulder.[85] Recalling that story in 1966, ten years later, "it has come to seem like a paradigm of community. Within Christ's body we seek a delicacy of community more careful of individuality," she wrote in *Stance*, "we do not really know that no one of us will be allowed by the others to fall in the desert. But somewhere on the other side of nakedness, on the other side of our last strength, lies the ability to walk and sing songs together as a people on the move, strangers and pilgrims at the frontiers of faith."[86]

Continuing in her life's pilgrimage, she observed that Christians have often focused on convincing others they are displeasing God. She came to believe that "divisions between the denominations of Christianity are all wrong." Instead, they are all versions of one truth.[87]

ৈ

In fall 1970, the Community called Dunstan to be copastor alongside John Schramm. "I was glad when Dunstan and I got to share the pastoral ministry," John said. Dunstan didn't go through any additional process to begin that role in a congregation that belonged to a Lutheran denomination. The Community simply accepted his Catholic seminary training and continued to treat him as ordained and called by God. The questions that did feel pressing were what it meant for the Community to call anyone as pastor. David wrote in *Stance*, "The Community has never been extremely articulate about the way it views the role of pastor within the Community's life nor the way it grants authority or develops leadership." Dunstan becoming pastor provided an opportunity to think through what that meant.[88]

85. Bateson, *Composing a Further Life*, 4–8; Bateson, "Strangers and Pilgrims," 1, 4.

86. Bateson, "Strangers and Pilgrims," 4.

87. Bateson, *Composing a Further Life*, 178.

88. Anderson, "Welcoming Dunstan," 2–3.

5

"Ministers to Each Other"

JOHN SCHRAMM THOUGHT SEVEN years was a good amount of time to be a pastor in one place. After that you either went on a sabbatical or you changed jobs. In the fall of 1972, John announced his resignation as pastor of the Community. He received a grant from the American Lutheran Church to start a peace and justice ministry. John and Mary also wanted more time to write, reflect, and tend to family life. They were making short trips to land they had in West Virginia. They moved to the old farmhouse there seven years after starting the Community.[1]

For most people in the Community, John had been different from other pastors they had known. To start, he did not "insist on the title of pastor, wear a clerical collar, or exercise authority in conducting business meetings," he wrote.[2] John Stewart recalled John saying, "People really want a bishop." What John Stewart understood from that was that "people want to be told what to do and he wasn't going to do that. So he thought it'd be best to wean his church from him earlier than later."[3]

David's childhood view of pastors was that they "were five hundred feet away from you, if not five hundred feet above you," he said. "You never saw them as people."[4] John started off on a different foot right away when David and Margaret Elsie came to DC. John picked them up at National Airport and they drove into the city at dusk, passing by the illuminated

1. John Stewart, in discussion with the author, January 2021; John Schramm, email message to author, March 25, 2023; Schramm and Schramm, *Things That Make for Peace*, 62–64.

2. Schramm and Anderson, *Dance in Steps of Change*, 15.

3. Stewart, in discussion with the author, January 2021.

4. David Anderson, in discussion with the author, March 2021.

monuments surrounded by cobalt sky. "The city seemed to glow with a radiance like nothing I'd ever seen before," David said. "We drove through the city to Cahill's, a bar and restaurant on P Street off Dupont Circle for a beer and a hamburger." The simple act represented "a kind of earthy hospitality that broke through some of the kinds of stereotypes of churches and pastors so prevalent at the time."[5]

From Larry's view as a theologically trained lay leader, John's leadership was well-suited for "a new congregation in the inner city." John's bivocational work for Lutheran Social Services during the years that he was pastor meant he was well informed about the needs of the city and how the Community might address those needs. "At the same time, he was never one to monopolize the Community," Larry said. "You have some leadership on important things that John did and then a way of the whole community taking responsibility for itself."[6] John encouraged Community members to think about the expectations they had for a pastor—especially a bivocational one—and to compare that with how they viewed anyone else in the Community and how they balanced job, family, and participation in Community life.[7]

To help Community members in that task, Valborg added a dose of humor with a poem in *Stance* attributed to a church calling committee:

> Thy car must be at least five
> years old and
> large enough to transport the
> picnic props; . . .
> We expect thee to study;
> to answer
> all questions relating to
> our problems.[8]

Though much of the poem lampooned traditional churches—with mentions of choir rehearsals, a building fund, and Toastmasters meetings—the Community was not immune from similarly unrealistic ideas. They needed a shepherd, not a religion expert or a psychiatrist, Valborg wrote. The Community wrote in its 1971 revised covenant that it called pastors "to share in the disciplines, ministries, and witness of the Community, regularly to proclaim the word of God, and to lead in the sacramental life of the

5. David Anderson, email message to author, March 20, 2021.

6. Larry and Nyla Rasmussen, in discussion with the author, June 2020.

7. Schramm, "Shared Responsibilities," 9.

8. Anderson, "Calling," 11. Same poem also in Anderson, *Thoughts, Faith, and Friends*, 8–10.

Community."[9] Valborg reminded the Community of the implications of the biblical model of Jesus as shepherd. "But how easily we forget the command that the same Shepherd gave to his disciples: Feed my sheep! Not me, the shepherd, but you—my followers—feed my sheep!" It was uncomfortable to take up that responsibility, Valborg wrote, and "it's easier to be told what to do, to hold daddy's hand."[10]

Likewise, Dunstan saw the goal of pastoral leadership as empowering laypeople. A pastor "can help people see things more clearly," to identify where mission work should be directed, where the obstacles lay, and how they might overcome them. It was the task of laypeople to do the work, though there was no reason the pastor couldn't also take part in it, as time and desire allowed.[11] This model for pastoral leadership was shared by like-minded Christians in the ferment of the 1960s. The Vatican II document *Gaudium et Spes* named clergy as guides rather than experts, and lifted up laypeople to engage in "the whole life of the Church" and live out their discipleship through their secular work.[12] To George Webber's *The Congregation in Mission*, which the Community read in its first year and regularly quoted in *Stance*, church had two dimensions: gathered life and dispersed life. The church is the people in worship and study, but they are equally being the church when they are working in the world.[13]

The Community of Christ initially used this language to refer to gatherings in Dupont Circle and those "dispersed" outside of the parish area. Then they picked up an agricultural metaphor, of the gathering of grain and the scattering of seed. The idea of being the gathered Community, later to be scattered, took root in the Community's common life. It was additionally strengthened through a liturgy that draws from the language of the Didache, an early Christian document. In its instructions on celebrating the Eucharist (giving thanks), it says, "Even as this broken bread was scattered over the hills, and was gathered together and became one, so let Your Church be gathered together from the ends of the earth into Your kingdom."[14] Walt incorporated similar language, from a eucharistic prayer by a Lutheran liturgist, into a liturgy commonly used in the Community. They became words many knew by heart.

---

9. Covenant of the Community of Christ, 1 January 1971, in Community of Christ Papers.

10. Anderson, "Shall We Share Our Shepherd," 4.

11. Dunstan Hayden, in discussion with the author, May 2021.

12. Flannery, *Vatican Council II*, 944.

13. Webber, *Congregation in Mission*, 58.

14. Riddle, "Didache," chap. 9.

In the early 1970s, when Korey Thompson met Walt, she was already part of conversations about the shape the church would take. She grew up Lutheran thinking that adults in the church gave more weight to reciting their preferred answers to the questions they posed, rather than youth understanding the message. Studying at Concordia College in Minnesota, the religion and ethics faculty opened up possibilities for the church in society. After graduation she served as a community worker in two congregations.[15]

Korey heard about the Community before she began attending. The Community was a celebrity in certain circles, with a reputation for being cool. "Community of Christ was held up as an example of a group that was strongly lay-led, even though there was clergy participation," she said. She was among those who were impressed by "the fact that it was an ecumenical and operational group that had had coherence and focus for many years, even at that point." Given its small size, the Community's presence in the wider church was larger in legend than reality, Korey said. Yet among those relatively few people, she found artists from many traditions who encouraged her to claim her gifts.[16]

Korey joined the group of forty-to-fifty adults and thirty-five children as John and Mary were leaving. Members such as Anna Mae struggled to accept the departure. "I was very attached to John and Mary," she said.[17] Within months of John's announcement, a group tasked with a plan for moving forward named "a very clear desire for calling a pastor." They leaned toward a full-time ordained person.[18] There was no interim minister trained to guide a congregation after a pastor leaves. "I think the Community kind of leapt into replacing John," Wendy said.[19]

After a pastoral search, the Community considered several final candidates in spring 1973, three men and one woman. Information on candidates mentions, in addition to the usual, items such as "involvement in local civil rights & politics has been limited, although study of and concern about 'the Third World' has been consistent. . . . Is comfortable with conventional terms such as 'Son of God,' 'Son of Man,' 'My Lord,' etc." They looked at a candidate who was a woman though not ordained—she worked as a consultant in an Episcopal church. Another candidate was listed as an "active participant in the peace movement since '65." One had a salary expectation of $17,000–18,000 (more than $116,000 in 2023 dollars). The person

15. Korey Thompson, in discussion with the author, February 2022.

16. Thompson, in discussion with the author, February 2022.

17. Patterson, in discussion with the author, June 2021.

18. "Second Report of the Process Committee," 14.

19. Wendy Ward, in discussion with the author, December 2021.

was "open to tent-making after a period,"[20] indicating willingness to have a second job through reference to the apostle Paul earning a living by making tents (Acts 18:3).

The Community chose a Presbyterian minister, Tom Luke Torosian, to be pastor. In a letter of call, Community members defined the role of pastor with ten points, many of them unsurprising: preaching and celebrating the Eucharist, providing initiative for studies and retreats, and participating in the Christian education of children. Indicating the Community's particular stance, the letter stated, "We would like our pastor to be someone who is willing to accept authority from us, but who is not willing to let us abdicate our own responsibilities as Christians and as members of this Community." Revealing even more about debates in the Community at that time, they wrote, "We feel that our pastor must be a Christian, confessing Jesus as Lord" at the beginning of the letter of call.[21]

Tom, like Dora, was only one generation removed from the terrors of the Armenian genocide. He was born in a public hospital in New York City and raised in the Bronx. His parents and a grandfather who lived with them were less assimilated than many immigrants. Yet, also like Dora, Tom received an education in notions of race and color in the United States when he went to the US South. "As a swarthy, first generation Armenian American," he wrote, he often felt out of place among people who were labeled white. He recognized his whiteness after he answered a call for ministers to go to Greenwood, Mississippi, to support the Student Nonviolent Coordinating Committee in spring 1964.[22]

When choosing Tom, the Community noted his ecumenical and interfaith background, and his "long history of social activism, including work with the East Harlem Protestant Parish."[23] Newly ordained in 1956, he coordinated youth ministry in six East Harlem congregations. Tom carried lessons from that time with him as he prepared to become pastor of the Community during the same years that EHPP was winding down. Tom felt strongly about the church not being merely a social club. With his experience in Harlem as well as being active with the Poor People's Campaign 1967–68, Torosian was attracted to the Community's commitment to a square-mile parish. He wanted to join in serving "an inclusive neighborhood of young

20. "Proposed procedure for the selection of a pastoral candidate," notes for Community meeting, 21 May 1973, in Community of Christ Papers. Today's dollars calculated with the US Bureau of Labor Statistics Consumer Price Index Inflation Calculator at https://data.bls.gov/cgi-bin/cpicalc.pl.

21. "Letter of Call for Tom Torosian," June 1973, in Community of Christ Papers.

22. Torosian, *Someday Yonkers*, 3–24, 95–97.

23. Anderson, "Tom Luke Torosian," 4.

and old, black and white, gay and straight, single and married, rich and poor."[24]

When Tom was installed as pastor in September 1973, he was forty-three years old, married to a woman named Peggy, and father to two teenage daughters, Tabitha and Rebecca. Unlike John Schramm, Tom received a salary. The initial agreement, for sixteen months, would include an annual payment of $17,400 covering income, housing allowance, pension, car allowance and medical insurance.[25] In 1974, the Community also gave them an interest-free loan of $12,000 for a down payment on a house, to be repaid monthly through June 1975.[26]

Tom was quite different in his style of pastoral leadership, preaching, and worship leading. Being Presbyterian, he didn't have the core of liturgical tradition that Lutherans, Episcopalians, and Catholics share. His homilies sometimes departed from traditional structure. For example, a sermon titled "Reassurance" wove together prose and poetry, ending with "We stand naked! / What do we do?"[27]

Another way he was not like John was that Tom didn't shy away from calling the Community "an experimental ministry." He continued the idea of supporting members in identifying their gifts and acting on their dreams. Tom also guided the creation of study groups, including on feminism and sexuality, and led the group examining gendered language in the liturgies.[28] Since the people skewed young, there wasn't as much need for pastoral visits to people who were homebound or hospitalized as occupies much of some pastors' time. But soon after Tom began as pastor, Wendy's mother died. Tom went to sit with her at her dining room table and read one of his poems as a way of offering pastoral care.[29]

Tom was candid, not pretending to be holy. After a retreat on prayer in April 1974, Tom said it was a time of growth, making him more open "to allow myself to think about prayer as a real possibility for my life."[30] No Community participant would have been surprised to hear that kind of statement from another in a small group or meeting, but coming from

24. Torosian, *Someday Yonkers*, 79–81, 127–28.

25. Torosian, *Someday Yonkers*, 90; "Letter of Call for Tom Torosian," June 1973, in Community of Christ Papers.

26. Minutes of Community meeting, 29 April 1974, in Community of Christ Papers.

27. Torosian, "Reassurance."

28. Torosian, *Someday Yonkers*, 127.

29. Wendy Ward, in discussion with the author, December 2021.

30. Hank Malinwoski, report on prayer retreat, 27 April 1974, in Community of Christ Papers.

the pastor it was unexpected. "Tom was honest about his struggles with the Christian faith," John Stewart said. "He talked about his doubts."[31]

Tom told Wendy, in an interview for *Stance*, that he experienced grace in his first year as pastor of the Community. "It has been a year when all the roles and pretenses of my faith were stripped away, and I found nothing there to hold on to," Tom said. "I began rebuilding my faith within the life of the Community. The Community allowed me—freed me—to do this." He cited Gal 5:1–13, freedom in Christ, as his scriptural basis for ministry. He saw possibility for the Community as a Spirit-based model of church. "The institutional church is tied to the American Dream," he said. "The times are ripe for a new church, and we are it."[32]

Tom asked for a review of his letter of call, and the Community evaluated his job description and performance. Some appreciated Tom's vulnerability and openness about struggling with faith. Wendy said that the Community did not want or need a charismatic leader, and that many in the Community found faith to be a challenge, not only Tom. Members raised that Tom didn't attempt to do all ten tasks they identified for pastoral leadership. Instead, Tom's year as pastor showed them their own capabilities. A major issue for some was whether Tom could affirm the lordship of Christ. They felt he was too focused on personal introspection and wanted him to be more biblically and gospel-oriented. Dora summarized: "The dominant question is feeling that our pastor should be a Christian preaching the word as revealed in the Old and New Testaments."[33] Valborg wrote afterward that while the discussion "brought out much of what people were thinking and feeling theologically, it must have been a horrible experience for Tom. He had asked for the review, but they can get more brutal than anyone realized."[34]

In the previous year, many people in the Community got along well with Tom, but some struggled. From what Margaret Elsie saw, Tom knew that he couldn't be John and that "the founder of something is always a unique person and is never really replicated." Still, she "didn't have the connection with him" that she had with John.[35] Anna Mae and Dunstan did not participate in choosing a new pastor since they were in Utah for several months with Dunstan teaching at Brigham Young University. After

31. Stewart, in discussion with the author, May 2022.

32. Torosian, "Tom Torosian Talks," 7.

33. Handwritten notes from Community meeting, ca. September 1974, in Community of Christ Papers.

34. Valborg Anderson to the Rev. Kenneth D. Baar, February 6, 1976, Community of Christ Papers, The Swarthmore College Peace Collection, Swarthmore, Pennsylvania.

35. Margaret Elsie Pearson, in discussion with the author, April 2021.

they returned, Anna Mae disliked Tom intensely: "It was a perfect example of when you live in a community, there's always one person who you wish wasn't there. And certainly when Tom was part of the Community, I was that person" for him.[36] She stopped going to worship for a while. Dunstan continued though he thought Tom's preaching was terrible.[37]

While Tom was pastor of the Community, he and Peggy ended their twenty-year marriage. For some in the Community, tensions in the family weren't apparent. For others, it felt as though they had to minister to Tom as much as he did to them. Some had side conversations about it, and a few attributed any deficiency they saw in Tom as a pastor to his marriage ending.[38] Dorothy Pohlman's first experience of the Community, in 1975, was an evening meeting in which members told Tom why they didn't like him as a pastor. At first, she was impressed, thinking, "This is a group that actually deals face-to-face with issues." She learned later that the level of directness that evening was unusual for the Community,[39] as with most congregations.

The Community in some ways was a "high-powered group: very highly educated, very opinionated people, and that's a tough situation to come into," Wendy said.[40] Some in the Community may not have given him a fair chance and he lost in comparison to John.[41] Nyla said, "There weren't clear expectations for us from him or for him from us."[42] Ann and Jim Doyle, members for several years, felt the Community placed great demands on its pastors. With Tom, "the pastor became the focal point for much of the frustration that exists (and perhaps will always exist) in a community as diverse as ours."[43] The Community was also bold to hire a full-time pastor, with the salary expectations that went along with that, amid its other financial commitments.[44] Members wanted to give away a substantial portion of their collected donations, as they did since their early days. Dora wrote, "It was a choice of either spending all our money on our internal life, or doing

36. Anna Mae Patterson, in discussion with the author, May 2021.

37. Hayden, in discussion with the author, May 2021.

38. John Stewart, in discussion with the author, January 2021 and May 2022; John Schramm, in discussion with the author, May 2020.

39. Dorothy Pohlman, in discussion with the author, February 2021.

40. Ward, in discussion with the author, December 2021.

41. Ward, in discussion with the author, December 2021.

42. Nyla Rasmussen, in discussion with the author, June 2020.

43. Ann and Jim Doyle to the Community of Christ, 16 March 1975, in Community of Christ Papers.

44. Minutes of Community meeting, 17 January 1975, in Community of Christ Papers; Judith Anderson Glass, in discussion with the author, May 2021.

without a salaried person and spending a good portion of the budget on external missions."[45]

Amid these struggles, Tom began looking for another job. He began another pastorate at a Presbyterian church thirty miles outside of DC, in a part of Maryland that was changing from rural to exurbs as developers bought up land from struggling farmers and turned it into housing complexes in the two decades prior.[46] "Weary and wounded," Tom felt "the need to separate myself from the freneticism of the city to reflect yet continue service," he wrote.

After Tom left, some said, "No, that was the direction we wanted and we wanted to continue being a seeker church." They embraced a seeker spirituality and were not comfortable calling themselves Christians.[47] The way Anna Mae saw it, some people saw their shared life "more as a commune than they did a Christian community."[48] Dunstan said, "Those who were less committed to Christianity, shall we say, and more interested in politics and women's liberation and socialism and some other things sort of drifted off the edges."[49]

Others in the Community wanted to be definitively Christian even as they saw themselves as non-dogmatic. They wanted to be able to ask questions from the basis of a Christian context.[50] Some people fitting that description stayed in the Community while others left for more traditional congregations. "The whole process was contentious, and I think people left because of the heated debates," Margaret Thomas said, as much as because of any stance they took within them.[51] In each case there was a different mixture of factors. By the end of the year, the Community had about twenty-five adults and eight children. Yet the change wasn't as dramatic as it might have been elsewhere, given the Community's structure in the preceding several years. Many who met in small groups didn't attend worship on Sunday mornings. One group continued to meet for years, even as half of them no longer worshiped with the gathered Community.[52]

45. Johnson, "Here We Are," 5–6.

46. Minutes of Community meeting, 27 January 1975, in Community of Christ Papers.

47. Pohlman, in discussion with the author, February 2021.

48. Patterson, in discussion with the author, May 2021.

49. Schramm and Hayden, "Community of Christ."

50. Dorothy Pohlman, in discussion with the author, February 2021.

51. Margaret Thomas, in discussion with the author, October 2021.

52. Schramm and Hayden, "Community of Christ"; Pohlman, in discussion with the author, February 2021.

Yet it was a loss when several leaders of small groups left, some by co-incidence rather than because of the falling out around Tom's pastorate. The small group constellations gave the Community vibrancy, Anne Yarbrough said. She joined the Community in Lent 1973 along with her husband, Doug Huron, and their infant daughter, Amanda. "There was this great sense of richness of the variety of worship styles," she said, "and worship traditions that were engaged in those small groups and the intimacy of those small groups."[53]

ﻉﺍ

Stephen White was a teletype operator for the press service where David Anderson was a journalist. Stephen also lived in three different group hous-es with David and Margaret Elsie. One they called St. Martin House, named after "St. Martin of Tours and St. Martin Luther King Jr."[54] Donald Bibeau and Marilyn Hoff joined them in practicing economic interdependence. Stephen was on the staff of *Stance*, writing about policy issues such as mili-tary spending or chemical and biological warfare, and pitching in with the typing. He took on specific roles as needed: carrying a heavy cross in a peace march, building a railing for Bill Anderson when he began having mobility challenges, and coming up with ideas for how to live more simply.[55]

He made forays into active involvement in the Community's religious life. One year he took part in the annual covenant ritual, committing to accept others in love and to "share the financial burdens of the Community of Christ and the needs of the world."[56] He was baptized on Christmas Eve 1969 along with two others. In Community meetings, he mainly listened. In one animated discussion, Dora said, "For some of us, after where we've been, the Community is the last ditch." Stephen replied, "Dora, for some of us, it's the first!"[57]

Bipolar disorder wasn't a common term in the Community's circles in the early 1970s. The illness didn't appear in mental health diagnostic

53. Anne Yarbrough, in discussion with the author, December 2021.

54. "St. Martin House," part of Covenant of the Community of Christ, ca. 1969, in Community of Christ Papers.

55. Covenant of the Community of Christ, n.d. ca. 1969, in Community of Christ Papers; David Anderson, in discussion with the author, February 2021; Margaret Elsie Pearson, in discussion with the author, April 2021; *Happenings*, 1 June 1975, in Com-munity of Christ Papers.

56. "Covenant of the Community of Christ," n.d. ca. 1969, in Community of Christ Papers.

57. Anderson, "One Man's Answer," 3.

materials until 1980.[58] "Much of Stephen's life was lived wide open, his ec-
static highs and his anguished lows visible to all," David wrote.[59] Yet at the
same time he hid parts of himself, "making him often a stranger to those
who thought they knew him best." Margaret Elsie remembered when Stephen "was up, he was so engaging." His charm shone. She said, "He was
unusually attractive as a person." Initially there wasn't an obvious pattern
with the times "when he was down." On one of those occasions, his mental
state altered by LSD, Stephen went alone into Rock Creek Park and ended
his life.[60]

Surrounded by that same park, the Community gathered on a June afternoon in 1975 on the lawn behind the space they were renting at the time.
Members created a liturgy "to both mark the death and celebrate the life
of our friend and acquaintance, Stephen, whose death touched each of our
lives—But more: whose life and works intersected our own and for many of
us helped shape the people we are." In litanies throughout the service, the
gathered responded, "We give thanks for Stephen's years among us, for the
gifts of his hands, his vulnerable heart." The service included readings from
Mahatma Gandhi, Thomas Merton, Henry David Thoreau, J. R. R. Tolkien,
and Kurt Vonnegut Jr., and a poem that Stephen had published in *Stance* in
1969. He ended with a mediation on "life, our only being." While they did
not celebrate the Eucharist, they shared a meal, "asking the blessing of the
Spirit that Stephen sought," the liturgists wrote. "If God was active in the
world for Stephen, it was in the community of people formed in the simple
but profound act of joining together to eat and drink."[61]

Though Tom was pastor at that time, John led the memorial service.
In part, it was because John believed that the Community members closest
to Stephen would want him there. John loved Stephen and felt he had been
a pastor to him, and he wanted to be the officiant. John spoke at length
about Stephen, his hopes and dreams. Instead of reinforcing the idea some
churches teach, that suicide is an unforgiveable sin, John preached about
the grace of God—as the notes still resounded from "Amazing Grace," sung
just before the homily. John said that God is more gracious than humans are
often able to be.[62]

58. "History of Bipolar Disorder," para. 11.

59. Memorial Service for Stephen White, 3 June 1975, Rosemont Center, in Community of Christ Papers.

60. Margaret Elsie Pearson, in discussion with the author, April 2021.

61. Memorial Service for Stephen White, 3 June 1975, Rosemont Center, in Community of Christ Papers.

62. John Schramm, in discussion with the author, March 2021.

On the grounds where the Community gathered, Wendy came upon John sitting and crying, saying, "This is so hard for me." Wendy wasn't accustomed to pastors showing emotion, let alone admitting something was difficult. The examples she had of ministers was that they were always in control or at least pretended to be. Amid the contrast, she was moved by John's expression of the pain of that day.[63]

❧

After Tom's departure at the end of 1975, the Community did not hire another pastor. "We decided it made more sense, at least temporarily, to experiment, to see if we could be ministers to each other."[64] It followed, Walt and David wrote, from the Community's involvement in "the twin movements of social activism and liturgical renewal that characterized the middle and late 1960s."[65] Through giving lectures to groups and writing for national publications, Walt contributed to the broader ecumenical conversation on liturgy and ritual based not only on his study but on what he saw lived out in the Community. Writing for *Liturgy* magazine, Walt and David described the Community's practice of small-group worship. They observed that a small group engaged the five senses more, including greater proximity to the bread and cup. Each person present shapes the whole gathering through their tone of voice as well as what they say, through their body language as well as their ritual actions. A small group also puts more pressure on leaders to come across as genuine, which requires preparation.[66]

Walt's faith that anyone in the Community could undertake that preparation and lead the liturgy was one expression of his robust theology of the ministry of the laity.[67] In a sermon on Jesus feeding the five thousand (Matt 14:13–21), Walt pointed out that "Jesus accomplishes much of what he does by working through his disciples." To those who might complain of having meager resources, Walt encouraged them to remember what Jesus said and did. "We might begin to say and do things differently."[68]

As the Community found its way forward, Walt and Dunstan each took some of the tasks usually carried by a pastor. Walt baptized the children born into the Community. He or Dunstan, or another person who

63. Wendy Ward, in discussion with the author, December 2021.

64. Schramm and Hayden, "Community of Christ."

65. Anderson and Scarvie, "Small Group Liturgies," 5.

66. Anderson and Scarvie, "Small Group Liturgies," 5–11.

67. David Anderson, in discussion with the author, February 2021.

68. Scarvie, Homily in the Community of Christ.

had formal theological training, consecrated the bread and cup for the Eucharist. Before beginning the eucharistic liturgy, the person put on a stole (while otherwise wearing their normal clothes) as a way of indicating their special authorization. If those individuals were absent, the gathered Community said the words all together. Several Community members noted the irony that in the Community laypeople interpreted Scripture and shaped their common theology yet reserved the role of celebrating the Eucharist for theologically trained people. Dora believed that consecrating the elements in the Eucharist involved "hocus-pocus" and thus was separate from the other tasks of leading worship.[69]

Some people had experience writing original liturgies or leading small group worship in members' homes. Yet incorporating language of social justice into a service is one thing, and creating a space in which people can connect with the divine is another. The Community jumped into the deep end, putting all of the regularly attending adults' names on a rotation to lead the service. They could opt out, but for the most part they began to do themselves what they had seen others do, in many cases for their whole lives.

After several years of the new practice, the Community continued finding ways to grow in their capacities as worship leaders. They created binders with their original liturgies, hymns and songs in a folk music style, and excerpts of prayers from sources other than the Lutheran Book of Worship, such as the Episcopal Book of Common Prayer. Walt and Dunstan, along with lay leaders David, Anne, and Larry developed a pair of two-hour workshop sessions on leading worship. They talked about how to avoid the dangers of ritualism, formalism, and "sloppyism." Anne noted that God's presence comes to us as it will in the liturgy. We can't control that and ought not pursue it through emotional manipulation. Original liturgies in the Community were wonderful, but the Community needed to see worship as embodied, not only "words, words, words," Walt stressed.[70] And worship is about more than being relevant, since it "both embraces and transcends time."[71] Ritual done well is a combination of the planned and the spontaneous.[72]

69. Dunstan Hayden, in discussion with the author, September 2021; Nyla Rasmussen, in discussion with the author, June 2020; Larry Rasmussen, email message to author, August 8, 2022.

70. Minutes of liturgy committee meeting, 1 January 1981, in Community of Christ Papers.

71. Scarvie, "Crisis of Belief and Liturgical Integrity," 18.

72. Scarvie, "Some Comments about Ritual," lecture series on aspects of the liturgy, in Community of Christ Papers.

Community practice of sharing worship leadership also included giving the homily. At Community Bible study, the group would talk together about the passages assigned—usually by the ecumenical lectionary, later called the Revised Common Lectionary, a compilation of texts for worship in Catholic and Protestant churches, with a Psalm, a reading from another book of the Old Testament, a Gospel story, and a selection from one of the New Testament letters. At its best, preparing a sermon allowed each person to practice listening for God's voice instead of expecting that to be mediated through the pastor or someone with special training. Dunstan saw the Community's approach to authorizing eucharistic celebrants as "a sensible way of proceeding," he said. "But having everybody or almost everybody take turns leading and preaching, that was an innovation."[73]

But great preaching it was not, most of the time. "There were a lot of bad sermons," Nyla said. "It helped me to understand that having a good sermon was not the essence of worship."[74] At times it was closer to the Community practice of a "shared word," expressing one's thoughts and feelings about some aspect of life or faith. Dora identified her talk as a shared word on an occasion when she spoke about difficulties in her work life, while saying, "I share because this Community has been very much a cornerstone from where I have taken that which I've learned and played it out in other arenas, principally in the workplace." Though apologizing that it was not a homily, Dora engaged the Bible lessons for the day, seeing a common theme of moving toward one's calling among Jeremiah, Jesus, and Paul.[75]

For some, it was intimidating, especially women who heard as children that they were not permitted to preach or teach a whole congregation. "The first time I preached, I was so scared," Bobbie said about joining the rotation the first year. But then she thought, "It's God's word speaking to the congregation." Like any homilist, her task was to be a channel for it.[76] Margaret Elsie was also terrified by "taking your turn," as they called it, a little ominously. After avoiding it for a while, she went all in and prepared a talk about religion and sex. She wore a light blue corduroy pantsuit. Her central point was that, contrary to what many of them had been taught, sex was not bad and there didn't have to be a conflict for a religious person. Everyone took her seriously, or at least "they didn't just laugh me out of the room." Dora responded in a group discussion, "speaking very directly to some of the joy

73. Hayden, in discussion with the author, May 2021.
74. Nyla Rasmussen, in discussion with the author, June 2020.
75. Johnson, shared word in the Community of Christ, in Community of Christ Papers.
76. Bobbie Stewart, in discussion with the author, May 2022.

of sex." Afterward, Margaret Elsie was amazed that she felt free enough with the Community to even think about addressing the topic.[77]

Sharing the task of preaching also transformed the practice of the Book of Disciplines (discipline being in the sense of spiritual practices) related to the Community's covenant. Disciplines included practices that shaped them as Christians, such as attending weekly study, going to a spiritual retreat once a year, or giving financial resources. One member, a city bus driver, fulfilled his discipline of praying for members of the Community while he drove along his bus route. It was a way of creating covenantal relationships, of accepting each other honestly and unconditionally. The book itself was a black loose-leaf notebook on the altar—itself a drop-leaf table—which was open every six months for people to sign or not.[78] "We committed ourselves to one another for six months, then it was all off and you decided whether you wanted to re-up again," Dunstan said.[79]

Initially, they symbolically dissolved the Community each six months. In theory, if no one committed to it again for six months or a year, the Community wouldn't have continued.[80] By the mid-1970s, the Community renegotiated the disciplines at a retreat twice a year. Larry recalled the conversation about what priorities were individually and collectively for the following period of time: "Keep this one. Don't keep that one. We should be thinking about something else."[81] To Dunstan, "it was just to motivate you to think again, What can I do in the coming six months?" In his view, the disciplines were options for growing in the Christian life, but not essential for everyone.[82]

If someone chose a discipline and didn't want to continue after a while, they simply stopped. There was no mechanism for accountability, especially if it was a solitary practice. Valborg noted, for example, that many in the Community said they lacked the ability to pray or time to go through each person's name one by one as named in the disciplines. "What would happen," she wondered, if all "let something else get squeezed out of our day" and set aside a regular time for prayer? Such repeated practices were necessary to build trust and acceptance among them. The notion that community is a gift had become "part of our rhetoric," Valborg wrote in *Stance*. She

77. Margaret Elsie Pearson, in discussion with the author, April 2021.

78. Schramm and Anderson, *Dance in Steps of Change*, 18–19; Ward, in discussion with the author, December 2021.

79. Schramm and Hayden, "Community of Christ."

80. Anderson, "Doing the Disciplines," 2.

81. Larry Rasmussen, in discussion with the author, June 2020.

82. Hayden, in discussion with the author, May 2021.

disagreed. "It seems to me to be something much more elusive . . . it might be described as a gossamer web—made up of many fragile threads—that binds us together."[83]

Throughout the 1970s, the practice of the Book of Disciplines became less and less formal. There was a gradual shift in emphasis from an individual moment of re-commitment to continued collective discernment. Some aspects were absorbed into the new shared responsibility of preaching and leading worship. It became a discipline for which people signed up by agreeing to be on the rotation again, or joining it for the first time. Most people took part in that. Small group worship petered out—at least as worship constellations of the Community. The Community began meeting as one group on Sunday mornings. On a weeknight, there was Bible study at Valborg and Bill Anderson's home.[84]

Pastoral care also became more of a shared task. This had been happening since John and Mary's departure, which "provoked people to become even more responsive to and relying on each other," Margaret Elsie said.[85] Dora was already a pastoral figure, the confidant of many who sought her out unique combination of making people feel loved and challenged at the same time: she was brave enough not to simply tell them what they wanted to hear. Dora encouraged Margaret Elsie and David to sort things out when they were unresolved after their relationship had ended. When they finally divorced, Dora supported everyone.[86] One of the earliest Community members, Linda, turned to Dora when her first marriage ended. Her mother told her, "No one in our family has ever gotten a divorce." Linda felt embarrassed and "didn't know what to do." Dora listened and then replied that she could see the marriage was never the right one for Linda anyway. "She told people for me, and that was that," Linda said. "Everybody accepted it."[87] When Linda married Charles Wells, in 1969, Dora was among the Community members who offered music and readings. The celebration was shaped by the Community's liturgical style—such as having the Eucharist be shared with bread and cup from person to person, and the passing of the peace with the words, "The peace of God is yours this day."[88]

83. Anderson, "Community: Minority Report," 5–6. Ellipses in original.

84. Anderson, in discussion with the author, November 2022.

85. Margaret Elsie Pearson, in discussion with the author, April 2021.

86. Pearson, in discussion with the author, April 2021; John Schramm, in discussion with the author, March 2021; Gail Taylor, in discussion with the author, February 2021.

87. Linda Wells, in discussion with the author, November 2021.

88. "Celebration of Marriage: Linda Fischer Alderman and Charles Talley Wells," 29 November 1969, in the author's possession.

6

"An Urban Village"

As an outgrowth of Dora and Bruce's commitment to integration, they felt strongly about moving into a neighborhood that had been abandoned during white flight. They chose Mount Pleasant, buying a home there in the waning months of the 1960s.[1] Once a wealthy neighborhood, with stately single family homes and brick row houses built in the Victorian era on its tree-lined streets, starting in the 1920s Mount Pleasant had a citizens association enforcing restrictive covenants that barred a house from being sold to anyone who wasn't white. The first African Americans to move into the neighborhood, a physician and his family, came in 1950, two years after the Supreme Court struck down such covenants. Many white homeowners moved away, both old-money families and more-recent European immigrants. Churches moved to the suburbs also, some selling their buildings to African American congregations. In the twenty years after that Supreme Court decision, DC went from being 35 percent Black to 71 percent. That was not the result of population growth; there were three quarters of a million residents from 1960 to 1970.[2]

In Mount Pleasant, the change was especially evident: it went from having one African American family in 1950 to being 70 percent African American two decades later. The perceived value of real estate changed during the same period, and the same houses and apartments now cost less. That attracted young adults such as those in the Community, most of them

1. Alicia Koundakjian Moyer, in discussion with the author, September 2021.

2. Cherkasky, *Mount Pleasant*, 78, 95, 101; Asch and Musgrove, *Chocolate City*, 245, 291, 383.

white,[3] who had a lot of education but not necessarily a lot of money. Bruce was in the real estate business and helped other Community members find homes among the two- and three-story row houses. He would give them a pitch: "We're all buying houses in Mount Pleasant. It's a great deal, you know, they're really affordable."[4] In the following several years, families who had been in the Community as well as newcomers all moved into the neighborhood. Several households even purchased homes on the same block of Monroe Street.

Community members were among the group of artists, social justice activists, new immigrants, and young professionals seeking a culturally diverse neighborhood.[5] Mount Pleasant and Adams Morgan were "Washington's only truly polyglot communities" in the mid-1970s, with a larger Latin American population than anywhere else in the city.[6] Activists and artists, including some in the Community, organized group houses on every block in the late 1960s and 1970s. Living together made housing even more affordable and involved some amount of community relationships. With the mix of cultural groups, some middle-class white people in other areas saw Mount Pleasant as dangerous.[7] For Anna Mae, as she commuted to and from work and walked around, there were "a lot of different colors of people, a lot of different ages on the street, and we felt very safe because there was just so much life."[8]

One of the area's major commercial corridors remained scarred after the "April 1968 riots left a trail of burned-out storefronts and wrecked apartment complexes" on 14th Street. Yet from such ruin and "the void created by white flight, against an inefficient and often indifferent city bureaucracy, DC residents sought to shape a new, racially egalitarian, and economically just city."[9] Some of the Christians among them were asking, "What is a way of being church in a society that is in the midst of so much change?" Larry said. Mission groups from the Church of the Saviour, which ran a coffee shop and bookstore, Potter's House, on another major stretch—Columbia Road—then bought and renovated two rundown apartment buildings nearby, turning them into affordable housing. A few blocks away, the

3. Cherkasky, *Mount Pleasant*, 101; Asch and Musgrove, *Chocolate City*, 383.

4. Anne Yarbrough, in discussion with the author, December 2021. Confirmed with Moyer and Martin Johnson.

5. Cherkasky, *Mount Pleasant*, 114.

6. Smith, *Captive Capital*, 14, 79

7. Cherkasky, *Mount Pleasant*, 101; John Stewart, in discussion with the author, April 2022; Morley, "Mount Pleasant Miracle."

8. Anna Mae Patterson, in discussion with the author, June 2021.

9. Asch and Musgrove, *Chocolate City*, 388, 391–93.

Community for Creative Non-Violence started in 1970, coming out of the radical Catholic tradition.[10] In 1975, two social-justice-oriented evangelical groups, the Sojourners community and Community of Hope, began neighborhood programs in Columbia Heights bordering Mount Pleasant and Adams Morgan. It was part of the ferment of the time, and it drew people such as Larry and Nyla to the area when they moved to DC in 1972, purchasing a home in the neighborhood.[11]

As the number of Community households in Mount Pleasant grew, and a worship group started there, it sparked the question of whether the square-mile parish model was still part of Community life—and if it was, if that was still in Dupont Circle. The Community ended the tutoring program for public school children in its parish area after several years. Valborg pushed them to think about why. "Did we let it die because it was not glamorous enough? Because there were no dramatic results? " she wrote. "Because someone called it a 'band-aid' operation?"[12] Community participation in the integrated neighborhood group also waned. Alexander Dobbins, a young Black attorney who joined the Community and became president of the Lincoln Civic Association, wrote in *Stance*, "Is the Lincoln Civic Association just another project in which the Community of Christ provided 'seed' participation and then dropped?" Dobbins called the Community to return more of its energy to the parish area it set out when it began.[13]

Complicating these questions further, the Community's landlady sold the house in Dupont Circle where the Community had been meeting in the basement since its early days. Dupont Circle was changing with developers constructing high-rises. One opened at 21st and N Streets in 1967 across from where the Community worshiped. The Community looked for a new rental space and settled on one two miles north, in a multicultural day care center called Rosemount.[14] It was in the northwestern corner of Mount Pleasant.

Several months later, an eleven-room storefront building came on the market in the main commercial stretch of the neighborhood. Among the businesses there were the landmark Heller's Bakery started by European immigrants, several Black-owned stores, and a growing number of shops

10. Sims, "Creative Non-Violence in Community," 7–8.

11. Asch and Musgrove, *Chocolate City*, 391; Nees, "What's in a Name?," paras. 1–2; Larry and Nyla Rasmussen, in discussion with the author, June 2020.

12. Anderson, "I've Got the Circle on My Mind," 6.

13. Dobbins, "Just a Reminder," 13.

14. Willmann, "High-Rise Living Area Grows"; Stewart, in discussion with the author, April 2022.

serving Latin American immigrants. The building named La Casa was previously a restaurant and nightclub. Its sign boasted "dancing nightly." Built in 1902 as a stately private residence, by 1973, it was empty and vandalized.[15]

A debate stirred up people in the Community. Would they stick to not owning a building out of principle? A decade earlier when the Community formed, they determined that remaining free to change their time, form, style, and place of worship gave them flexibility and openness.[16] To support that, the Community's original covenant stated, "We will worship the Lord in homes or in rented space, and no church building shall be constructed for the worship services of the Community." At that time, they believed "that God has called us to this particular square mile"—from the National Mall to P Street NW and from 17th Street to the Rock Creek Parkway—and a commitment to all who lived there, transitional though some residents were.[17] Though the Community updated its covenant in 1971 and removed the geographic boundaries, those ideas remained strong for some. Would it be abandoning those commitments? Or was it a sign of the flexibility and openness they also held dear to reevaluate even the few characteristics they thought would not change?

The Community gathered at Rosemount Center, where they were renting space, and settled in for a long meeting about whether they'd buy La Casa.[18] "It was not a conventional church building," Doug wrote, but many initially objected to owning any building where they worshiped.[19] Phil Wheaton, an Episcopal priest who lived in the neighborhood and knew various Community members through religious activist groups, came to speak in favor of the Community buying La Casa. Phil argued that if the Community didn't buy the property, a developer could snatch it up and possibly demolish it to build apartments or condos. At that time such practices were beginning as some developers sought to make their income from turning an affordable neighborhood into a gentrified one. Phil's argument convinced Bobbie, who had moved to Mount Pleasant with John earlier that year.[20] Anna Mae agreed: "We decided not only that we didn't want the

15. Cherkasky, *Mount Pleasant*, 114; "Information about Community of Christ and La Casa," 24 April 2016, in the author's possession; D'au Vin, "NW Group Shows Big Deeds," D8.

16. Schramm, "Community of Christ," 21.

17. "Covenant of the Community of Christ," 21.

18. Judith Anderson Glass, in discussion with the author, May 2021.

19. Huron, "Putting the Burden Behind Us," 5.

20. John and Bobbie Stewart, in discussion with the author, January 2021; Patterson, in discussion with the author, June 2021.

developers to develop it," but they wanted it to be a place for ministry and mission for the Community and others.[21]

Another persuasive factor was the storefront space with large windows opening out onto Mount Pleasant Street. The Sign of Jonah art and gift shop would nearly double its square footage.[22] "Ultimately all agreed that La Casa, with its many rooms, could serve as a worship area for the Community," Doug wrote, and provide low-rent space for a "potpourri of alternative shops and offices" for nonprofits.[23] Dunstan saw that as mitigating the Community's concerns. "That was what was the big counterbalance against the original decision not to buy a building, because then you put all your resources into the building and we weren't going to do that," Dunstan said. "We were going to make the building available to others."[24] The building would be a community center, not a church, but "the fact that we gathered in worship there would be a testimony," Margaret Elsie said.[25]

Though committed to not owning property, the Community had already compromised once to own the parsonage where the Schramms lived. After they moved, the Community sold it for $50,000 in early 1974. That was the total cost to buy La Casa, though the Community had other expenses, including a full-time pastor at the time. They took a loan of $45,000 from a friend of the Community, Jesse Aiken. The $5,000 down payment came from its dream fund. It was Margaret Ann Hoven's dream to start a day program for adults with developmental disabilities. It would be a place for them to discover their capacities and engage with others, and not merely be babysat—and even that wasn't a widely available option at the time.[26]

❧

Antelope, Montana, in the 1950s was about as rural as it gets. To Margaret Ann, it was also an idyllic place to grow up. On their family farm, where they raised wheat and cattle, chores were not too heavy or out of balance with time to explore and play outside. Farms were often small in those days. The second of five children, she especially enjoyed riding in the grain truck

21. Patterson, in discussion with the author, June 2021.

22. Judith Anderson Glass, in discussion with the author, May 2021.

23. Huron, "Putting the Burden Behind Us," 5–6.

24. Dunstan Hayden, in discussion with the author, May 2021.

25. Margaret Elsie Pearson, in discussion with the author, April 2021.

26. La Casa building report, 14 February 1974, in Community of Christ Papers; Margaret Ann Hoven, in discussion with the author, August 2021; Hoven, Life Skills Center report to the Community, March 25, 1974, in Community of Christ Papers.

at harvest time. The small Lutheran church in town and the Sons of Norway fraternal organization were central to life. The social and religious aspects of church were intertwined. She thought of Easter as the day she received a new bonnet and dress, ate breakfast in the church basement, and waited with her grandmother for their turn at the Communion rail. She felt God watching over her.[27]

As a student at Concordia University, a Lutheran school, she entered an exchange program with a historically Black school, Virginia Union University. She and some of the other Concordia students in Virginia who were part of an effort called Listening Witness went into DC and visited the Community of Christ. Margaret Ann joined those visits in summer 1969.

She loved to sing since she was a child and she dreamed of moving to New York City or Hollywood, California. She saw them in the movies. She spent a summer as a nanny on Long Island, and she was drawn to the city, but she felt timid. When she visited the Community in DC, she found a small, friendly group of people. Even though it was the big city, it was easy to be part of the Community. It offered a path that felt safe, even for "a scared person from Montana." In 1970, after graduating from college, she moved to DC along with a few classmates, among them Wendy Ward, and joined the Community when she was twenty-one years old.

Margaret Ann found a job with children and youth with developmental disabilities. She learned that by the time her clients reached her age, there weren't continuing services for them. There were approximately five thousand adults with developmental disabilities in DC without work or educational opportunities.[28] They were labeled as having "no vocational potential."[29] Margaret Ann thought, "I could start a program for those folks."[30] She resigned from her job in fall 1973 and began planning for a program that would be in La Casa after the Community purchased the building. She asked for two rooms on the second floor, along with a small kitchen, which would have to be put in. She was unsure where the boldness came from that made her think she could do it, being twenty-four years old and with limited experience.[31] But the Community didn't see anyone as too young to discern their gift.

27. Hoven, in discussion with the author, August 2021; Hoven, email message to author, August 16, 2021; Hoven, untitled selection in *Lenten Booklet 1987*, April 18.

28. D'au Vin, "NW Group Shows Big Deeds," D8; Hoven, Life Skills Center report to the Community, March 25, 1974, in Community of Christ Papers.

29. "Life Skills Center," program brochure, ca. 1980, in Community of Christ Papers.

30. Hoven, in discussion with the author, August 2021.

31. Hoven, report to the Community, November 26, 1973, in Community of Christ Papers; Hoven, in discussion with the author, August 2021.

Margaret Ann started Life Skills Center with those two rooms and two clients: their parents saw her newspaper ad, interviewed her, and trusted her with their sons. The Community was her only source of income initially, giving her $1,800 annually, partly so that she could be paid some salary, even $100 a month.[32] Getting grant money proved difficult—"for the most part, institutions (private and public) continue to pat Life Skills on the head and say it's doing a good job, and refuse funds to allow it to grow," Dora wrote.[33] The Community continued to give donations to Life Skills in addition to rental space at well below market rate. Life Skills also asked for assistance from the Community with advocacy, writing to the DC city council in support of a bill to aid people with developmental disabilities.[34]

Like the Community as a whole, Life Skills never intended to get large. Instead, it provided "a small, home-like setting" as its learning environment.[35] At first participants learned survival skills such as writing their own names, calling 911, and crossing the streets. Later the program expanded to include computer basics and creative expression through music, art, and drama. The staff became bilingual, speaking English and Spanish, as the neighborhood changed. They helped families navigate getting services for their loved ones with disabilities.

Through getting to know the adults in Life Skills, Margaret Ann engaged the world with a deeper ability to see "the differences and the value in every human being." One day as she walked with a few of the clients, someone on the street made fun of one of them. Another client recognized what happened and said to the man who had been mocked, "Don't pay them any mind. That's what I do." Margaret Ann saw clients who had previously been abused, angry, or afraid blossom as they grew in their capacities to express themselves and learn new activities—like making grilled cheese sandwiches for eight without help. These accomplishments came after struggle, with many struggles for Margaret Ann along the way, too. "I have learned a serious lesson—it is not what you know or how you behave that makes you a whole person, but how fully you use the gifts you possess and how you share love and friendship. My life would be less whole" without the people of Life Skills, she wrote.[36]

32. Hoven, in discussion with the author, August 2021; Life Skills report for Community meeting, 27 January 1975, in Community of Christ Papers.

33. Johnson, "Here We Are," 5–6.

34. Life Skills report for Community meeting, 9 October 1978, in Community of Christ Papers.

35. "Life Skills Center," program brochure, ca. 1980, in Community of Christ Papers.

36. Margaret Ann Hoven to the Community of Christ, 11 October 1978, in Community of Christ Papers.

While she worked in La Casa during the week, Margaret Ann was also the primary music leader on Sunday mornings. Seated and playing guitar on one side of the worship space, she led the small group of other musicians and brought in the congregation from among the people rather than the front. Her style was dynamic with call and response and other interaction. The songs they chose—weaving together bluegrass, spirituals, and folk hymns written in the 1970s by composers such as the St. Louis Jesuits—and the way Margaret led them changed how the Community was singing and how music shaped the service.[37]

It was also a way of relating to their neighbors outside of the building. There were many people who were homeless living on Mount Pleasant Street near La Casa, some listening as Margaret and the others sang. One winter, during a cold stretch, three people died on the street in Mount Pleasant. Margaret recorded the Stanley Brothers song "Who Will Sing for Me?" and dedicated it to them. During Holy Week, Margaret Ann and others from the Community took part in a Good Friday Stations of the Cross with other neighborhood churches. Margaret would sing "Tramp on the Street." When Hazel and Grady Cole released the song in 1939, the word *tramp* meant someone who had no permanent address. The lyrics compare such a person to the biblical Lazarus at the rich man's gate and to Jesus. The final verse alludes to Matt 25: 35–45, asking present-day listeners how they would respond if Jesus knocked on their door. Would we let him choose what he wanted from our pantries? Or would we turn him away hungry? Would we leave Jesus to die on the street?[38]

David and Margaret Ann, who married in 1976, led the Good Friday service together for many years. David would preach for the evening Tenebrae service punctuated with silence and ending in darkness. "These are Caesar's hours," he would say, inviting listeners to dwell in the pain after the crucifixion without the assurance that resurrection would come. Margaret would sing "Were You There When They Crucified My Lord?" After the service ended, those who had gathered would exit onto the sidewalk on Mount Pleasant Street and watch the procession from the Shrine of the Sacred Heart, the Catholic church in Mount Pleasant. Parishioners filled the street, carrying candles, a statue of the Blessed Virgin Mary, and a figure of the crucified Christ presented as though he was the deceased at an open-casket funeral.

---

37. Community of Christ hymn binder, in the author's possession; Andrew Wells-Dang, in discussion with the author, December 2021.

38. Cole and Cole, "Tramp on the Street."

One year as she prepared for Lent, Margaret Ann struggled to find time to write down her reflections to share with the Community about waiting for Easter amid the mess and stress of life. "It is a little hard to be thoughtful these days—these years." She recalled how she felt God's care as a child. "Does God watch over me like he used to? Maybe it just feels different because God is not a He anymore." Nevertheless, she concluded, Easter gives the chance to try again in the life of faith.

                                            ❧

With no steeple, cross, or stained-glass, people passing by La Casa might think it was still a restaurant. Or so some in the Community feared.[39] Rudy set to work designing a sign to place near the front door at street level, visible to people passing by. He considered several options, including a flower symbol and the words "celebrating life" or the distinctly Christian message "He is risen" along with three crosses on a hill. The final sign simply named the new owners, the Community of Christ, accompanied by a blue fish.[40] The symbol, used by Christians since early centuries, stood in for more obvious marks of being a place of worship.

Rudy shared his gifts as an illustrator in nearly all aspects of Community mission. In 1971 he left a Lutheran church in suburban Virginia because of "our conflicting interpretations of Christian life and action, particularly in response to the social needs of our times."[41] And in 1973 he retired from the US Forest Service, where he had worked since 1933 and was the primary person responsible for Smokey Bear, a humanlike figure who educated people through television, posters, and magazine advertisements about preventing forest fires.[42] As he looked at images he drew of Smokey, "his eyes especially haunt me with a reproachful look, saying something like, 'Why are you people doing all this horrid stuff to God's Creation?'"[43]

Rudy found in the Community a place where he could connect with others for whom environmental politics and faith were intertwined. As the 1970s began, Community members spoke aloud their "visions and nightmares" for the decade. Members raised concerns about pollution,

39. Valborg Anderson to the Rev. Kenneth D Baar, 6 February 1976, in Community of Christ Papers.

40. Rudolph Wendelin sketches, private collection of Elizabeth Wendelin.

41. Rudolph Wendelin to Our Savior Lutheran Church, 24 December 1969, private collection of Elizabeth Wendelin.

42. Sierra Club, "Rudolph Wendelin."

43. Wendelin, "Trinity Sunday."

overpopulation, and starvation in the developing world.[44] They were already engaged in consciousness-raising efforts about hunger and nutrition through weekly "poverty meals," in which the people cooking sought to put together a meal with the same amount of money that a person receiving welfare assistance in the United States at that time would be getting. For example, it could be 37 cents per person for the meal. This opened up participants to a deeper understanding of global economics and the role of US policy in protecting profits while many remained malnourished and at the mercy of market prices for food. The Community sought to avoid being another comfortable American church ignoring uncomfortable times.

The Community's efforts flowed into its desire for a deeper shared life: economic interdependence was a way to use resources more wisely and strengthen community bonds. From the beginning, the Community had an undercurrent of cooperation and communal living,[45] expressed largely through having a square-mile parish area and sharing the costs and profits from the Third Day and the Sign of Jonah. The Community was the first group Larry and Nyla were part of where some people moved to a new city to join the common life. Larry and Nyla were impressed by "the level of commitments on all fronts."

Yet members raised the need to become more economically interdependent if the Community was to continue being countercultural, given the overconsumption of resources all around them.[46] Dunstan wrote, "Though we are Christians, the economic dimension of our lifestyle is scarcely different from other middle class Americans; and that leaves us uneasy."[47] They asked how they could responsibly use the world's resources and engage in mutual support in the Community at the same time. First, they broke a taboo for most groups: "we took turns stating explicitly how much money we make, how we spent it, how we feel about how we spend it," Dunstan wrote, "and it was surprisingly pleasant to be candid."[48] Then they looked at how far they wanted to go. At the one end of the spectrum was pooling their salaries entirely or in large part.[49] Some peer communities followed the model seen in the New Testament book of Acts, turning over their whole paychecks to

44. Anderson, "Ecology Is Where It's at," 3; one of many examples of those themes in *Stance* in those years.

45. Mosher, "Signs of the Times," 15.

46. Huck, "Community of the Empty Garbage Can," 7.

47. Hayden, "Economic Interdependence," 13.

48. Anderson, "Mission and Economic Interdependence," 7.

49. "Alternatives Project," 2 September 1973, in Community of Christ Papers.

be distributed by collective agreement. (They also argued, for example, about whether a particular member really needed a new pair of socks).

Holding possessions in common (Acts 2:44; 4:32) did not have to be all or nothing. It was not the Community's style to "plunge everyone into a commune," David wrote. What was the Community's style was to encourage each other, as Dunstan wrote, "to be open to the call of the Spirit."[50] That might lead to dramatic changes for a household, and members could reach out to others in the Community to see if they felt the same call. For everyone, they could save resources by sharing goods and skills, which would allow them to give away more money to needs outside the Community. Dunstan gave a prime example of a shareable item, asking, "Unless someone is a waffle freak, you could easily borrow one for the occasions when you develop a yearning for waffles."[51] Another collective possession was an aluminum extension ladder. Another relatively easy conclusion for the whole Community was to create an emergency borrowing fund giving interest-free loans for any unexpected need.

In Mount Pleasant, where about two dozen Community people lived by the early 1970s and were meeting for midweek worship, some yearned for an alternative lifestyle but at first were stuck on the idea that it was only possible in rural areas. Then they saw they could have it in the city, too. Dora wrote, "our imaginations slowly came alive—something began to make sense," and they could envision sharing washers and dryers as well as worship. It was not only about having less stuff and more money to give away, but also about striving for a wholeness in their fragmented lives.[52] They canned food together, especially enormous quantities of applesauce and tomatoes. Dora and Margaret Elsie, and sometimes Nyla and Anna Mae, would buy bushels of fruit and put the jars in a hot water bath to seal them after the children were asleep. "We'd be up 'til 2:00 and 3:00 in the morning canning," Margaret Elsie said. "We'd get giddy."[53] They baked many loaves of bread and made their own yogurt. They created a co-op in the Rasmussens' basement, buying goods at wholesale prices and sharing them. As a child, Andy was especially impressed by the jumbo wheels of cheese. Eventually that cheese included brie and they bought white wine in bulk, Larry said. They laughed at themselves for their bourgeois tastes, even as they continued to work to end hunger and poverty for others.[54]

50. Minutes of Community meeting, 6 January 1975, in Community of Christ Papers.

51. Schramm and Schramm, *Things That Make for Peace*, 67.

52. Johnson, "For the Archives," 7–9.

53. Margaret Elsie Pearson, in discussion with the author, April 2021.

54. Andrew Rasmussen, in discussion with the author, December 2021; Larry and

Perhaps the biggest step was that several families in Mount Pleasant began sharing a car. Most of the adults took buses to work. The car could be parked on any of their blocks in the neighborhood. Even without cell phones, somehow they found the communal car when they needed it. Until one occasion when no one had seen it for a few days. They figured out that the car was stolen, but no one could tell the police where it had last been seen.[55]

With the half-dozen children in the Community who had been born in the late 1960s and early 1970s, their parents formed a childcare sharing arrangement they called the kid co-op. There was also another family who lived in the neighborhood who didn't attend the Community of Christ but whose two children were part of the kid co-op. Each school year, the parents would sit down and look at the schedules they had in their variety of professions: bookkeeper, lawyer, professor, realtor, scholar-activist. Each adult would choose a day when they were responsible for the children after school. Part of why it worked, Anne said, is that most of the adults had flexible jobs with a fair amount of input into their work conditions. Only Nyla, who was a nurse, had firm expectations for start and stop times.[56] For Larry, his day to have all of the children meant a break from the world of academia to have snacks with a group of young children.[57]

Community families also recycled together, seeing it as another way to share resources and counter the wastefulness of the US lifestyle.[58] They opened up a recycling center serving their neighbors as well, receiving aluminum and newspapers on Saturdays. Bruce was one of the main coordinators and he stored the materials in their family's basement. When they could stuff no more in the space, he hauled it all down to the city collection site.[59]

Even as the Community got closer to an Acts model of interdependence, only a few members actually lived in a commune. The Community purchased a large, rambling stucco house at 1701 Newton Street—one of Mount Pleasant's grand homes built in the late 1800s.[60] The Community paid $18,000 in May 1973 to purchase the house from the Department of Housing and Urban Development. It had been vacant for three years and badly

Nyla Rasmussen, in discussion with the author, June 2020; Larry Rasmussen, in discussion with the author, May 2022.

55. Yarbrough, in discussion with the author, December 2021; Rasmussen, in discussion with the author, May 2022.

56. Yarbrough, in discussion with the author, December 2021.

57. Larry and Nyla Rasmussen, in discussion with the author, June 2020.

58. Huck, "Community of the Empty Garbage," 7.

59. Multiple archival documents, e.g., *Happenings* in 1976; Moyer, in discussion with the author, September 2021.

60. Cherkasky, *Mount Pleasant*, 21, 69.

needed repairs.[61] Bruce Johnson used his connections to get a low price, and the Community put up the seed money for it, taking cash from its dream fund. The Community paid the mortgage and the group of people living there paid them back. When the members of the Johnny Appleseed Memorial commune moved in, they planted an apple tree in the yard, of course.[62]

In Community fashion, Johnny Appleseed Memorial commune sought to connect "the dreams of the people living there" with "the needs of the neighborhood," wrote Wendy Ward, whose dream was the commune itself.[63] The commune provided affordable housing near others in the Community for its residents, who worked in low-paying jobs at social service organizations or for Community ministries The Third Day and Sign of Jonah. They grew some vegetables with their neighbors and provided child care for a few local families. "There was an older woman who lived about half a block away who was very upset that this group of hippies was moving in," Wendy said, but later she was sympathetic when Wendy's kitten got lost. Ultimately, this group of people in their twenties didn't have a concrete plan for being a positive presence. "At best, Johnny Appleseed was just a resting place or stop-off place for people in the midst of their lives to assess what was going on and share some cooking and have debates over whether or not to keep the bananas in the refrigerator," Wendy said.[64]

As of 1975, the commune had ended, and the Community had to decide whether to keep 1701 Newton with a nonprofit organization as a tenant. Initially, members tried to keep and rent it. Judith, Bill, and Valborg Anderson expressed interest in buying it if the Community did not find another purpose it supported. In mid-1976, the Community decided to sell them the house. They became one more household to move from Dupont Circle to Mount Pleasant. They continued to host Bible study.[65]

All of the interconnections in the neighborhood beyond Sunday mornings created a sense of Mount Pleasant as truly "an urban village."[66] The

61. R. Bruce Johnson to Mr. H. R. Crawford, HUD assistant secretary for housing management, 12 July 1973, in Community of Christ Papers; Real estate deed recordation tax return dated 26 July 1973, signed by Rudolph Wendelin (Community president), in Community of Christ Papers.

62. Reports for Community meetings, 23 March 1974 and 4 November 1974, in Community of Christ Papers.

63. Wendy Ward, untitled document on JAM commune, 4 February 1973, in Community of Christ Papers.

64. Ward, in discussion with the author, December 2021.

65. Minutes of Community meeting, 27 January 1975, in Community of Christ Papers; Judith Anderson Glass, email message to author, November 12, 2022.

66. Mara Cherkasky, *Mount Pleasant*, 101.

older cohort of Community children didn't see much distinction between the Community and the neighborhood. Amos, the youngest of the kid co-op group, noted the blending together of the people in his life, especially in his earliest years. It was another way that the Community continued to live out a vision of Christian discipleship that didn't segregate the sacred and the secular. To Amos Huron, "there were elements of Christianity woven into everything," but without zealotry or taking religion too seriously, he said.

Andy's observations about life in the Community and Mount Pleasant overlapped with his growing understanding of race. It seemed to him that most of the white liberal families in the neighborhood attended the Community of Christ, and that his parents knew all the rest.[67] While Community families were friendly with their Black and brown neighbors, for the most part they didn't know each other at the same level. Andy remembers one Sunday when an African American woman came to visit the Community. She had gotten a list of congregations in the area and was visiting them all. She sat politely, looked around, and never came back.

People in the Community talked openly about race and class. Adults were conscientious and realistic, Andy said. They didn't romanticize the possibilities for togetherness and acknowledged cultural differences within groups of people rather than painting others with a broad brush. They recognized racial injustice and the complexities of city politics and the neighborhood. Parents didn't attempt to shield their children from the tensions among Latin American immigrants, established Black families, and white residents in the neighborhood. The conflict had racial and class-based aspects, and "had a social justice component to it at multiple levels," Andy said.[68] To hear adults confronting these issues in all their messiness was unusual for him and other white children.

There was also discussion and debate around the question of neighborhood schools. When Community members moved to Mount Pleasant, they talked about getting involved in the public elementary school, Bancroft. Rose Whiteside, a Community member, was highly involved in neighborhood activism, including as a Bancroft parent.[69] Lydia Mosher, whose family was among those who moved to Mount Pleasant and met for weekly meals together, looked at Bancroft with Dora. They had sons the same age. "There had started to be some gang culture," Lydia said. She feared one of her sons would be bullied and the other would succumb to pressure

67. Rasmussen, in discussion with the author, December 2021.

68. Rasmussen, in discussion with the author, December 2021.

69. Cherkasky, *Mount Pleasant*, 102; Happenings and Miscellaneous, 1975, in Community of Christ Papers.

to join.[70] Dora to some extent still wanted Martin and Alicia to attend Bancroft, though when she sat in on a class, she saw that many children were behind in learning to read. Bruce felt that their children "shouldn't have to be guinea pigs" to see if they could thrive at a struggling school.[71]

Even stronger than such concerns was the appeal of the Montessori method of education with its play-based, hands-on exploratory approach. Lydia was a Montessori teacher, as were Sanford and Martha Braden Jones. The Community supported Sanford in his dream of starting a Montessori school that would accept many of its students on scholarship. Mount Pleasant Montessori was for several years a beneficiary of Community benevolences, its name for its giving to partner ministries and nonprofit organizations. For the group of children who were part of the kid co-op, also attending Montessori school together was one more way their lives were intertwined with others in the Community.[72]

⁊⋒

La Casa badly needed renovation of the building when the Community bought it. The Community put an estimated $10,000 toward renovations. Since the building had been a restaurant, it came with a deep fat fryer, bar sink, and booths, which the Community sold as part of the fundraising for renovations. Each adult in the Community was asked to give one Saturday or evening a month.[73] The work and the building code requirements were challenging, and renovations ended with La Casa being "habitable, nothing more," Doug wrote.[74]

Tenants began moving in, first Life Skills Center and then the Sign of Jonah in September 1974. It rededicated itself in its new space, and the Community lent $6,500 from its dream fund. Yet within two years, it closed. In Dupont Circle, the Community and the people who came in shared a mutual desire for conversation at the Sign of Jonah. Mount Pleasant Street at that time had a higher bar for getting people from different backgrounds

70. Mosher, in discussion with the author, February 2023.

71. Moyer, in discussion with the author, September 2021.

72. Mosher, in discussion with the author, February 2023; Moyer, in discussion with the author, February and September 2021; Report of ad hoc budget committee, 1975, in Community of Christ Papers; Rasmussen, in discussion with the author, December 2021.

73. Summary of Budget Meetings, compiled by Sanford Jones, 26 November 1973, in Community of Christ Papers; Minutes of Community meeting, 29 April 1974, in Community of Christ Papers.

74. Huron, "Putting the Burden Behind Us," 5.

to interact, Margaret Elsie thought. The largely white clientele in Dupont Circle—where real estate prices had risen by the mid-1970s and they now saw it as a respectable neighborhood—mistrusted Mount Pleasant. The lack of parking on Mount Pleasant Street additionally meant customers didn't follow the Sign of Jonah to the new location. (The Third Day, which the Community called "a not-for-profit business"—it paid taxes but gave away its extra income as a nonprofit would be compelled to do—remained in Dupont Circle. Margaret Elsie and Oakley, who fell in love at the plant shop and married, bought the business along with two other longtime employees.)[75]

Other tenants came and went in La Casa. There was studio space for a silkscreen artist and a candlemaker, and office space for the United Farm Workers and the Women's Ordination Conference—a Catholic group advocating expanded leadership roles for women. A toy lending library was open to families four days a week. When DC gained home rule in late 1973 after a century of control by Congress, it created advisory neighborhood commissions, a form of participatory democracy with unpaid elected officials, and they opened an office in La Casa in what had been the Sign of Jonah space in 1976. Accustomed to worshiping in a basement from its first seven years, the Community did the same in its own building for a while.[76]

By 1977, the Community devoted some of the proceeds from selling the Johnny Appleseed house to a fuller remodeling of La Casa. But the work was slow. "It was an unhappy time," Doug wrote about the Community, "which had once prided itself on being free from material concerns—and which had always sought to spend most of its money on external benevolences."[77] By fall 1979, the work was complete. There was a new worship space on the middle level, with stained-glass blocks in shades of dark blue, gold, purple, and orange.[78]

For all of the investment of time and money in La Casa, Mount Pleasant did not become the established parish area as completely as Dupont Circle was. Many active members never lived there, commuting on Sundays from other parts of the city and suburbs. A few who had been in Mount Pleasant moved without leaving DC. When Walt and Korey bought a house across town in 1978, Dora was upset. "You didn't consult with us. What

75. Minutes of Community meeting, 2 December 1973, in Community of Christ Papers; Margaret Elsie Pearson, in discussion with the author, April 21 and August 2022; Asch and Musgrove, *Chocolate City*, 391; John Stewart, in discussion with the author, April 2022.

76. Asch and Musgrove, *Chocolate City*, 379–80; July 11, 1976 meeting. Community archives. Huron, "Putting the Burden Behind Us," 6.

77. Huron, "Putting the Burden Behind Us," 6.

78. Ward, "Through a Glass Lightly," 13.

were you thinking?" she asked. Korey replied, "I didn't know we were supposed to consult with you."[79]

Around the same time, the Mount Pleasant core group had another loss when Anna Mae moved to New York City after she and Dunstan divorced. At that time, by some estimates "10 percent of all priests in the United States had left the active ministry" and commonly entered married life.[80] Like Dunstan, many who had taken vows in Catholic religious orders struggled in the years after Vatican II and found it impossible to stay in their monasteries, convents, or parish rectories. In "first relationships of a nun or a priest leaving their vowed life," Anna Mae said, there was "much adjustment to be made on both partners' part." Anna Mae came to realize "the breadth, the depth, and the intensity of the transition that Dunstan had had to go through" after two decades in a monastery with its rigid hierarchy. Coming from her own background of being "a Protestant minister's daughter, I had no clue what the reality was that he was experiencing and not only no clue, but very little patience." When they divorced, "we both assumed equal responsibility for that." Though Anna Mae moved away, she stayed connected to the Community. And she remained in Dora's orbit. "She kept track of everybody, both gathered and scattered," Anna Mae said.[81]

૨ન

When Bob Klonowski arrived at La Casa, he couldn't find the door. The building didn't have an obvious entry the way a church usually does. He had taken two buses across the city that morning from Georgetown University, where he was a student in the mid-to-late 1970s. Bob's pastor at Community of Christ the Servant, a Lutheran group in the Chicago suburbs, encouraged him to visit the Community while in DC.[82] At twenty years old, Bob went through a painful breakup and decided to give the Community a try. The people of the Community drew him in, especially Rudy and Carrol, and Dora. One Sunday Bob and Dora had a conversation about disappointment. Three days later Bob received a letter in the mail, with Dora's further thoughts about the conversation they had. "It was just unbelievable to me that somebody would take me seriously enough to be thinking about that

79. Korey Thompson, in discussion with the author, February 2022.

80. Tentler, *American Catholics*, 316–17.

81. Patterson, in discussion with the author, June 2021.

82. The author found no direct connection between the Community in DC and the Community of Christ the Servant in the Chicago suburbs, started by Jack Lundin in 1968.

and to write down her thoughts," Bob said. It was mildly corrective, conveying that she heard him but giving him a few more things to think about.[83] Bob interviewed Dora for *Stance* and she shared her approach to social action that went beyond elections and protests: "It's when the marching ends that the hard work begins. The job is to celebrate your daily life in a way that expresses concern for your neighbor."[84]

Bob joined the preaching rotation, giving his first sermon in the Community. It was a step towards his vocation as a Lutheran pastor. He also "almost immediately got drafted into being a Sunday school teacher" with junior-high youth. When he was that age, learning about sin, grace, and redemption at church with his family, it hadn't gripped him. But after seeing more of the broken human condition in himself, it was life-giving to hear that message in the Community.[85] It was "the place where Christian faith and community started to make sense."[86]

83. Robert Klonowski, in discussion with the author, December 2021.

84. Klonowski, "Community Sketches," 12.

85. Klonowski, in discussion with the author, December 2021.

86. Robert Klonowski, email message to author, June 30, 2021.

Dora Koundakjian Johnson in the mid-1960s in New York City, where someone brought their pet monkey to a park. Photo by Philip Koundakjian

From left, Judith Anderson, Kathleen Keating, and Valborg Anderson at a Community party in 1969. Photo courtesy of Community of Christ 2016 reunion planning committee

Dunstan Hayden, center, celebrates the Eucharist in Community worship in 1969. Anna Mae Patterson, left, and Kathleen Keating, right, contribute to leading liturgy. Photo courtesy of Community of Christ 2016 reunion planning committee

Rudolph Wendelin created the Community's logo in 1985, inspired by a phrase in a Community litany that became the title of John Schramm and David Anderson's 1970 book, *Dance in Steps of Change*. Photo courtesy of Sandra Wojahn

From front row left, Alden Almquist, and Barbara and Dunstan Hayden sing as Margaret Ann Hoven leads with guitar at the Community of Christ twentieth anniversary celebration in August 1985. Photo by Bert Glenn

Community members dressed as clowns welcome worshipers into La Casa in the mid-1990s while neighbors on Mount Pleasant Street look. Photo courtesy of Sandra Wojahn

Lindsey and Bob Pohlman work on the Advent calendar that Sandra Wojahn created
for the children with felt figures of symbols and biblical characters, in 1990.
Photo courtesy of Sandra Wojahn

The Community's Palm Sunday celebration in 1991 includes both cloaks and
branches (Luke 19:36; Matt 21:8) for a biblically complete reenactment.
Photo courtesy of Sandra Wojahn

From left, Larry Rasmussen, Sally Hanlon, and Carrol Wendelin in December 1985.
Photo by Bert Glenn

Sally Hanlon's calligraphy depicts a thread in the writing of liberation theologian
Gustavo Gutiérrez on the incarnation, translated to "Jesus is God made poor." Image
from untitled selection in *Lenten Booklet 1999*, March 28, used by permission of
Sister Colette Hanlon.

Dorothy Pohlman and Doug Huron in conversation in 1987. Photo by Bert Glenn

Doug Huron talks with Gail Taylor through his DynaWrite speech synthesizer in 2004. Photo by Bert Glenn

Dianne Russell leads worship on Easter Sunday in La Casa.
Photo by Bert Glenn

Sandra Wojahn and Dora Johnson laugh together at a Community party at Alden
and Nancy Almquist's home in August 2006. Photo courtesy of Sandra Wojahn

Dunstan Hayden, left, prepares to baptize Alex, Christopher, and Dorothy Beane at the Community of Christ reunion and final retreat in September 2016. John Schramm, center left, assists, while Jaret Beane and Robin Pedtke, back right, join as parents. Photo by Martin Johnson

Alicia and Isadora Moyer sing at the Community of Christ reunion and final retreat in September 2016. To the right are Sanford Jones, John Stewart, and Sandra Wojahn. Photo by Martin Johnson

7

"The Kids Will Get It through Osmosis"

INDOCTRINATION WAS A BAD word to Community adults who came of age in the 1940s and 1950s. Instead, they often prided themselves on raising their children to be free-thinking. Dora told the Community, for example, about a time when her daughter, Alicia, as a young child, when sent to her room as a punishment, looked Dora in the eye and said, "You know, Mom, you can make me do things with my body, but you can't make me do them in my mind."[1]

From the early days, even the pastor's children didn't feel that they were on the sidelines, expected to be perfectly behaved. Instead, they were in the thick of Community activities with adults who cared about them and engaged with them. In the summer before he entered seventh grade, Mark Schramm gave the Shared Word in Community worship, a practice of talking about part of one's faith journey or struggles. Mark spoke about his thoughts on race and class relationships in DC as he prepared to commute from a multiracial, mixed-income neighborhood and school to private St. Anselm's Abbey boys school across town. Mark also said how much he loved the Community. "The way I would describe it is like a giant family."[2] The only coldness the children and youth felt was from the light brown metal folding chairs the Community put up in a circle in the basement that always smelled like coffee.

On Sunday mornings and at Community gatherings, children were fully involved and yet not much was specifically geared toward them, Alicia observed about the second and third decades of the Community. Dora's

1. Dora Johnson, untitled selection in *Lenten Booklet 1990*, March 23.
2. Mark Schramm, "Shared Word," 6.

friend Mary Catherine Bateson, a linguist and cultural anthropologist who worshiped with the Community while she lived in DC, wrote that many spiritual communities that started in the 1960s didn't have a model for raising children in the faith. (These were not only or even primarily Christian communities.) Adults in these communities were raised with religious backgrounds that they may have left behind but never fully rejected. Then they formed communities in "the more specialized parts of wider traditions, and I don't think they always did a good job of figuring out how to include children."[3]

Bateson herself was raised similarly to children and youth in the Community. Her mother, Margaret Mead, perhaps the best-known American cultural anthropologist, was an Episcopalian who thought that, in Mary Catherine's words, "You should take a child to church but not to Sunday school."[4] Mary Catherine wrote, "One of the things that my mother believed was that if children have shared the experiences of worship with a group of believing, engaged adults, they will have the capacity to empathize and participate later in life, so she wanted me beside her rather than in a Sunday school class, where I might memorize easily forgotten bits of doctrine with no connection to experience." Building "awe and devotion around ritual" was more important to her.[5]

Whether or not the Community parents expressed that directly, they pursued a similar approach much of the time. Children usually remained for all of the worship service and participated as they were able, Dora wrote. She noted that they also "sat through interminable meetings with us."[6] Dora often said, "The kids will get it through osmosis."[7]

Children and teenagers also joined in Community publications without much distinction from the adults. For several years before *Stance* petered out in the mid-1980s, older children offered short stories and articles occasionally. And even young children contributed many years to the Lenten booklet, a curated collection of original reflections, poems, and art as well as quotes from thinkers respected in the Community. Some years they had parameters. One year they drew Jesus and the two thieves crucified. One child, taught by his mother about the saints, identified the penitent thief by the name Dismas given to him by tradition, likely educating much of the Community on that point. Other times they could contribute whatever

3. Bateson, *Composing a Further Life*, 167.

4. Bateson, *Composing a Further Life*, 116.

5. Bateson, *Composing a Further Life*, 167–69.

6. Johnson, "Here We Are," 5–6.

7. Alicia Koundakjian Moyer, in discussion with the author, February 2021.

they liked, a sketch of a puppy, for example. In 1987, the year Lois McArdle started the booklet, her daughter Marguerite submitted an unpunctuated poem with a mystical ending, "New life / a journey everyone must take"[8]

Though Sunday school was not consistently offered, the Community did not eschew the idea. Many of the core people grew up in Protestant congregations that inherited the tradition, which began in the late 1700s. Sunday school was initially concerned with imparting both secular skills and religious teachings. With the creation of public schools, Protestant children usually didn't attend parochial schools and instead had approximately one hour a week of instruction on Christianity and their specific denomination. Many parents felt it sufficed for teaching the essentials to their children.[9] Beyond prayer before dinner or at bedtime, faith might not be part of home life.

With mixed feelings about that tradition, Community adults wrestled with what to do about Christian education. From the beginning, they asked, "How do you pass the faith on, if that's something you can pass on?" David said. For a stretch of months or years, they had some version of Sunday school or a specific discussion, for example about the meaning of Communion, before it would lose steam. In the early years, they had four age categories and four locations, though they were finding education more difficult than worship to hold in a rented space.[10] In the 1980s for a while they collaborated with a small house church with two families in Mount Pleasant. Ryan Good, who was one of the children in that cooperative Sunday school, observed the way the adults involved had a tension with their inherited beliefs. They are a gift, connecting us to past generations and grounding us, he said. Yet with any tradition there's "also all that it brings that is resistant to change."[11]

One of the challenges for Sunday school was a common one in most congregations: finding teachers. Part of it was that adults wanted to remain in worship.[12] Anne Yarbrough acknowledged that she was not interested in corralling the children and teaching them the Bible. "So they heard the stories, but sporadically."[13] John and Mary Schramm's daughter Karen, when

8. Marguerite McArdle-Pettee, untitled selection in *Lenten Booklet 1987*, March 18.

9. Marty, *Righteous Empire*, 75–77.

10. John E. Schramm to the members of the Eastern District Mission Committee, Summary report for 1966, Community of Christ Papers, The Swarthmore College Peace Collection, Swarthmore, Pennsylvania.

11. Betty Good, email message to author, December 9, 2022; Ryan Good, in discussion with author, November 2022.

12. Hayley Hoffman to the Community of Christ, 21 September 96, in Community of Christ Papers.

13. Anne Yarbrough, in discussion with the author, December 2021.

she took a biblical literature class in college, checked a children's Bible out of the library to fill the gap in her knowledge. As an effort to remedy that lack, perhaps, at some point the Community bought a stack of Bible story coloring books. By the 1990s, sometimes Sunday school was gathering around a long conference table in one of the side rooms used by nonprofits during the week, using crayons and markers to fill in the outlines of the illustrations.

Community children may not have memorized Scripture, but they had faith modeled for them by adults who lived it out alongside them. "We have covenanted with each other that we are all responsible" for the children, Dora wrote. Parents were grateful that "we trust our children with each other—that they have adults influence their lives other than their immediate parents."[14] Children came to demonstrations for various justice causes and were part of the teams serving Saturday lunch with the Community's partner ministries at St. Stephen and the Incarnation Episcopal Church or Christ House. Anne saw that as a strength of the Community, and an experience of learning to care for one's neighbors.[15] During the 1980s, Andy thought of it as being as natural to see Christians at a protest of nuclear weapons as it was to see them in worship. The Community had taught him that Christianity had the potential to be a radical force in society, Andy said. "When I think about what's important and where and how I should be guiding my life, I think about that group of people."[16]

The importance of social relationships was evident to the children of the Community. Anyone who didn't connect socially to the Community didn't stay long, Andy recalled. The relationships felt organic. The social component was prominent both in terms of social justice and in terms of gathering in each other's homes. In the older cohort of children, going to church was primarily a social experience. During fellowship time they would get sticky glazed doughnuts from Heller's Bakery—a neighborhood fixture since 1940[17]—and they'd get to see their friends. Alicia wrote for *Stance* when she was eleven, an article titled "A Normal Day at Church—for the Community of Christ." It begins with liturgical language (Christ is risen indeed!) and ends with the gathered being sent with the Trinitarian formula. In between, she describes fellowship time and the children's relationships.[18]

Nevertheless, the children were attuned to what was happening in worship. Singing together was an essential part of worship to the children.

14. Johnson, "Here We Are," 5–6.

15. Yarbrough, in discussion with the author, December 2021.

16. Andrew Rasmussen, in discussion with the author, December 2021.

17. Cherkasky, *Mount Pleasant*, 80.

18. Johnson, "Normal Day at Church," 10.

Andy picked up that "this is what you're supposed to do in church. You're supposed to sing." A song that resonated for him was the spiritual "Motherless Child."[19] Amos Huron thought of singing as something that especially bound them together. "There's a vulnerability to singing in front of people," he said. His father, Doug, would sing "loudly and proudly and terribly." To see people in the Community around the neighborhood, when they sang together, made the relationship more intimate. Another child born into the Community, Cyrus Hampton, noted that the singing showed the strength of the communality. He observed that there was no notion of "'Who are the good singers? We're only going to look to them. But instead all these folks, everyone in the Community, we want all of you to be involved.'"[20]

Marguerite heard the message that Christianity wasn't just about coming to worship but that "it's important to make this world a better place and fight for the things we believe in." She was impressed by the worship-leading rotation and the idea that "you could lead a service if you wanted." It meant variety in styles of leading liturgy, of preaching, and the topics that people spoke about. She noticed the differences in Dunstan's and Walt's homilies, and she liked them both. Walt was calm and collected; Dunstan joked more,[21] though it wasn't always possible for the children to understand the humor when the adults were laughing. (An example of the kind of practical, pastoral thoughts Dunstan shared, on prayer: "What should we expect of God in meditation? Not flashes of lightning. God tried that once near Damascus, with mixed results. Since then, God has given every person periodically a tiny peek at reality—enough to instruct but not so much as to dazzle."[22])

As he entered preteen years, Andy would look at the rotation of people leading the liturgy and giving the homily. "You sort of knew what to expect, whether you were going to be bored in the sermon, whether it was going to be good," he said. If it was a particular person who tended to go long, he brought an bring an extra toy or zoned out. But there were also preachers he looked forward to hearing. Doug Huron, an attorney, had well-thought-out arguments and spoke eloquently. Andy was impressed by David Anderson's leftist politics. He admired the countercultural people who were politically radical and stayed Christian.[23]

And Andy was interested in what Dunstan had to say when he preached, and always liked him. "He's so charismatic in his own curmudgeonly way,"

19. Rasmussen, in discussion with the author, December 2021.

20. Hampton, in discussion with the author, September 2021.

21. Marguerite Lee, in discussion with the author, December 2021.

22. Dunstan Hayden, untitled selection in *Lenten Booklet 1987*, March 5.

23. Rasmussen, in discussion with the author, December 2021.

Andy said. When Andy's birthday was coming up, Dunstan offered to make a special meal as a gift. Andy asked for macaroni and cheese and chocolate pudding. Dunstan, who had taken up gourmet cooking, prepared the main course with special French cheeses and the dessert was chocolate mousse. The quality of the ingredients was lost on Andy as he enjoyed the birthday meal several years in a row, but he knew Dunstan cared about him.[24]

Children in the Community of Christ had experience with other churches when they visited extended family, or for other reasons, so they knew how different worship in the Community was. The hymns were photocopied pages in a three-ring binder and no one wore vestments beyond a stole while celebrating the Eucharist, and that could be missed if you weren't thinking about it. There would occasionally be incense. Andy's impression was that it was as much to mask smells from other uses of the building as it was liturgical. The smell of La Casa and the carpeting that was there for many years also stood out to Amanda Huron. The person who was named the pastor at that time—mainly in documents shared by the adults with entities such as the denomination—did not take a central role in worship, so to children it felt like there was no pastor.[25] (And to adults a lot of the time, too.) In 1986, the Rasmussens moved to New York City, where Larry was Reinhold Niebuhr professor of social ethics at Union Theological Seminary. They started attending a more traditional Lutheran church. Andy protested going, partly because he was a teenager and didn't want to get out of bed early. But he also knew he could strike a chord with Larry and Nyla by asking, "How can I go to a church like that after going to church like Community of Christ?"

ેગ

David Anderson carried an extra-large tray half-filled with decorated cookies as he moved around the tables set up in La Casa's main room. "David, I need you over here!" one child called. "It's nice to be needed," he said as he picked up the freshly iced bunch. The annual cookie decorating party of the Community of Christ was not only a holiday celebration but neighborhood service, since the trays of iced cookies were for the meal programs for the hungry where Community members served. The rule was that cookies could only be eaten if they broke, and sure enough, each child always ended up with a few broken ones.

24. Rasmussen, in discussion with the author, December 2021.

25. Rasmussen, in discussion with the author, December 2021; Amanda Huron, in discussion with the author, September 2021.

Throughout the year there were several intergenerational activities tied to the liturgical calendar. There was baking lion and lamb bread for Holy Week. Bobbie had a vast rectangular baking pan for the occasion. They would make enough dough for five loaves, with the children helping shape it to look like a lion cradling a lamb.[26] And there was the Epiphany party on the closest weekend to January 6. Anyone who wanted to be involved acted out the Christmas story. After my family joined in 1990, my father sang harmony with Margaret Ann on "Star of Bethlehem" and "Bright Morning Stars." Harmonizing was a gift he carried from growing up in traditional Mennonite congregations.

One year in the short nativity play, I agreed to be Mary. I was eleven years old. None of the boys would be Joseph. I wasn't so sure I wanted to be Mary anymore. Then Rudy, who was eighty-four years old, offered to take the role. After that, I didn't want to risk hurting his feelings. Rudy was beloved by the children and youth. He made us all Smokey Bear calendars. Amos saw all people his parents' age as uncool, but since Rudy was a generation older, that made him fun to be around, like a Community grandparent.[27]

Several of the adults debated whether it would be a historically accurate play. The Bible does not give Mary and Joseph's ages. Mary was likely an adolescent or possibly prepubescent. A strain of early Christian tradition—and a lot of religious art—depicts Joseph as being an old man. Some dismiss this as only needed to bolster the doctrine of Mary's perpetual virginity, with Jesus's siblings being children of Joseph from an earlier marriage.[28] I was accustomed by this point in the Community to adults telling me biblical scholarship alongside church tradition but not presenting either as absolute truth.

With Rudy as Joseph, the show went on. Lydia, a baby a few months old, was in a wicker laundry basket with a blanket around her, starring as baby Jesus. Being a bright and curious child came naturally to her. As Mary, I wore one cloth on my head, and another wrapped around my striped shirt and denim overalls. Rudy, in a plaid bathrobe and a patterned cloth tied around his head, really committed to the role, adding outstretched arms to his reading of the lines.

Parties in general were an intergenerational activity with theological underpinnings (however uneven the awareness of that was). Then and now, Christianity isn't generally associated with parties, even though Jesus's first miracle was to keep the festivities going at a wedding reception (John

---

26. Christina Nichols, in discussion with the author, November 2021.

27. Amos Huron, in discussion with the author, December 2021.

28. Ruether, *Mary—The Feminine Face*, 34, 54–55.

2:1–11). In the Community, in addition to the Epiphany party tied to the church calendar, other parties had a purpose, such as writing letters to members of Congress for a campaign to end hunger. In all cases, they were about celebrating and making a space to receive community as a gift rather than something made by human effort. This also connected to the Community's idea of mission. If Christian service in the world is only work and not play—with no enjoyment—it can become drudgery and feed into the idea that we as humans are saving ourselves.[29] God's grace involves the freedom to play and to have fun.

Community parties were also a primary way of introducing newcomers to its people. People stood or sat in small groups or one-on-one in the living room, dining room, kitchen, and porches of a house. Parties created a relaxed setting for conversation, for people to share their thoughts on a Saturday evening so that there was a fuller sense of what they brought on Sunday morning. There was often live music by Community musicians. Parties were also a way to include partners and housemates apart from worship. More than a few Community members were in interfaith relationships or had a spouse who was done with church—even one like the Community striving to be distinct from traditional organized religion.

During Community parties at members' homes and in the La Casa building on Sundays, children were free range with the minimum necessary adult supervision. It was also part of the Community being interwoven with family and neighborhood and always being happy to celebrate with people. "It was a very safe place," Anne said. "So a lot of one's social life and parties, birthday parties, everything had to do with that group, and it made it really easy to have a social life because it just fit with your church."[30] Especially on Monroe Street, where several Community families lived, during parties children would run around between backyards and on the block. They were joined by neighbor children from families outside the Community. If it was one of DC's relatively rare too-cold evenings, children would find some nook or cranny of the house. At La Casa, a former restaurant, the stairwell that ran from the storerooms of the basement to the second-floor kitchen became a hide-and-seek course.

Many of the youth who grew up in the Community stopped attending worship when their parents gave them that option. Yet social gatherings were a way to continue relationships with adults and other youth in the Community. For Amos, that period of life coincided with attending Sidwell Friends, a Quaker school. His peers lived in wealthier neighborhoods and were "not

29. Schramm and Anderson, *Dance in Steps of Change*, 58–60.
30. Yarbrough, in discussion with the author, December 2021.

going to storefront churches," he said. Anne became a United Methodist minister and pastored more-traditional churches. He started thinking of the Community as an oddball place his father was involved in. Seeing people around the neighborhood simultaneously elicited warm familiarity and a bit of embarrassment. Yet he felt comfortable with Community people and continued attending parties, especially if watching football was an activity.[31]

Parties were a place to explore rituals in continuity with worship but also a time for pushing the edges. That was especially true at the Solstice party, led for many years by Korey and later Hayley. During the years when the party was at Korey and Walt's home, a tradition began of singing the Christian folk song "Lord of the Dance." When this happened at Hayley's home, she grabbed someone's hand and started a chain until everyone was caught up in the dance. As they continued singing, the chain went out of the back door and to the backyard in the dark. Hayley introduced more pagan rituals into the celebration. When Hayley lived in a house with a large backyard, she built a fire. A group of people took pots and pans to the edge of the yard that was not adjacent to houses and banged them to ward off evil spirits. She also created a labyrinth by laying a large spiral of pine branches with apples and candles. The children walked through to light a candle and then walked all the way around the spiral. This continued with each successive candle until the whole spiral was illuminated.[32]

The porousness between adult and children's activities went both ways—the adults explored play, perhaps most so with clowning. "It's a combination of mindfulness and humor," said Korey, who introduced clowning to the Community. This was especially powerful for those raised in conservative homes and taught that church was a place to be prim and proper. Clowning illustrates that grace doesn't depend on us, Korey said. She took classes with a Lutheran pastor in Maryland and then taught in DC.[33] Several Community people joined. Clowns led the Easter Sunday procession around La Casa for several years or welcomed people at the door.

One of the clowns was Sandra Wojahn, who went by Sandi. Like Korey, she had work experience in lay ministry and ample artistic gifts that she brought into the Community when she joined in 1977. Through the years she planned rituals to recognize milestones in the children and youth's lives and to bring faith into family life. A woman with German Lutheran heritage, Sandi trained in theology in order to instruct children in the faith.

31. Amos Huron, in discussion with the author, December 2021.

32. Hayley Hoffman, in discussion with author, September 2021.

33. Korey Thompson, in discussion with the author, February 2022.

She taught in Lutheran parochial schools for two years before her life took a different direction.

ॐ

Sandi's parents were farmers in Oklahoma who married in 1932, during the Great Depression. The land they worked was hard and dry with few trees, and wind blew through in great gusts. Sandi's mother gave birth to five children in six years. There were four girls and one boy, who died as an infant of what was called dust pneumonia.[34]

After several pregnancies in rapid succession, a doctor advised Sandi's mother to avoid conceiving another child. They used birth control, but then Sandi came as a surprise in 1944. She was six years younger than her next oldest sister. At that time they lived in a community that was Lutheran and Catholic, with a sense of competition between them. They later moved to northeast Oklahoma, at the bottom of the Ozarks, which was primarily Baptist and Methodist.

Her parents had a small farm, 200 acres with alternating crops of wheat and soybeans. They had a small herd of cattle they milked by hand; the milk truck would come by daily to pick it up. It was unaffordable to hire people, so the girls did the farm work along with their parents. Chores came before school or any fun activities. They also had huge gardens, which meant no summer vacation. Sandi considered it an achievement to get a week off to go to Lutheran summer camp when she was a young teenager. By then, most of her older sisters were out of the house so the need to grow and preserve large amounts of food had lessened.[35]

The first Lutheran church they attended seemed huge to Sandi as a child. "The pipes of the organ and the ascending Christ statue loomed large at the altar and the vaulted ceiling was high in the sky beyond all reach," she wrote. Her childhood faith was strong. "Nothing shook my belief; God took care of me and my family and the steady participation in Sunday school and church provided any needed reassurance."[36] She learned about grace and a loving God rather than being instilled with a fear of damnation.

In high school her church hired a new pastor who modeled a faith connected to justice. It was the early 1960s, and he supported the civil rights movement. Merely talking about race in church offended some members. After the pastor did that, Sandi started noticing more of the reality around

34. Wojahn, in discussion with the author, September 2021.
35. Wojahn, in discussion with the author, September 2021.
36. Sandra Wojahn, untitled selection in *Lenten Booklet 1995*, March 8.

her living in a sundown county, where Black people could come inside the county line during the day only. Sandi's pastor noticed her gifts and commitment to the church, and he encouraged her on the path to becoming a Lutheran teacher. She studied at Concordia Teachers College in Nebraska and took courses on religion. Some were specifically about doctrine—the official teachings of the Lutheran Church Missouri Synod.[37]

Yet when she started her job at a parochial elementary school in North Carolina, the pieces stopped fitting together. As she taught six- and seven-year-olds about the Triune God, "it sort of hit me, to be very honest, that I don't understand this," she said. She had learned all the content of her theology and doctrinal courses without it soaking in, she said. "It made me step back a bit."[38]

At the same time, around the South the civil rights movement was gaining strength. It was twelve years after the 1954 Supreme Court decision that desegregated schools, and she sensed that many families were sending their children to the Lutheran private school because it was essentially still segregated. In her conversation about renewing her contract, she asked why there were no African Americans among their students. The school board leader told her that African Americans were happy in their own schools and "we're happy with ours." She taught for one more school year, 1967–68, and then left.[39]

Curiosity about the wider world led her to join the Peace Corps,[40] serving in Sarawak, Malaysia, in 1968–70. Then she moved to DC to work at the Peace Corps headquarters. She got an apartment in the Adams Morgan neighborhood. Moving into a new season of life after the end of a relationship, she called Lutheran Social Services and asked if they knew any congregations in the city that were socially active. She hadn't been part of any church for three years. The LSS staff member suggested she try the Community. She walked over to La Casa in early June 1977. She began tithing immediately, writing a check as her first donation.[41]

The next year, Sandi started dating John Hampton. He grew up Episcopalian and shared Sandi's appreciation for the liturgy of their traditions. They signed their wedding invitations "yours in love and faith in the future"

37. Wojahn, in discussion with the author, September 2021.

38. Wojahn, in discussion with the author, September 2021.

39. Wojahn, in discussion with the author, September 2021.

40. Sandra Wojahn, "The Patchwork of Life," in *Lenten Booklet 1990*, March 12.

41. Wojahn, in discussion with the author, September 2021.

and married in 1980. "All of the Community of Christ folk were there" for the ceremony and potluck. Their son, Cyrus, was born in December 1984.[42]

Sandi continued to hold leadership roles in the Community and on the board of Life Skills Center. If John wasn't available for the board meeting or during worship, Sandi would lead with Cyrus as a baby or toddler beside her. Sandi preached on the Sunday that Cyrus was baptized, Easter 1985. Drawing on her Lutheran teacher training, she addressed the children present, asking them to name the four sources of celebration: baptism, confirmation, the Eucharist, resurrection. Baptizing Cyrus meant that he was officially welcomed into the community of believers and adopted into God's covenant people, she explained. "He is forgiven and free to live without excuses and to explore the gift of the Holy Spirit," she said. She then talked about how confirmation is a choice to confirm baptismal vows, in this case for Aaron Anderson. In describing the Eucharist, she noted the origins of the name in the Greek word for thanksgiving. Wisely, Sandi made no attempt to explain resurrection.[43]

Sandi also shared her artistic gifts with projects for all ages but accessible to the children. She would find an idea in a home-and-garden-type magazine or from someone in her extended family, but then she adapted it. One project was making Advent calendars with felt figures and symbols illustrating the stories of Advent, such as John the Baptist. Children would lift the flap for each day and learn about that Bible character or image. She wanted to create something for her own family with more than little trinkets, toys, or candy. Once she had made a calendar that satisfied her, she shared it with other families in the Community to mark Advent in their homes. Another project was a paper angel that could grace the top of a Christmas tree, with the names of all the people in the Community.[44] She also revived an illustration Rudy had done of Rom 16 and 1 Cor 12, one body with many members. Names of people in the Community made up the body parts: "Marguerite" and "Catherine" were the feet, for example, and "Cyrus" and "Amos" were among the toes.[45]

Cyrus compared his mother to the spine. Sandi was "a backbone person," Cyrus said, holding up the Community. He saw it as natural for someone who grew up on a family farm to work hard without perfectionism. Even if the end result wasn't pretty, it needed to get done.

---

42. Wojahn, in discussion with the author, September 2021.

43. Wojahn, Easter homily in the Community of Christ.

44. Wojahn, in discussion with the author, September 2021.

45. Rudy Wendelin, "Salute You . . . Brethren and Sisters!," in *Lenten Booklet 1989*, February 9.

What Cyrus experienced at home from his parents and what he experienced in the Community of Christ both modeled the same view of the world. That perspective was distinct from what he saw in school, on television, and in the broader society. It was a way of navigating life contemplatively, to think and talk about what's happening rather than "strong arm your way through life's problems," Cyrus said. From his father, Cyrus learned to be analytical. And with Sandi, "everything was very conversational, very contemplative." Even when Sandi disciplined him, punishment was to sit down and talk about what he was thinking and what caused him to make the choice he did. In the Community of Christ, Cyrus saw the shared task of giving homilies as having a similar approach, looking at new events and information and comparing that with one's touchstones. In the Community's case, that was the Bible and Christian teachings, "but always constantly engaging those with whatever was happening in the news." He observed Community worship and life together:

> Here are all these adults here, all these people around you and what they're going to do is every week they're going to get together and they're going to bounce ideas around and they're going to talk about the things they've seen and they're going to talk about the shared ideas they have. And there might be disagreement about it, and it might be smooth and agreeable. Sometimes it might be, you know, tumultuous and you can see so-and-so is angry at such-and-such because they said this thing the other day or they have ongoing friction about their philosophies. But it has solidified for me that what you do is ask questions and contemplate an answer to those questions. That is what adults do. That's what people do broadly. That's a natural way to navigate the world, . . . to navigate the difficult parts of life and of making sense of, What are we doing in small communities? What are we doing in larger communities of nations and international communities?

He recognized "how distinct and unique and also how big that probably was in me conceiving of adulthood and responsibility and community."

⋅⋅⋅

During its middle decades, when many of the core people were raising children, the Community provided opportunities for the children to bond with adults and primarily with each other. A lot of it was activities in a positive, caring environment, but without a component of religious teaching.[46] For the older group, attending Montessori school together—with an educational method the parents embraced—stood in for children's programming in the Community in some ways, Alicia said.[47]

For a few years in the late 1980s and early 1990s, a young woman who came to the Community gave focused attention to children at retreats and on Sunday mornings. Cathy Hays Smith went to DC planning to be a lawyer and instead discovered her gift was teaching children. The activities she led were developmentally appropriate and encouraged reflection. They might make a mobile with a stick, attaching drawings and pinecones. She'd ask, "What was important to you?" The themes weren't directly religious. A guiding question could be "What's a good friend?" Or "My family is _____." Cathy said, "As far as the deeper themes of the formation of their faith, it just seemed sort of organic."[48]

Around the time that Cathy moved away, several Community parents decided they wanted something for the older children. It would not be led by those parents, and there would not be siblings in the same group.[49] Hayley Hoffman, Bert Glenn, and Norajean Flanagan agreed to lead. To the youth, the three thirty-somethings seemed young and cool in comparison with their parents.[50] The request from the parents was simply to lead fun activities for the children and provide an opportunity for bonding. The group rode bicycles through Rock Creek Park, baked bread at Dora's house, and went on a hayride in the fall.

The group went on weekend retreats, with Hayley taking the lead after Bert and Norajean moved. Younger adults in the Community jumped in when in DC: one was Amanda, part of the older cohort, after she returned from college. Another was Talley Wells, whose parents Linda and Charles were married in the Community in 1969 and who was baptized there. He was in DC 1994–95. He stayed with Dora, who immediately recruited him to work with the youth. Since his mother was one of the earliest Community members, he knew some of the teenagers' parents. "You could just see the various personalities of the Community coming out" in their children, he said, the next generation "questioning their faith and questioning what it meant to be growing up in an urban environment in the nineties."[51]

46. Nichols, in discussion with the author, November 2021.
47. Moyer, in discussion with the author, February 2021.
48. Hays Smith, in discussion with the author, March 2021.
49. Bert Glenn and Norajean Flanagan, in discussion with author, December 2021.
50. Amos Huron, in discussion with the author, November 2021.
51. Talley Wells, in discussion with the author, November 2021.

In later years, a primary activity was going to Shakespeare plays in which the oldest member of the group, Lindsey Pohlman, acted. They were at her school, which was especially for students with learning disabilities. The youth group felt like a safe place to her, as did services at La Casa. "I felt very loved and supported every Sunday," Lindsey said. "I could find other adults that were not my mom and dad to go to and talk to them about stuff that was going on in my life, particularly Hayley."[52]

While it built caring, lasting relationships, the youth group's time together was not preparation for confirmation, though group members were the usual age for such classes. "They never wanted us to do any religious education at all, nor did we," Norajean said of the initial request from the parents. She added with a hint of humor, "I mean, hopefully we acted according to Christian values. But no, I wasn't thinking in theological terms at all."[53]

Another father in the Community wanted specifically religious education for his children. Alden Almquist grew up as the son of a Swedish Covenant missionary doctor in Congo, immersed in African Christianity. Raising children in the United States, Alden wanted them to have a buffer from the messages being marketed to them. For him, that was Christian faith, but he would have accepted any other tradition they chose, Alden said. "I wouldn't have objected if they had turned out to be devout Buddhist—anything to counter this breathtakingly individualistic, materialistic culture."[54] Alden and Nancy were grateful for the positive experience their son had in confirmation classes.[55] The Community's named pastors at the time—Phil Wheaton, a retired Episcopal priest, and Bill Wegener, a retired Lutheran pastor—led sessions in a wonderful way, not just going through the motions, Alden said.[56]

After the oldest member of the youth group went to college, adding new children under the Community's initial parameters posed a problem. Unlike the two previous cohorts of Community children, the five children came from only two families. In addition to Alden and Nancy's two children, three of them were Hayley's sons, so they would have to find another leader. Even if the Community had been willing to shift from the idea of a youth group without siblings and without parents of those youth as leaders, the few youth born in the mid-to-late 1980s didn't share interests. Alden

52. Lindsey Pohlman, in discussion with the author, November 2021.

53. Glenn and Flanagan, in discussion with the author, December 2021.

54. Alden Almquist, in discussion with the author, December 2021.

55. Nancy Almquist, in discussion with Laci Barrow, Christina Nichols, and Martin Johnson, September 2016.

56. Almquist, in discussion with the author, December 2021.

lamented that, while recognizing that "kids bond how they bond."[57] Another factor was the Community's size. "That's where small is maybe not so beautiful," Margaret Ann said.[58] Perhaps if the Community had attracted more families with children that age, the group dynamic would have been different.

Years later, Hayley and some of the other parents of younger children restarted Sunday school. She was reading a book by Anne Lamott about Sunday school with her church in California, and it made Hayley want to offer an experience like that to her children. "We made a very colorful room with all kinds of things for the kids to play with and whatnot in the room beside the kitchen," she said. Families donated toys and created a space just for the children on the second floor of La Casa, and met there on Sunday mornings. "It was like the exact opposite of the youth group," Hayley said. "All the parents who wanted to have Sunday school volunteered and took turns rotating, doing Sunday school."[59]

❧

The Community's nondogmatic approach proved both a weakness and a strength. "Everything was so open to interpretation, we didn't know what we believed," Alicia said. Cyrus understood that "the point was not 'we are going to indoctrinate you with a singular vision,' but rather, 'we're going to be open to questions and doubt.'" As an adult, Cyrus spends more time in activist spaces than religious ones. He encounters disdain for religion, especially Christianity, and agrees that "much of our present day interaction with public religion is really, really nasty and awful." Yet because of the Community, he knows that Christian faith can be a tool of "exploration, questioning, embracing self-doubt, embracing self-criticism." Cyrus connects strongly with a philosophy "viewing Jesus as a sort of revolutionary, some sort of a social malcontent, someone who is pointing out, 'Here's what's really going on. You know, here's what the leaders are saying, but here's what's really going on. And let's be honest about it, and let's be honest about ourselves.'" And he learned as central to Christianity the idea of giving of oneself so that others may thrive, with Jesus' death on the cross being the ultimate example.

Children and youth in the Community also absorbed, through osmosis or otherwise, that the Community was a place where people could be vulnerable and receive support. Dora regarded as precious that joys and

57. Almquist, in discussion with the author, December 2021.
58. Margaret Ann Hoven, in discussion with the author, August 2021.
59. Hoffman, in discussion with the author, September 2021.

concerns were shared out loud during the Sunday service. Alicia observed that people could speak without strict boundaries about what topics were not allowed. People would open up and be heard with intensely personal stories as well as sometimes equally intense feelings about global issues. "Here we are in this little room together on these foldout chairs," Alicia said, and in the world "people are starving and there's war." Alicia learned that suffering was not something to be feared. "There was a lot of space around sadness in our community; there was never a numbing of it or a fleeing from it," she said. "We did hard things together as a result. Nobody abandoned anyone else to go through it alone."

Amos likened the Community to a group of superheroes. When someone was threatened by hardship, a Community member would sound the call: "Activate!" This started in the days of phone chains and shifted to email. "The community had this ability to act both as a bunch of individual people and as an organization," Amos said.[60] Andy noted that the Community modeled that Christian life together was not limited to Sundays: "It's a community that was happening the whole week. It was about relying on one another."[61] While there were strong friendships in the Community, people and families also had bonds that transcended mere affinity, Amanda said. "They were committed enough to each other to work through whatever challenges."[62] A faith community is able to give a level of support that is hard for a group of friends to organize or sustain. And it's difficult to find a place outside of a religious community not only for thoughtful conversation but sharing life's sorrow and delight, Cyrus noted.[63]

At times the sharing during worship was intense for the children. Alicia sometimes felt "a little bit of a bracing," she said. Her nervous system went on alert, as if asking, "'What's going to happen? Is somebody going to start talking and crying?' And, yes, somebody was going to start talking and crying." She saw that the tears among this group seemed to help them work through what they were feeling. "There was this kind of feeling that as long as we weren't afraid to speak it, there was no shame around it," she said. "There was still space for that person. They were embraced by the group." Walt and Korey's daughter, Krista, similarly perceived waves of emotion at church. This was most profound when her family was going through one of

---

60. Amos Huron, in discussion with the author, December 2021.

61. Rasmussen, in discussion with the author, December 2021.

62. Amanda Huron, in discussion with the author, September 2021.

63. Moyer, in discussion with the author, February 2021; Hampton, in discussion with the author, September 2021.

the most painful times of their lives. Korey wept every Sunday in worship, and Krista associated going to church with her mother crying.[64]

A few years after Krista was born, Korey and Walt conceived twin boys. Just over halfway into the pregnancy, Korey started bleeding a little, and the doctor recommended that she be admitted to the hospital. Without anyone telling her she was having contractions, the situation careened out of control, she wrote, "then suddenly a wide crescendo of excruciating pain, mass confusion, physical relief, a hurried and hushed birth, and finally the feel of an anesthesia mask filled with the cool, welcoming vapor that led to a tunnel of oblivion."[65] When Korey awakened, after a hemorrhage, the hospital was finally forthright: the boys would not survive because they were too small. But if she hadn't delivered them, she likely wouldn't have survived herself. They were in a Catholic hospital, and the nurse asked if they wanted the infants to be baptized. Korey's first thought was, "How could we get the Community of Christ here tonight?"[66] But there wasn't enough time, and the Community's pastor was Walt. The boys were the spitting image of him. Walt replied that baptism was not magic—it couldn't save the boys' lives, and their souls didn't need to be saved. They were already under the cover of God's grace. Korey, still stunned by all she endured that evening, longed for some ritual with the Community to bless the boys in the moment of transition.[67]

The Community had a moment of lifting up their lives the following Sunday, yet in the following months members struggled to recognize the deep wound opened by the infants' death. As in any congregation, it can feel easier to feed people than to accompany them in the kind of pain that is hard to even speak about to others. Adding to that, Walt was a deeply private person. In the ambiguous space between a person in grief asking for care and others offering support, Korey and Walt did not receive what they needed. Complicating it further, a few months after the boys died, two other women in the Community delivered healthy babies. Their due dates were within weeks of the one Korey had.[68]

A few years later, when Bert and Norajean were struggling with infertility and pregnancy loss, Korey cared for them from a place of deep understanding. Bert and Norajean's first baby died six months into the pregnancy,

64. Krista Thompson Scarvie, in discussion with the author, December 2021.

65. Korey Thompson, untitled selection in *Lenten Booklet 1987*, March 12.

66. Thompson, in discussion with the author, February 2022.

67. Thompson, email message to author, January 2, 2023.

68. Thompson, in discussion with the author, February 2022.

and Korey shared about the value of rituals. Norajean appreciated Korey's encouragement "to commemorate the life and the death."[69]

It happened that the Community was gathered at Walt and Korey's home for the Solstice party in December 1994 the night after Norajean gave birth to a healthy girl. Bert and Norajean lived in San Francisco and called with the news. No one picked up the phone initially, but Korey listened to the message later. She then organized the group to sing "Angels We Have Heard on High" to Bert and Norajean's answering machine, replacing the refrain "in excelsis Deo" with the baby's name: Mary Kate Elizabeth.[70] Scattered and gathered united to share in the joy.

69. Glenn and Flanagan, in discussion with the author, December 2021.

70. Glenn and Flanagan, in discussion with the author, December 2021; Hoffman, in discussion with the author, September 2021; Thompson, in discussion with the author, February 2022.

8

"A Friend of the Street People"

SALLY HANLON WAS A clown at protests. There and elsewhere, she would put on face makeup and a costume and act out her persona, often using her hands as a beating heart. It was a twist in her reputation for ardor as an activist in DC leftist circles, in the Catholic Worker movement, and in the Latin American nations where she had lived. She was one of the few who spent many days in a row protesting in front of the White House, marking a person among those most committed to their message.[1]

John and Bobbie Stewart first invited Sally to visit the Community when she was living across the street from them. She was the most truly religious person Bobbie ever knew. She chose not to preach, but she conveyed her faith with her presence. "She was always doing her knee work, as she called it," John said.[2] Her spiritual disciplines, she said, "things that I really don't enjoy doing but that I feel called to do with a certain regularity" as a peacemaker were clowning, fasting, participating in civil disobedience, praying alone with arms outstretched, and spending the night on the streets. "Much as I struggle with myself before doing any one of the above, experience has taught me that these practices are necessary for me in order to maintain my sanity and even to find hope and joy in the world today."[3]

As in Sally's approach to the life of faith, the Community's activism was grounded in prayer and communal discernment of God's will. From its early years, Community leaders sought to hold their involvement in balance with knowledge that any human effort might fail. They tried not to make

1. Kim Klein, in discussion with the author, December 2021.
2. John and Bobbie Stewart, in discussion with the author, January 2021.
3. Sally Hanlon, untitled selection in *Lenten Booklet 1989*, March 10.

any cause an ultimate concern. They knew that God's reign does not depend on the outcome of any particular issue. This allowed them to have a sense of humor amid their serious political work.[4]

Sally's combination of playful creativity and political-religious earnestness made her a singular soul, even among the unusual characters who made up the Community of Christ. She had a disarming sense of humor among her coworkers in social service work caring for people with the least resources in the city, often a cause of over-seriousness. Sally commanded everyone to take a break at staff retreats and do silly dances. She made up silly songs and goaded everyone to sing with her until they were laughing.[5]

Around DC and beyond, Sally was known for her calligraphy, which she put on banners, posters, note cards, and little brightly colored slips of paper one could keep in a purse or wallet. She'd hand them out to tourists when protesting in front of the White House. In photos and videos of marches and protests, whether in independent activist publications or the *Washington Post* and television evening news, Sally's calligraphy stood out on signs and banners. They proclaimed messages such as "FYI: Drones Are Always Tools of Terrorism" or "Lord, Make Our Lives a Prayer for People Everywhere."

In the Community, her calligraphy expressed her theology. One Lenten Booklet contribution reads, "Practicing Resurrection = Dying to myself, that the new me may be."[6] Another year, each Monday included a Lenten assignment from her, such as "Meditate on the Agony (Read: Humanity as Crucified God) in the Garden (Read: Planet Earth.)."[7] A poster she made for my husband and me as our wedding card from the Community reads, "For Josiah and Celeste, May Your Love Be a Healing Balm for People and the Wounded Earth. May You Be a Blessing on the Land!" Surrounding that message are images she cut out of a magazine, including a photo of children living on a garbage heap and a bird covered with oil.

Some of Sally's art was lighthearted. One calligraphy image, accompanied by a smiley face, declared, "Life's Four Basic Lessons: 1. Show Up. 2. Pay Attention. 3. Speak Truth. 4. Be Open to Possibilities." And for a collage card, she clipped a photo from a magazine of a seagull with red legs and feet. The calligraphy caption read, "In fashion, beautiful shoes are very important."[8]

4. Schramm and Anderson, *Dance in Steps of Change*, 112–13.
5. Alicia Wilson, in discussion with the author, April 2022.
6. Sally Hanlon, untitled selection in *Lenten Booklet 1992*, March 5.
7. Sally Hanlon, untitled selection in *Lenten Booklet 1994*, March 28.
8. Klein, in discussion with the author, December 2021.

Sally was born in 1935 in Needham, Massachusetts, the second youngest of six children. She was christened Sarah Judge Hanlon. She disliked her middle name, a family name from their Irish and Scottish ancestors. She did not want to judge other people or be judged by them.[9]

Her mother, Frances Hanlon, taught her children not to be afraid of God. She was a devout Catholic but didn't think it was the only way. "There are many paths to God," Frances told her children. She taught them about the Trinity with the illustration of her multiple identities as wife, mother, friend. And she talked about what the Trinity meant to her. "When I need a friend, I talk to Jesus," she said. "When I don't know what to do with the six of you, I talk to the Holy Spirit." She wanted them to go beyond memorizing the catechism. Frances asked her children, "What does it mean to you that God made you?"[10]

Sally had epilepsy as a young child. A family friend told her parents that it was a variety she would outgrow. The seizures stopped when Sally was six years old. By then, her intellect and musical and artistic gifts were apparent. She could play the piano by ear and was largely self-taught. She also had a knack for languages. Latin was taught in public school and she picked it up quickly. French was next. She eventually achieved fluency in half a dozen languages, as well as variations within Spanish. "She could adopt the accent of a Chilean speaking to a Chilean, or a Guatemalan speaking to a Guatemalan," her sister Susie said.[11]

Sally could have been a fashion designer. As a child she won a contest in a girl's magazine with a dress she designed. On the trip to New York City they awarded, they showed her the dress they had produced from her design. They had taken out the most interesting part, a v-shaped piece of fabric that overlaid the rest of the dress. When it was up to Sally, she didn't let anyone dull down her sartorial sensibilities. Money wasn't an obstacle to her fashion either: she'd get castoffs from others and then hand-sew them into what she wanted them to look like. A scarf would be the final touch on any outfit.[12]

While Sally was at college at Notre Dame of Maryland, the sisters on the faculty thought Sally would become a nun because she willingly

9. Colette Hanlon, in discussion with the author, September 2021.

10. Hanlon, in discussion with the author, September 2021.

11. Hanlon, in discussion with the author, September 2021.

12. Klein, in discussion with the author, December 2021; Hanlon, in discussion with the author, September 2021.

attended daily Mass. But she also went to parties and liked to be the center of attention. She dated young men from the nearby naval academy.[13]

Sally worked as a teacher back in New England and learned about a Catholic mission work position available to laypeople. She volunteered to go to Latin America. After WWII, the number of Catholic missionaries increased greatly, including laypeople, especially in Central and South America.[14] Sally went to Honduras and learned the language and then went on to Peru. It was a three-year commitment to be a papal volunteer. "After two years, I joined the Maryknoll Order—not so much that I wanted to be a nun, but I thought that was what God wanted me to do," she said.[15] The pull into a religious vocation was also in part from her siblings, Susie and William, called Chip. Chip long felt a call to be a missionary and joined the Franciscans. Susie took her vows with the Sisters of Charity, adopting the name Colette. Sally traveled from Lima, Peru, to Chip's ordination. Colette was there also. "I think she saw Chip as happy and me as happy, and she thought if you just become a priest or a nun, you could be happy," Colette said. Sally took her final vows as a Maryknoll sister in 1963.[16]

In her ministry in Peru, she would travel by horse in the mountains, praying that she wouldn't fall off a cliff in perilous passages. Sometimes she accompanied a priest who was going to say Mass in the remote villages. People who were hosting them often put them in the same house, assuming that they had a sexual relationship. That was nerve-wracking for Sally.[17]

But she was much more deeply troubled by the poverty of the people. She developed solidly left-of-center politics. She taught youth to question the state of the world they lived in: wealthy landowners lived in luxury while the farmers who worked their land had little more than a roof over their heads.[18] Catholic missionaries across Latin America were making similar connections and "denouncing repressive governments that were often supported by the United States."[19] Maryknoll priests were expelled from Guatemala in 1968 after they supported student protests against the government. Some saw armed struggle as necessary to bring about freedom. Maryknoll fathers and sisters joined or aided leftist combatants, as did some local

13. Hanlon, in discussion with the author, September 2021.

14. Tentler, *American Catholics*, 234.

15. West, "Three Samaritans," F6.

16. Hanlon, in discussion with the author, September 2021.

17. Klein, in discussion with the author, December 2021; Hanlon, in discussion with the author, September 2021.

18. Hanlon, in discussion with the author, September 2021.

19. Tentler, *American Catholics*, 234.

clergy.[20] One Colombian priest, Camilo Torres, asked to be laicized before he joined the guerrilla, saying, "The Catholic who is not a revolutionary is living in mortal sin."[21] A popular song compared his death in 1966 at the hands of the Colombian military to the crucifixion of Jesus.[22]

After his death, one of his close friends, Gustavo Gutiérrez, a Peruvian priest and a sociologist like Torres,[23] continued the struggle in the realm of theology. In the summer of 1968 Gutiérrez gave a talk called "Toward a Theology of Liberation," which influenced the conference of Latin American bishops in Medellín, Colombia, that began a month later. They also drew on the Vatican II document *Gaudium et Spes* on the church in the modern world, which called on Christians to bear witness to their faith through their work in society.[24] The Latin American bishops declared that God had a "preferential option for the poor" and blessed the ecclesial base communities that were forming. These grassroots church groups gave Christian workers and farmers a chance to read Scripture for themselves and connect it to their experience of economic and political oppression. One of the core principles of liberation theology is that sin is the root of injustice, oppression, and exploitation.[25] Therefore Christ's liberating work affects not only souls but the physical conditions in which people live.

As with Vatican II's reforms, not all local bishops and priests embraced liberation theology. In the area where Sally was working, members of the Catholic hierarchy heard rumors that she was a radical. She received a one-way ticket to visit her brother in Brazil, and then she was to return to the Maryknoll motherhouse in New York. Sally felt heartbroken and betrayed.[26]

At the Maryknoll convent, Sally saw retired nuns eating three meals a day. She was aghast that they received Christmas presents; she saw even a bar of perfumed soap as a luxury. This was not the vision of the level of sacrifice that Sally expected from religious life.[27]

20. Gail Taylor, untitled selection in *Lenten Booklet 2012*, March 6; Pacatte, "Blase Bonpane"; Gerassi, "Introduction," 3.

21. Gerassi, "Introduction," 28–29.

22. Victor Jara, vocalist, "Camilo Torres," by D. Viglietti, compact disc of 1973 album *Te Recuerdo Amanda*.

23. Gerassi, "Introduction," 17.

24. Bettenson and Maunder, *Documents of the Christian Church*, 379–82; Flannery, *Vatican Council II*, 943–44.

25. Hennelly, *Liberation Theologies*, 11, 17, 25.

26. Hanlon, in discussion with the author, September 2021.

27. Hanlon, in discussion with the author, September 2021.

It wasn't the vows of chastity or poverty that were a problem for Sally.[28] "I could give up anything or do anything that would be for the good of people," she said. "Faith has been a key thing for me all along. I said, 'Oh, Lord, you're the one who has been there during the tough times.'" After a decade in Latin America and disillusionment with life at the motherhouse, she went on leave from Maryknoll. She was in Finland for a summer and swept the floors in a factory for a year, receiving minimum wage and living in a basement room. Sally kept extending her leave, and Maryknoll was understanding when she resigned and left the convent permanently, she said. "So now I'm an ex-con. That's what ex-nuns are called."[29] At least, that's what Sally called herself, again identifying with people who are marginalized.

Sally found her way to DC and moved into Tabor House, one of the group houses in Mount Pleasant, along with other former missionaries who were politically active on behalf of the people they had served alongside in Latin America. For a while she was dating a man at Tabor House. They talked about marriage, but then Sally decided not to marry.

She was a teacher's aide at Rosemount, the bilingual daycare center where the Community had worshiped for a while in the mid-1970s. There she met Kim Klein, whose daughters went to Rosemount. They began a close, lifelong friendship. Sally rented a room from Kim and her family for a while, giving Kim a chance to witness Sally's level of commitment to living simply. "She had such respect for limited resources and the hard life of where there's not enough water," Kim said. Sally would bathe with a thermos of hot water left over from the kettle when she made her morning tea. She also refused free tickets to a performance at the Kennedy Center for the Performing Arts that Kim had gotten from her job, saying that someone else would appreciate it more than she would—even though Sally was a musician.[30]

Such tendencies, and her aquiline face, could make Sally seem severe. Yet that was not the full picture. "She would just stride out into the morning, absolutely beaming," Kim said, "radiating the sheer joy of living and being part of this world and being able to make a difference."[31]

While Sally had a singular spiritual life, she wanted to be part of something larger. She was part of innumerable activist groups and two congregations. She went to Mass at the Shrine of the Sacred Heart, Mount Pleasant's Catholic parish, on Sundays. Then she walked a few blocks to attend the 10:30 a.m. service at the Community of Christ. To Norajean, a Catholic who

28. Klein, in discussion with the author, December 2021.

29. West, "Three Samaritans," F6.

30. Klein, in discussion with the author, December 2021.

31. Klein, in discussion with the author, December 2021.

joined the Community in 1984, Sally was an exemplar of an ecumenical Christian. "She was just such a joy and a delight," Norajean said, an "embodiment of the joy and love of God."[32]

Sally also had a rap sheet that exceeded many ardent activists. DC gives many opportunities for civil disobedience, and Sally availed herself of many of them. One time she was strip-searched, which was traumatic. After that, she didn't go out of her way to risk arrest.[33] In 1980, Sally was featured in the People-Fashion section of the *Washington Post* as one of three especially committed activists. (Unfortunately, it wasn't for her sense of style.) Sally summed up her life this way:

> I want to be one of those who identify with the people and help others to do it, too. I never want to forget that there are political prisoners. I never want to have a savior complex. I need people to laugh me out of my seriousness. A lot of my life I spent in the prayer of desperation. It makes for a good night's sleep. I try to make my life a permanent prayer.[34]

From 1987, Sally's Lenten booklet contribution is a prayer, "After hearing a heart-rending lecture on US policy & Central America." "We have just heard the real truth, Lord, about what is being done in our name," Sally wrote. "How can we stand before you in prayer, how face your wounded world?" She compared contemporary Christians to believers in Nero's Rome, the people of Nineveh when Jonah removes "the mask of blindness," and German Christians during Hitler's mass murder.[35]

During the 1980s, the United States government gave millions in military aid to El Salvador, even though the decade began with the nation's military agents assassinating Archbishop Óscar Romero and four US churchwomen.[36] Two of the women, Maura Clarke and Ita Ford, were Maryknoll sisters working among some of the poorest people in Latin America, as Sally had. In the months before their deaths, they provided medical supplies for a surgeon, Juan Romagoza Arce, who risked his life to treat people injured by the police and army.[37]

On December 12, 1980, ten days after the sisters were killed, soldiers fired machine guns on a crowd of people being served through one of the

32. Norajean Flanagan, in discussion with the author, December 2021.

33. Hanlon, in discussion with the author, September 2021.

34. West, "Three Samaritans," F6.

35. Hanlon, "After Hearing a Heart-Rending Lecture," in *Lenten Booklet 1987*, April 10.

36. Markey, *Radical Faith*, 203, 209, 253.

37. Markey, *Radical Faith*, 237–39.

rural clinics Romagoza set up with Catholic churches and Christian base communities. Soldiers detained him at the National Guard headquarters. He endured twenty-two days of torture, sustaining wounds that achieved the torturers' goal of ensuring that he could no longer perform surgery.[38] Romagoza was one of thousands of laypeople who were tortured. Many of them were also executed, along with hundreds of nuns and priests across Latin America. Catholic theologian Rosemary Radford Ruether wrote in the Community's magazine, *Stance*, "The price of the 'option for the poor' for the Church is written starkly in the blood of many martyrs."[39]

When Romagoza arrived in the United States in 1983, he was shocked to learn that most people thought the war in El Salvador was about communism. "I walked almost the whole country of El Salvador on foot—and I never met people who talked to me about communism. What I did see was hunger, unemployment, premature deaths, epidemics, injustice, massacres. This was what made the majority of Salvadorans denounce the government, organize, and resist." Romagoza became executive director at La Clínica del Pueblo, a nonprofit clinic serving Spanish speakers, providing care in all the ways he still could. Continuing the work he did in El Salvador, "this helps me live, survive, and inspires me to overcome my physical and emotional limitations," Romagoza said.[40]

Sally was one of the people who accompanied Romagoza as he persevered in pursuing his vocation. She could do simultaneous interpretation—which only the most fluent speakers can do, and Sally did it without notes—and knew her way around DC and had connections in the Central American community there. Alicia Wilson, who worked at La Clínica del Pueblo, saw Sally's relationship with Romagoza as being a symbiotic one. Sally did more than translate and type as Romagoza's assistant,[41] she embodied liberation theology's religious grounding in solidarity and social justice. Romagoza, who was a torture survivor but also "100 percent fundamentally committed to health care" as human rights work, helped Sally channel her faith into a specific action. Together, they formed the organization's moral compass, making it more than simply a social service agency. "This was their mission, their vocation," Wilson said.[42] To Sally's friend Kim, their

38. "Client: Dr. Juan Romagoza Arce," para. 1–5; Romagoza, *No Safe Haven*, 2–3.

39. Ruether, "Latin American Church," 6.

40. Romagoza, "Tortured Path to Justice."

41. Klein, in discussion with the author, April 2022; Wilson, in discussion with the author, April 2022.

42. Wilson, in discussion with the author, March 2023.

collaboration reminded her of St. Clare and St. Francis of Assisi.[43] They aided each other in overcoming obstacles to pursue their callings, and they brought about transformation far beyond the individuals they met.[44]

Like women of St. Clare's order, Sally lived below the poverty line and encouraged contemplation. And like the Franciscans, she went out around the city to preach with her example and care for the most neglected. She spent one day a week at the Dorothy Day Catholic Worker House, she prayed in protest at the Pentagon, and she worked at La Clínica. But she would not accept enough salary to have to pay taxes that would have gone largely to warmaking with its military interventions she so despised. When people gave her money, she gave it away. She often bartered for what she needed, such as haircuts.[45] She volunteered at a shelter. "I'm a friend of the street people," she said.[46]

During the 1980s, people living on the streets needed more friends. After two decades of growth in public housing, much of it sponsored by the federal government, new construction came to a halt with the Reagan administration. Most US cities saw increased homelessness from year to year as large as 50 percent during the 1980s. The effects were readily seen in the part of DC where the Community of Christ was located. Their neighbor in the Church of the Saviour, physician and author David Hilfiker, wrote that while it's difficult to take an accurate census of homeless people, "What is clear is that nationally, as in Washington, the problem of homelessness has been growing for several decades, slowly in the sixties and seventies and exponentially in the eighties and nineties."[47]

Hilfiker was one of the founders of Christ House, "a thirty-four-bed medical recovery shelter for homeless men too sick to be on the streets yet not sick enough to be in the hospital." It was the result of one of the Church of the Saviour's mission groups, up to ten people meeting to pray about a specific idea. A donor gave $2.5 million to the Church of the Saviour "to create an infirmary for the homeless. At the same time, a vacant, decaying apartment building across the street from Columbia Road Health Services went up for sale." The Church of the Saviour purchased it in early 1984, and Christ House opened in early 1985.[48]

43. Klein, in discussion with the author, [Zoom interview]

44. Sweeney, *Light in the Dark Ages*, 11, 22, 68, 75.

45. Hanlon, untitled selection in *Lenten Thoughts, 2004*, February 29; Wilson, in discussion with the author, April 2022.

46. West, "Three Samaritans," F6.

47. Hilfiker, *Not All of Us Are Saints*, 82–84.

48. Hilfiker, *Not All of Us Are Saints*, 13, 60–63.

Once Christ House was established, Community members joined the volunteer rotation of this ministry of their mentor-partner congregation. Volunteering at Christ House made practical sense. So did partnering with the nearby Episcopal congregation St. Stephen and the Incarnation with its Loaves and Fishes program. A Community group volunteered each Saturday. Shepherd's Pie was the standard—a dish of ground meat, carrots, celery, and onions topped with mashed potatoes—cooked in enormous trays. People from the Community often sat down to eat with the people they served. At Christ House one Saturday, Bobbie shared a meal with one person who had no teeth and another who was blind. She thought of Jesus' Parable of the Great Banquet (Luke 14:16–21), where the host of a feast is turned down by the guests he initially invited. He then extends the invitation to everyone in the streets and alleys of the town: people who are poor, who are blind, who cannot walk.[49]

With its partnerships, the Community bolstered the efforts of others instead of feeling that it needed to own or control a particular ministry. "We had a little bit of wisdom in that you don't always have to do everything yourself," Dunstan said. "We didn't feel we had to run our own soup kitchen when others were doing it and probably doing a better job."[50] It was also a way for the Community to do something about the needs in its square-mile parish without the level of sacrifice of Christ House doctors and nurses, who lived together on the top two floors of the building where they worked. And even the families at Christ House kept some middle-class comforts. Not like the Christian activists in the nearby Community for Creative Non-Violence, whose work the Community of Christ also supported with prayers, donations, and volunteers.[51]

CCNV was committed to poverty as a sign of true community, founder Ed Guinan told *Stance*, "because of the need and importance of sharing and interdependence."[52] Initially focused on the Vietnam War, they realized that "we were blindly stepping over the bodies here in DC," Guinan said. By the mid-1970s, dozens of people were sleeping on the floor of CCNV's row house each night.[53] CCNV activists and people coming off of the streets lived together. Carol Fennelly, who was part of CCNV for seventeen years, said, "We ate out of the soup kitchen, dressed out of the clothing room, slept

49. Dunstan Hayden, in discussion with the author, May 2021; John and Bobbie Stewart, in discussion with the author, May 2022.

50. Hayden, in discussion with the author, May 2021.

51. Hilfiker, *Not All of Us Are Saints*; Community of Christ Papers, The Swarthmore College Peace Collection.

52. Sims, "Creative Non-Violence in Community," 8.

53. Asch and Musgrove, *Chocolate City*, 390–92.

at the shelter, and got our medical care out of the free clinic that we ran at the building." (Hilfiker was one of the doctors providing that care.) CCNV had payphones in its building, and, as with other buildings with a payphone in them, the owners received a portion of the money. CCNV activists divided the monthly check amount into "something like $5 apiece," Fennelly said. That was their only source of spending money.[54]

Mitch Snyder, CCNV's most-prominent member, gave up a comfortable life as a Madison Avenue management consultant. He saw his work as a religious vocation, and he dreamed of a world without homelessness. Working for money was selling oneself "whether you're standing on 14th Street or in a boardroom for AT&T," he said, the former referring to a corridor in DC where sex workers met customers. Snyder grew up with atheist Jewish parents in Brooklyn, New York. He converted to Catholicism after reading the Bible and meeting radical priest brothers Philip and Daniel Berrigan in a Connecticut prison in the early 1970s. (Snyder was convicted of car theft; he maintained his innocence.)[55] In the tradition of Gandhi and Catholic Worker cofounder Dorothy Day, Snyder learned hunger strikes as a form of protest.[56]

Snyder made a scene many times to expose the wrongs of society. He held public funerals for the dozens of people who froze to death on the street each winter after refusing to endure degrading treatment in city-run shelters—if they could even find space there. In 1978–79, he led protests in Holy Trinity parish in Georgetown, which had many high-level business and political leaders in the pews. CCNV and Holy Trinity were exploring working together when the church began a capital campaign to raise $400,000 to restore its historic building and organ. CCNV asked Holy Trinity to ask donors for an additional $80,000 to help CCNV renovate its shelter. The parish council wouldn't agree to that. Snyder, Fennelly, and several other CCNV members stood silently (as opposed to kneeling or sitting) throughout Mass on Sundays for months. Snyder and others fasted, some while living in the church courtyard. Snyder denied himself food and water to the point of serious illness but ended the fast after the parish council refused to reconsider. To continue after that would have been symbolic, he said.[57]

54. Fennelly, in discussion with the author, June 2022.

55. National Coalition for the Homeless, "Remembering Mitch Snyder," paras. 4–7.

56. Kernan, "Mitch Snyder, the Wayward Shepherd."

57. Fennelly, in discussion with the author, June 2022; Kernan, "Mitch Snyder, the Wayward Shepherd."

As homelessness worsened, CCNV broadened its fight to change city-wide and federal policies. In 1984, Snyder estimated there were thousands of homeless people in DC, possibly as many as 10,000.[58] Fennelly called every church in DC to ask them to open their doors. They argued that their insurance didn't cover that, and besides, they needed their fellowship hall for church dinners. Luther Place and St. Stephen and the Incarnation Episcopal, the two churches that offered temporary shelter, were at capacity. CCNV looked to the old Federal City College downtown, which was large and vacant. "We had gotten legislation passed to make federal buildings available for people," Fennelly said. They got access to the building in December 1983, but the government wanted them to leave in the spring, as if people only need shelter in the winter, despite the city exceeding 100-degree temperatures for stretches in the summer. Fennelly realized, "If we leave here, we lose the building." They refused to leave, and the federal government tried to evict them, threatening to shut off the water. CCNV members went on hunger strikes.[59] In fall of 1984, as President Reagan ran for re-election, Snyder fasted from food for fifty-one days, almost to death. Two days before the election, Reagan agreed CCNV could renovate the building to use as a shelter with 1,350 beds, which they did. CCNV believes it to be the largest and most comprehensive facility of its kind.[60]

Fennelly described such public actions as employing "good old-fashioned embarrassment," she said. "We worry about hurting people's feelings who are in power instead of making them do the right thing." Fennelly, Snyder, and others saw that in action for social change, people who are poor have the least power. "They don't fund campaigns," she said. "They tend not to vote." Without power or money, CCNV sought to "equalize the dialogue" by using their bodies and freedom. They were willing to be arrested, even to die in hunger strikes.[61]

That level of commitment was inspiring and challenging for the Community, spurring self-examination about their own discipleship. When CCNV members were publicly fasting, Valborg wrote about it in the Community's internal newsletter, *Happenings*. Sometimes Community members joined in solidarity. They broke their fast with the Eucharist.[62] CCNV was regularly in the Community's budget starting when CCNV began its efforts against hunger, a primary topic of concern for the Community at that time

58. Kernan, "Mitch Snyder, the Wayward Shepherd."
59. Fennelly, in discussion with the author, June 2022.
60. "History of the CCNV," para. 6.
61. Fennelly, in discussion with the author, June 2022.
62. *Happenings*, 25 August 1974, in Community of Christ Papers.

as well.[63] The Community finished its renovations of La Casa in 1979, not long after Snyder's fast at Holy Trinity, and many of them sympathized with calling a wealthy parish to account for spending so much on its building. "On a per capita basis the Community is spending as much on La Casa," Doug admitted, though noting that the Community gave away $15,000 the previous year and loaned $10,000 each for housing projects to CCNV and the Community of Hope, another neighboring Christian group.[64]

Once, when Snyder came to a meeting with the Community, Dunstan recalled that "he basically lay on the floor and kind of looked at us." Dunstan imagined that Snyder thought the Community "didn't meet his standards."[65] Fennelly disagreed. As long as a group was "out there doing their best," they were all right with him. As for Community members, she said, "He always appreciated all of you, and so did I. Frankly."[66]

In the mid-1980s, Larry gave a homily in Community worship about how prophets were not well-liked in their time. They were obnoxious to the people around them. They wouldn't give people any peace while there was injustice glaring. Larry gave Snyder as an example of a prophet in the biblical tradition. Dunstan noted that he was taught in his Catholic education that many saints were to be admired but not imitated, "because they are such a pain in the neck."[67]

Barbara Hayden, who joined the Community and married Dunstan in 1985, saw Snyder as highly effective as an activist: the city would have far less commitment to homeless people if it weren't for Snyder. "He was pushing, pushing, brilliantly pushing, just pushing the government to face up to the homelessness we had," Barbara said. "This was the Reagan administration. And you had all the riches that were being paraded around the city and the contrast with the homelessness because of the deinstitutionalization of mental hospitals and economic downturn." Snyder embodied identifying in the extreme with the mission of one's community and religious life. Barbara thought about how the Community described itself in the 1960s, "The Community seeks to *be* mission, not merely to engage in mission work."[68] She took that to mean doing more than simply helping with the meal program at St. Stephen's or Christ House, then saying, "'Oh, I've done my good deed for the month,' and you don't let it in." The Community sought to deepen

63. Financial records, 1973–74, in Community of Christ Papers.

64. Huron, "Putting the Burden Behind Us," 5–6, 8.

65. Dunstan Hayden, in discussion with the author, May 2020.

66. Fennelly, in discussion with the author, June 2022.

67. Barbara and Dunstan Hayden, in discussion with the author, May 2020.

68. Schramm and Anderson, *Dance in Steps of Change*, 18.

an ability to "share the anguish of the hungry and the broken and the disenfranchised," she said, even as it remained primarily a worshiping body. In contrast, Snyder "was the mission," Barbara said. "He was just so driven."[69]

⁊⬤

Need for affordable housing in the Community's square-mile parish of concern increased in the 1980s because of the arrival of thousands of people from Latin America. "Mostly young, male, and poor, the new immigrants packed into dilapidated, overcrowded apartments," and worked in unstable industries such as restaurants and construction.[70] Mount Pleasant and Adams Morgan already had the largest concentration of Latin Americans in DC by the mid-1970s, though they were less than 10 percent of the city's population. At the end of the 1980s, Latin Americans made up more than a quarter of Mount Pleasant residents. To many of them, it felt like a village with other newcomers who were far from their homes, many having left their families as teenagers or young adults. It was also a place to mix with people of other cultures.[71]

Many of them fled violence in their home countries, especially El Salvador. Some were tortured by government agents or saw family members executed in front of them. Frequently, men coping with trauma turned to alcohol and drugs. Some would pass out in the alley behind La Casa.[72] On Sunday mornings, walking to church meant stepping over men on the sidewalk who had not yet sobered up from the night before. Sometimes it was necessary to make sure they were still breathing and if it wasn't clear, to call paramedics. One day a man who was intoxicated and in need of medical attention opened the door to La Casa during worship but couldn't make it up the stairs to the main gathering space. A few Spanish speakers went to talk to him in the doorway while others called 911.

Margaret Ann, who had worked in the La Casa building with Life Skills Center since 1974, felt increasingly saddened and frustrated on Mount Pleasant Street. She wrote, "Day after day after day I face the poverty and hopelessness of the people who walk on the street; very young children walking themselves to school eating potato chips for breakfast; people in line at the grocery store trying to buy groceries with limited cash or food stamps; and elderly people with thin coats struggling to get their one bag of groceries home." Seeing the contrast between their lives and her own tore at her soul and her faith, she

69. Barbara Hayden, in discussion with the author, May 2020.

70. Asch and Musgrove, *Chocolate City*, 413–14.

71. Smith, *Captive Capital*, 79; Morley, "Mount Pleasant Miracle"; Walton, *La Manplesa*.

72. John and Bobbie Stewart, in discussion with the author, May 2022.

wrote. "As I walk on the street I step over bodies, bodies of young Hispanic men with no homes, who drink until they drop. I step over them and I sin."[73]

Margaret Ann created a set of guidelines for herself to make those moments less painful. She would help up someone struggling to stand, give money to those who asked if she had some handy, and look for others nearby to help if someone was unconscious. One day Margaret Ann saw a man lying not on the sidewalk but in the gutter. A police officer was standing perhaps twenty feet away, laughing with a civilian. The officer told Margaret Ann she had already called for a police wagon, and then she returned to her conversation. Calluses grow as we are exposed to the abrasion of suffering, not only on hands and feet but on the ability to feel compassion.

Yet even as sin abounded on Mount Pleasant Street, Margaret Ann wrote, grace abounded also. She saw it in the owners of the 7-Eleven convenience store who handed out unsold sandwiches at the end of the day to men preparing to spend the night on the streets. She saw it in the shop owners who treated her clients from Life Skills, who had developmental disabilities, with respect and patience. Neighbors noticed when a client, Leticia, was dropped off at La Casa on a day when Life Skills was closed, and waited with her until the police contacted Margaret Ann at home. All this despite the language barrier, since Leticia spoke only Spanish.[74]

As Margaret Ann and others in the Community struggled with how to respond to the men on Mount Pleasant Street, many homeowners, Black and white, felt the newcomers threatened the character of the neighborhood.[75] People who had lived in the neighborhood during the 1970s and early 1980s noticed the police were increasingly rough with young men. The majority African American police force was not trained to understand cultural differences. If young men hung out in Mount Pleasant's central park after work the way they would have in a plaza back in El Salvador, the police called them vagrants. And in many cases the police responded differently to similar behavior. Children of all cultures in the neighborhood spent long hours outside. When the children and teenagers were Latino, police would break them up for hanging out in groups, even if they had no weapons or drugs and weren't arguing with each other. One officer came up to a group of boys sitting outside of their apartment building and pressed a pistol against a boy's temple. The officer said something in English, which they didn't understand.[76]

73. Margaret Ann Hoven, "Sin and Grace on Mt. Pleasant St," *Lenten Booklet 1989*, February 13.

74. Hoven, "Sin and Grace on Mt. Pleasant St," *Lenten Booklet 1989*, February 13.

75. Asch and Musgrove, *Chocolate City*, 414.

76. Cherkasky, *Mount Pleasant*, 69; José "Chico" Diaz, in discussion with Patrick Scallen, December 2017; Walton, *La Manplesa*.

ટ્જ

May 5, 1991, was one of those spring evenings in DC when it already feels like summer. It was a Sunday and Daniel Enrique Gomez, thirty, who worked as a dishwasher in a Georgetown hotel after arriving in the city from El Salvador in 1989, was out drinking with his friends, as many young men do after work. On this balmy evening, there was a fight in Don Juan's, a Salvadoran restaurant, and Gomez went across Lamont Street to the small park in the center of Mount Pleasant. Two female officers arrived and moved to arrest Gomez and three friends for public intoxication. Some witnesses said Gomez told the officers, "This is unfair. Take my handcuffs off." Officers said that one of his hands was free and held a knife. Angela Jewell, a Black officer, yelled, "Freeze!" Neither she nor Gomez were speaking the other's language and neither responded to the other's command. Jewell shot Gomez in the chest.[77]

Others who were on the street at the time heard the shot, and Gomez was taken away in an ambulance, his fate unclear. A crowd gathered and some shouted that the police had killed a man for no reason. Word spread, adding that the man was handcuffed when shot. It was reminiscent of the murderous government agents they had fled in El Salvador.[78] Young men flocked into the streets. Some pelted the police with rocks and bottles. The mayor called on the police to "contain rather than confront the rioters,"[79] but that still meant a large police presence in riot gear. Officers brutalized some of the men, and they arrested 230.[80]

The next day, even as local news reported that Gomez was alive in critical condition, conflict reignited for a second night. One officer described the street the night of May 6 as being like a war zone. Some homes of Community members were only a couple of blocks away from the center of the conflict. Tear gas traveled down the streets and seeped inside at the edges of the old wooden windows with their rope-and-pulley systems. On Mount Pleasant Street, some of the young men shattered windows on thirty storefronts, burned vehicles, and torched a fast-food chain restaurant a block away from La Casa.[81]

At one point in the chaos, someone tossed a Molotov cocktail toward the door of La Casa. Dr. Romagoza was nearby with one of the teams from La

77. Asch and Musgrove, *Chocolate City*, 414; George Derek Musgrove, email message to author, February 20, 2023; Morley, "Mount Pleasant Miracle"; Walton, *La Manplesa*.

78. Morley, "Mount Pleasant Miracle"; Walton, *La Manplesa*.

79. Asch and Musgrove, *Chocolate City*, 414.

80. Walton, *La Manplesa*; Cherkasky, *Mount Pleasant*, 124.

81. Asch and Musgrove, *Chocolate City*, 414; author's memory; Cherkasky, *Mount Pleasant*, 124.

Clínica del Pueblo providing water and medical care to the injured. A member of the medical team grabbed the Molotov cocktail and moved it away. They saw La Casa as a place that served the community, not like the other institutions where people had ignored and mistreated their neighbors.[82]

In the aftermath, John Stewart and Bob Pohlman were part of a group who surveyed Mount Pleasant residents to find out about unmet needs. They learned that the Vietnamese Americans, largely living in one apartment building on the north end of Mount Pleasant Street, needed a space to gather for meetings and events. This was a signal to the Community to make La Casa available to a more-diverse set of groups.[83] La Casa came to be known as one of the main community centers in the neighborhood.[84]

ॐ

Valborg, who sometimes said she moved to DC to be able to protest the Vietnam War in front of the White House, marched for many causes. In her seventies, she was arrested at the South African embassy along with others from the Community calling for an end to apartheid. For decades she hosted the Community's weekly Bible study, one evening proclaiming her discovery, "Paul didn't write all those letters, did he?"[85] Near the end of her life, Valborg envisioned "continuing creation" when violence and environmental destruction

> will not drape dreams
> of mine. The legacy I leave
> will not be much: some tattered words,
> and here and there a stake set down:
> a clown, a fool, some bright balloons
> of laughter and love. This old buffoon
> awaits impatiently the open door.[86]

Valborg died in 1996 at the age of eighty-seven. In the bulletin for her memorial service at La Casa, her family wrote, "She is probably now leading the angels in a demonstration and demanding answers from God about all sorts of things that happened on this earth."[87]

82. Wilson, in discussion with the author, April 2022.

83. John Stewart, in discussion with the author, May 2022.

84. Ellie Walton (*La Manplesa* documentarian), email message to author, June 1, 2022.

85. David E. Anderson, Valborg memorial homily, January 4, 1997, in the author's possession.

86. Anderson, *Thoughts, Faith, and Friends*, 82.

87. Valborg D. Anderson memorial service bulletin, January 4, 1997, in the author's possession.

In the late 1990s, the Community began a sister-church relationship with Christians in Nicaragua. Phil Wheaton, who was the Mount Pleasant neighbor who spoke in favor of buying La Casa in the 1970s, later lived in Nicaragua. He and his family met the Christian ecclesial base community in the mountain village of Jiñocuao. After Phil joined the Community, he led delegations to Jiñocuao with Community members to meet the base community and see the economic aid projects the Community helped to fund, including with livestock and carpentry.[88]

On the first delegation, in June 2001, Community members saw another embodiment of ministry flowing from the gifts of laypeople. Base community leaders are called delegates of the word, trained to preach (but not administer the sacraments). Eighty such leaders founded 120 base communities in northern Nicaragua in the mid-1970s, the same time that the Community became primarily lay-led. At that time, there were tens of thousands of Latin American Christian base communities. During the 1980s, US-funded Contra militants crossing the Honduran border targeted rural lay leaders as elsewhere in Central America. Conflict with the Catholic hierarchy caused many base communities to close. The Jiñocuao community continued without license.[89]

By 2001, Jiñocuao's Iglesia San José was still gathering, with seventy-five to a hundred people on Sundays singing in strong voices and reflecting on Scripture together in light of their everyday experiences. They saw the Community as "so much in solidarity with us," connecting their *hermanamiento* (sister relationship) to one of the core concepts in liberation theology.[90] Phil wrote, "Like all of us, the faithful of Jiñocuao have their vices and virtues, but their unique *fidelity* has emerged in their struggles as an integrated community—in its work and worship together—to replicate the small communities of the Early Church and strive to follow Jesus' example with his disciples in building a new humanity."[91]

88. Wheaton, *Faithful Community*, 3, 156.

89. Ruether, "Latin American Church," 6, 14; Bettenson and Maunder, *Documents of the Christian Church*, 382–88; Wheaton, *Faithful Community*, 3, 65–70, 156.

90. "Church of the Poor in Jiñocuao, Iglesia San José," ca. 2001, in the author's possession; Base community in Jiñocuao to the Community of Christ, January 2001, in the author's possession; Bettenson and Maunder, *Documents of the Christian Church*, 379.

91. Wheaton, *Faithful Community*, 233. Italics in original.

9

"The Promise of Radical Inclusiveness"

ANOTHER WORLD IS POSSIBLE. That was the rallying cry for activists in the 1990s struggling for a democratic globalization, one that put people over profits. Protesters gathered at the World Trade Organization meetings in Seattle in 1999, and near the World Bank and International Monetary Fund buildings in DC. Faith-based groups drew religious and nonreligious activists to declare 2000 a Jubilee year, demanding the cancellation of onerous debts placed on countries in the global South, often agreed to by dictators and leading to a draining of resources needed for public health and education. Hands linked in a human chain around the Capitol in the fall of 1999 then let go to symbolize the breaking of the chains of debt.

While not stopping the momentum built, the US presidential election of 2000 and the attacks on September 11, 2001, were sobering. The forces of racism, militarism, and global economic exploitation were as potent as ever. Had anything changed since Martin Luther King Jr. named those three evils of society three decades earlier? If anything, it felt like things were getting worse, as we began to wrap our minds around how economic exploitation was harming not only people but the earth itself. Amid such questions, people of the Community entered a new season of a practice they had in various ways since the beginning: holding in tension their differences with their desire to be in relationship with each other. Even when it was difficult to understand each other, was it still possible to care deeply and vulnerably for each other?

When Andrew Wells-Dang arrived in DC in 1995, he "was a committed Christian with progressive-leftist tendencies" looking for a community to join. In conversation with his housemates and friends, he learned that "there's this really cool, progressive Christian group that's kind of hard to get in and get to know that meets up on Mount Pleasant Street." He previously visited a Church of the Saviour worship group, but it was even "harder to get to know people," and it was less openly political than he was looking for in a congregation. So he tried the Community.[1]

He was twenty-four and thought, "we were going to have a new progressive movement and do the sixties right this time." They would learn from the mistakes of that period, including the rampant sexism in other movements that made the women's movement all the more necessary. "After the Cold War, we didn't have to worry about the whole anti-communist nonsense anymore—that was the mood of the anti-globalization movement in the nineties, which I was in the middle of," he said. "We really thought we were making a difference." And they were, as the movement "did stop some of the worst aspects of the neoliberal project at the time."[2]

Despite his critiques of movements in the 1960s that shaped many in the Community, the people drew Andrew in and kept him coming back, along with joining the musicians led by Margaret Ann. Homilies spurred further reflection. David Anderson and Doug Huron especially imparted "the idea that the world isn't becoming a better place." Instead of a trajectory of progress, "it definitely can decline and fall apart and is indeed doing so," Andrew said, "whether it's ourselves, our own lives, or our society and the world as a whole." David's and Doug's doubt, and their "cynical, jaded view of the world in the context of a church and our faith was something new and different and challenging to me." Doug further pushed Andrew on his "naive optimism about liberal progressive values advancing and that we were past some of the more negative aspects of history." In Doug's homilies, Andrew heard a message: "This is how it's always been and how they treated the prophets," it went. "The church has also oppressed people through its history and yet we're still here. . . . You recognize all the obstacles, but still, we have a chance to do this."[3] The world could be changed.

As a young man, Andrew treasured the example of men a generation older than him who had careers they cared about but didn't let that be the trait that defined them. He learned from them that "you find something hopefully meaningful and contributing to society—at a minimum not harmful. What really mattered is family and relationships, and who we are as people."[4] Andrew grew up seeing his parents' neighbors in Springfield, Virginia, working for the military and the FBI and similar institutions. "I

1. Andrew Wells-Dang, in discussion with the author, December 2021.
2. Wells-Dang, in discussion with the author, December 2021.
3. Wells-Dang, in discussion with the author, December 2021.
4. Wells-Dang, in discussion with the author, December 2021.

knew I didn't want to be like them. And a lot of them seemed sort of beaten down by the system." The people in the Community provided a contrast to that. Andrew learned from men in the Community "that it was possible to have a job working for a local or even federal government and still be cool." Yet these men at the core of the Community didn't have overblown egos. "I didn't know about all this stuff Bob Pohlman did" in the DC government and as an affordable housing advocate, Andrew said. "Same for Doug."[5]

Doug was an influential civil rights attorney. Doug and a legal partner successfully argued a landmark employment rights case at the US Supreme Court, *Price Waterhouse v. Hopkins* (1989). "It was one of the top five employment rights cases of the last century," said Josiah Groff, who attended the Community while he was in law school. Doug knew Josiah was studying employment law, yet he didn't regale him with the story of that case even once, let alone countless times as others might have. Instead, when they talked after worship, Doug wanted to hear what Josiah was working on and thinking about in law school and his internships. Since attorneys' names aren't the focus in court opinion documents, Josiah didn't know Doug litigated the case until many years later when Doug's daughter, Amanda, shared video footage from the 1980s with Doug being interviewed on C-SPAN.[6]

❧

Doug was a skeptic, like his father before him. Walter Huron expressed reservations about the creeds and the idea of a heaven. Walter said, "The idea of annihilation is unthinkable to me, but I cannot latch on to any palpable concept of everlastingness." Walter believed in God but didn't think God could be explained. The family attended church during Doug's childhood, first a Presbyterian one—Doug's mother was a Christian—then Unitarian. Growing up, Doug had a push-and-pull relationship with religion. When he was twelve, he went to a revival at a nearby Baptist church with a friend. "At the close of a fiery sermon, the preacher beseeched us sinners to come up to the altar and be saved," Doug said. His friend "wanted to go up, but I was either embarrassed or skeptical—probably both—and I blocked his way."[7]

At the Unitarian church Doug's family attended while he was in high school, there was an annual Youth Sunday, and Doug was chosen from among his peers to speak. "For some time, I had been put off by the smug, self-congratulatory atmosphere at the church, as if we knew that we were a

5. Wells-Dang, in discussion with the author, December 2021.
6. Josiah Groff, in discussion with the author, July 2022.
7. Huron, "Third Sunday of Advent."

cut above the worshiping masses. And I found it ironic that Unitarians—the champions of skepticism and free and open debate—would act like we had a corner on the truth." He candidly addressed that and ended by asking, "Surely we don't believe that ours is the one true faith?" A member of the congregation told him, "You really gave us hell."[8]

Doug was about to start college in August 1963. He and a friend took a bus from suburban Maryland to the National Mall to attend the March on Washington. Doug wrote, "I remember thinking this was the most spiritual moment I'd ever experienced. It wasn't just the smiling, although there was plenty of that. This was a glimpse of heaven—free from alienation, feeling at one with the universe. It's the only time I felt that way."[9]

Doug held a similar tension with church as his father did in his career. Walter was as close to a pacifist as Doug knew, though he spent his career in the US Air Force. Doug "believed in the teachings of Jesus, but he didn't necessarily believe in Christianity." Yet he was devoted to his Christian community.[10]

Initially joining a church was his wife Anne's idea. She grew up United Methodist, in a socially active congregation, and wanted to find a similarly engaged community that also had more formal liturgy and followed the church seasons. After they moved to DC, they tried a number of churches but found them too polished and grand. In 1973, Anne talked with a Roman Catholic friend who was teaching at Wesley Seminary with Larry, a relatively new member of the Community. Anne's friend said: "You should really check out this ecumenical, kind of off-the-grid group. It's half Catholic, half Lutheran. And Larry Rasmussen says a lot of nice things about it."[11] On the first Sunday of Lent, Anne and Doug attended the Community with their infant daughter, Amanda. They found a home.

Within a year, Doug and Anne were woven into the religious, social, and neighborhood life of the Community. Bruce Johnson convinced them to move to Mount Pleasant. In 1978, the Community celebrated with them when they had a son, Amos. When Doug and Anne divorced in the early 1980s, Community members were kind and supportive to everyone in the family. Dora especially made sure that Amos and Amanda received caring attention.[12] Their divorce was not acrimonious, as Bruce and Dora's would be a few years later. Anne observed that the late thirties to mid-forties are

8. Huron, "Second Sunday in Lent."
9. Huron, "Race," 7.
10. Amos Huron, in discussion with the author, November 2021.
11. Anne Yarbrough, in discussion with the author, December 2021.
12. Amos Huron, in discussion with the author, November 2021.

"a vulnerable period." When congregations have a lot of people around the same age, it can be dramatic when the core group reaches that stage.[13]

As Doug navigated that season of life, he continued to be accomplished professionally. He began his career at the Department of Justice in the civil rights division, taking part in several successful legal efforts against racial discrimination in employment settings. He continued his work for the US government with President Jimmy Carter. Part of his role was advising the administration on whom to nominate as federal judges. He recommended Ruth Bader Ginsburg for the US Court of Appeals for the DC Circuit.[14]

After joining the inclusive club of DC-area residents booted from a job when the presidency switched parties, Doug entered private practice and by the end of the decade won a case at the Supreme Court. He wrote the legal briefs on behalf of Ann Hopkins, who was rejected as a partner at the accounting firm where she worked for being "too macho," "pushy," and in need of "a course in charm school." The 6–3 Supreme Court decision established as a form of unlawful discrimination the use of "expectations of gender-related behavior" for hiring and promoting individuals.[15] Amy Wind, an attorney who worked with Doug at the same firm in the 1980s, identified as "Doug's brilliant innovation, starting in the lower courts," that he brought in evidence from social science that was new in the 1980s on how sex-based stereotyping worked. "If someone goes against the prevailing stereotype for behavior they will then be perceived negatively," Amy said. "It's the same with race or other categories." People could see how it was true anecdotally, but Doug brought in evidence to back it up. The legal victory later helped gay, lesbian, and transgender people seeking legal redress for mistreatment.[16]

᠈᠊

Amy didn't think she wanted to date a coworker. Then, in the summer of 1986, she gave notice that she would be leaving the firm where she and Doug were attorneys at the end of the year. She would travel across the African continent for six months with a backpack, then return to her hometown of San Diego and start a civil rights law practice there. Amy went on a date with Doug, thinking it would be short-lived summer fun, but it turned out

---

13. Yarbrough, in discussion with the author, December 2021.

14. Huron, "Race," 29.

15. Schudel, "Douglas B. Huron."

16. Wind, in discussion with the author, July 2022.

to be more. "It was high romance," she said. "I figured I better explore this before I leave forever."[17]

Early the next year, she went to Africa as planned. They communicated by telegrams that Amy would pick up at stops along the way. Doug met her halfway through the trip, in Senegal and the Gambia, and proved to be a great travel companion. They rode on the backs of trucks, crossed borders in the desert, and swam with crocodiles. Amy sent Doug back to DC with a letter to the firm asking if she could come back to her job in the fall. They said yes, and the trip became known as a sabbatical.

Amy faced a decision. She was thirty-two and her life was still one of adventure, of going out dancing until the early hours of the morning. She had another relationship with a swashbuckling, world-traveling type of guy working in international relations such as one can meet on the DC dating scene. Doug was forty and the kind of person who'd nurse a cat with leukemia—which he did for Amy's pet for six months while she was abroad.

And Doug went to church. What's more, the Community of Christ was the bulk of his social life. The concept wasn't totally unfamiliar to Amy. She grew up in a Reform Jewish home and much of her parents' social group was from the small, progressive temple they belonged to in San Diego. At the same time, she had a bias that churches were oppressive. "I was pretty skeptical of these church people," she said. "They were older and not necessarily more conservative, just more staid, more settled."[18]

Doug also engaged with Christian practices and theology in the Community. He gave the same kind of focused attention to his homilies as he did legal briefs.[19] Bert, another attorney in the Community who made beer with Doug in their spare time one year, found Doug's homilies "particularly insightful."[20] One that stood out among all those he heard in the Community as "fabulous theology" was when Doug noted that while Christianity's "big-ticket item" is often seen as eternal life, "really it's how you live your life today. Live it as Jesus tells you to live."[21]

At times, expressing doubt allowed Doug to find what he could affirm, or at least to a new way of looking at some religious idea that others rejected. The celebration of resurrection, for example, felt disconnected from "the values I prize most—justice and mercy and love," he said. Then, one

17. Wind, in discussion with the author, October 2021.

18. Wind, in discussion with the author, October 2021.

19. Amos Huron, in discussion with the author, November 2021.

20. Glenn, in discussion with the author, December 2021.

21. Bert Glenn, in discussion with Laci Barrow, Christina Nichols, and Martin Johnson, September 2016.

year it was Doug's turn to share the homily on the second Sunday of the Easter season. In the Gospel, John 20:19–31, the disciple Thomas wants to touch Christ's wounds before he could believe Jesus was alive again. Doug could have preached about the value of empirically verifying testimony or any other angle praising skepticism. Instead, Doug turned to Acts 4:32–35. There was also an easy out: skip from verse 32 to 34 and 35, all of which focus on economic sharing and providing for the needy in the early community of believers. Yet Doug highlighted verse 33: "With great power the apostles gave their testimony to the resurrection of the Lord Jesus, and great grace was upon them all." It is illogical, Doug said, to have verse 33 interrupting "the explanation of the economic system devised by the people in Acts. But the reason to have it there has nothing to do with logic. It is because the Resurrection was inspiring their whole lives, all the time." While the fear of death can stop people from following their calling, Doug said, faith that death is overcome imparts courage to act for justice.[22]

Yet Doug acknowledged the limitations in how much any of us do this, because of our human frailty:

> I have been assuming that the people in Acts were living in a just manner. I believe they were. In this Community, we have talked, now and again, about pooling our resources. It never happens, and it never will. But even if it did, it would not be sufficient, because we would only be taking care of our own crowd. The same was true of the early Christians. It was believers—and only believers—who were not needy. . . . Inattention to justice is a universal condition. But we have the capacity to be free—and an obligation to do something with our freedom. As for me, having finally seen the connection between the Resurrection and the pursuit of justice, maybe Easter will actually resonate next year.[23]

Doug knew plenty about human frailty. After having been in great shape for decades, he started to say, "My feet don't feel right. I think there's something off." One day he was throwing a ball with his son Amos, as he often did, but he tripped and fell. He chalked it up to his knees bothering him. Another day, he was with Amy and other coworkers on their law firm softball team. Playing first base, he fielded a ground ball. But then he couldn't get his legs to move so that he could tag out the runner before he made it to the base. Their other coworkers said, "Oh, well. Good try, Doug!"

22. Huron, "Second Sunday of Easter."
23. Huron, "Second Sunday of Easter."

But since Amy was on the field as well, she knew how unusual it was for Doug. Afterward, they talked and agreed it was time to go to a doctor.[24]

A year of tests resulted in a diagnosis of Primary Lateral Sclerosis. It is related to the better-known ALS but progresses less quickly. If it had been ALS, he likely wouldn't have lived beyond two or three years. He was forty-seven years old. The next time Doug and Amy were hosting a Community party, he told everyone he had an announcement. He wanted everyone to know rather than to have it make its way through the grapevine or to have the news be sugarcoated.[25]

As the decade went on, Rudy also confronted the loss of cherished abilities. The artist was going blind. In 1999, at a retreat center room with a large white board, Rudy discovered he could still see enough in high contrast to draw with a black marker. Rudy drew a deer, a rabbit, a squirrel, a quail with her chicks, an owl, and of course, Smokey Bear. The owl—like the squirrel and Smokey, wearing a hat—stands on a trash can and says "Give a Hoot! Leave this beautiful retreat as clean (or cleaner) than you found it)." The Community shared the joy of this epiphany, memorializing it by printing photographs of Rudy with the drawing, which he autographed to various Community members.[26]

In older age, Rudy found prayer imbued with greater meaning, "moving from a ritualistic recitation level to a sort of metaphysical spiritual plateau, where body and mind strain toward constant communication with God." Prayer felt more like a gift. It was also a lifelong practice of self-surrender, an emptying of the ego.[27] Rudy died at age ninety in August 2000, having been an essential part of the gathered body for twenty-nine of the Community's thirty-five years.

❧

The morning of September 11, 2001, brought panic across the DC area. The news sliced through commutes, workplaces, and classes that morning: airplanes crashing into the Pentagon and the World Trade Center, the twin towers collapsing into dust. A cloud of fire and smoke rose from the military headquarters, where nearly 20,000 people work, many of them civilians.[28]

---

24. Amos Huron, in discussion with the author, November 2021; Wind, in discussion with the author, October 2021.

25. Wind, in discussion with the author, October 2021.

26. Photograph in the author's possession.

27. Wendelin, "Probable Submission."

28. Merry, "Just Like Korea."

We could only imagine that the White House and US Capitol were next and that our loved ones who worked there or nearby would be buried in rubble as thousands were in New York. People evacuated buildings downtown and we scrambled to locate each other without ubiquitous cell phones or people checking in as safe on social media.

Three days later on Capitol Hill, Congress was in session and the United States was moving toward military action in Afghanistan. There was one dissenting voice. Rep. Barbara Lee (California, 13th district) was the only person in both houses of Congress to urge restraint, saying, "I am convinced that military action will not prevent further acts of international terrorism against the United States."[29] Rep. Lee was a hero to many in the Community of Christ.

That Sunday, the Community gathered for worship and then for further discussion and response in the evening. Doug was the lone dissenter, supporting military action as necessary. "War should always be the last resort," he said, and in this case he thought it was. "Right or wrong, it was a legitimate viewpoint," he said. "Usually when I say something, people respond; they might agree or disagree, but there is feedback." For the first time in nearly thirty years in the Community, Doug felt like a pariah. "No one even bothered to try to engage me."

Bill Wegener, who joined the Community after his retirement as a Lutheran pastor, preached about dissenters to the mainstream response to September 11. He praised as a strength of the Community that such dissenters are welcome. Doug listened to the homily and to a prayer from Joy Kauffman, a Mennonite in the Community, among the shared joys and concerns giving thanks that in Kabul women who did not choose to wear burqas could stop placing the full-body covering atop their regular clothes. To Doug, Joy seemed apologetic and fearful that she would be criticized for naming a positive effect of the war in Afghanistan. After worship, Bob Pohlman asked Bill if he thought the Community would welcome a dissenter from its own majority viewpoint. Bill said he didn't know.

Doug responded to Bob's question the next time it was his turn to lead Community worship and preach. "The answer is no," he said. It was the season of Advent, he noted, when God's people await the coming of the kingdom as described in the Scriptures for that Sunday. "We are obligated not only to wait but to act," Doug said. "We know that, in the end, only the Lord can bring a world of love, of harmony, of justice. But that does not relieve us of the obligation to do what we can to hasten the day of the Lord."[30]

29. Brockell, "She Was the Only Member."
30. Huron, "Third Sunday of Advent."

A dramatic response is necessary "when thousands of people are killed at their offices," he said. Had circumstances been different on September 11—if the passengers on the fourth plane had not caused it to crash in Pennsylvania, if the Pentagon building had completely collapsed—the number of deaths in DC could have easily exceeded what they were in New York.[31] The threat struck Doug deeply, and it didn't end on that day. "Does anyone doubt that Osama bin Laden or his allies would detonate a nuclear device a few blocks from here, in Lafayette Park, if only they could?" Yes, it was necessary to deal with the political and economic root causes of terrorism, but Doug also believed that a limited amount of military force was necessary in the short term. The initial bombing campaign in fall 2001 was an act of liberation from the Taliban, Doug said, and worthy of celebration. "The problem is not that we acted as we did but—rather—that we did not do it sooner. Our shame is that we act to free others from oppression only when it suits our own interests."[32]

The Community did not officially hold a position on nonviolence. From the early years, it belonged to the broader peace movement, and many held pacifist or near-pacifist stances.[33] Dora, who grew up "in an environment of war" in the Middle East, expressed her disquiet with the whirring blades "of the helicopters and the sonic booms of military planes" in DC after September 11.[34] In Dunstan's view, "One of the great virtues of the Community was that unanimity of opinion was not required. So I could see that some people were terribly strong on pacifism and that's fine. But other people weren't. And some people were just kind of uncertain." Dunstan never considered himself a pacifist and thought decisions must be made in each context. "Any sensible person hates war. But on the other hand, the desire for justice sometimes, as you must, says you must do something. And so then it gets down to a question, is this a place where you should do something? And if so, can you do something so dramatic as a war? And you can't solve that in the abstract." At times he found pacifists in the Community intolerant and told them so. It wasn't necessarily that he disagreed with them in a particular instance, but he opposed being strident. At times he felt that they must think he was terrible because he wouldn't adopt their position. "It was just kind of left as an uneasy topic."[35]

31. Merry, "Just Like Korea."

32. Huron, "Third Sunday of Advent." Lafayette Park was two miles away.

33. Linda Wells, in discussion with the author, November 2021.

34. Dora Johnson, untitled selection in *Thoughts on the Lenten Season 2002*, March 21.

35. Hayden, in discussion with the author, May 2021.

The day after Doug's sermon in December 2001, Dunstan wrote to the Community email list expressing his agreement. He did not speak up at the meeting in September because he felt the Community "carefully avoided discussing" pacifism in the prior few years. Dunstan advocated both-and rather than either-or thinking. He hoped that the United States would "change the way it treats other nations," he wrote. Yet he believed the US military was the only force capable of preventing "at least the most outrageous acts of terrorists" given the absence of a viable international police force. He respected pacifism, but he argued that "sometimes all your choices are bad choices. . . . I think we have selected the least bad choice."[36]

This debate spilled over into the Community's relationships in its building. An adult with developmental disabilities who was a Life Skills Center client put a US flag in the window of one of the rooms where they had Life Skills activities. That window was at the storefront level looking out at Mount Pleasant Street. Some in the Community saw the US flag as a symbol of nationalism and objected vociferously to such a symbol being in the window of a building where there was also Christian worship. What if neighbors saw it as a nationalistic display at a church? To Dunstan, La Casa was clearly a multipurpose building and not a church.[37] Furthermore, displaying a flag "does not mean you approve of everything the country has ever done," he said. Instead, it can show that "you have a basic faithfulness and commitment to the country."[38]

It was one of the occasions in the Community when consensus-based decision-making was a struggle. Eventually, the Community agreed to a compromise: the flag could be considered an expression of the person who was part of Life Skills Center. What was in the windows represented the Community to some extent. But ultimately, respecting everyone in La Casa and not only the Community's wishes meant that they permitted the US flag to stay.[39]

❧

In early 2002, Doug's ability to speak became unpredictable because of Primary Lateral Sclerosis. His mind remained that of a man who wrote legal briefs that convinced Supreme Court justices. In the US Supreme Court

36. Hayden, email message to the Community of Christ, December 17, 2001.

37. David Anderson, in discussion with the author, March 2021; Hayden, email message to the Community of Christ, February 9, 2002.

38. Hayden, in discussion with the author, May 2021.

39. Anderson, in discussion with the author, March 2021.

case he argued in the 1980s, he and his legal partner Jim Heller made a strategy decision to have Heller argue in court. He had more gray hair. In the mid-2000s, Doug worked on another case that was appealed to the Supreme Court. It was for a Senate staff member who was fired after he said a medical condition made it inadvisable for him to work late hours. Sen. Mark Dayton (D-Minnesota) sought immunity from laws prohibiting workplace discrimination. In this case, again, Doug's legal briefs were declared brilliant by his colleagues. This time, Doug had plenty of gray hair. But he could no longer speak. A younger partner argued the case, and their firm prevailed for its client.[40]

Even as it was unreliable whether Doug could get words and sentences out, he remained on the rotation to lead Sunday services in the Community, including writing a homily. Then one week he called up Margaret and said, "I can't do it." After he placed the phone in its cradle, he cried. Ten minutes later, Dora called. "You are not getting out of this," she said. "You're going to do it, you're going to figure it out." She wasn't going to let him stop sharing his interpretation of Scripture and the world through his homilies. After the call Doug cried again, this time because he felt loved and supported. His community wasn't going to let him go through this alone.[41]

Doug prepared a homily, and on that occasion Amanda read the manuscript. The homily began by telling that story—of not being allowed to drop off of the worship leading rotation. Amanda paused to cry. After she resumed speaking for her father, there were few dry eyes in the room. Initially Doug wondered, as most people would, if people still wanted him around. Doug's older son Amos saw Doug's faith in the Community stay strong even as what religious faith he had as a skeptic wavered. Doug believed "in the good that comes out of people coming together and loving each other and being there for each other," Amos said.[42]

The next year, Doug began to communicate using a machine called a DynaWrite speech synthesizer,[43] which was attached to his power chair and allowed him to type and then press a button to generate a voice saying what he had typed. In early 2003 he used it for the first time publicly at a conference at American University Law School. One of the speakers was the expert witness Doug called for *Price Waterhouse v. Hopkins*. Susan Fiske, a social psychologist, had given testimony about gender-based stereotypes that was essential to the victory in the case and Doug wanted "a chance to

40. Wind, in discussion with the author, July 2022; Schudel, "Huron," para. 21–23.
41. Amanda Huron, in discussion with the author, September 2021.
42. Amos Huron, in discussion with the author, November 2021.
43. Wind, in discussion with the author, July 2022.

praise her publicly for her contribution to the Hopkins case." The two colleagues had not seen each other in at least a decade when he introduced her to the audience. As they talked one-on-one afterward, Doug said, "I noticed a pained expression on her face, which I recognized. I had seen it before on the faces of friends who have not seen me in some time, a mixture of sorrow and pity."[44]

That experience, combined with having a homily coming up, caused Doug to finally read a series of articles about disability and faith shared by Jim Bowman in the Community. The articles resonated with him in that, like the authors, Doug did not want to be told he was special in God's eyes and would be made whole in heaven. He definitely didn't think God had given him this disability to build his character. At the same time, he objected to what he saw as

> a refusal to accept the hard reality that accompanies being disabled. For example, one writer objects to people saying that someone is "afflicted" with a disability, on the ground that such language implies pain and evokes pity. I cannot speak for others, but I sure as hell feel afflicted, and there are times when I hate what has happened to me. I don't want pity, but there certainly is pain. . . . So when someone says that, "because of deeply inculcated ablist [sic] norms, we cannot fathom when persons with disabilities say they do not want to be changed or cured"—well, I cannot fathom it myself.[45]

Another core message was that many people see themselves as welcoming, but only "as long as you are just like us." Christianity holds a "promise of radical inclusiveness," Doug said, "a promise that is always being broken." Still "the good news is available to all. So it is possible for all people, even those who are disabled, to live a rich and full life—and on occasion to glimpse the eternal." When Doug saw colleagues and friends unable to believe that, they failed to keep the promise.[46]

When Amy and Doug married, they began navigating life in the Community as an interfaith couple. When Doug was leading the service, Amy helped him carry in the wine and bread for the Eucharist. Then she left. Amy never felt that anyone in the Community was trying to convert her to Christianity.

44. Huron, homily in the Community of Christ.
45. Huron, homily in the Community of Christ.
46. Huron, homily in the Community of Christ.

Her informal title was the Jewish Auxiliary. "The Community of Christ was really flexible and welcoming and ecumenical and all that stuff, but the bottom line was they were Christian," she said. "I was making a conscious effort to separate myself from the religious part of it." She joined in every other aspect of Community life: attending and hosting parties, serving food at St. Stephen's, and bidding in the annual auction. Amy went on the Community's annual retreat each January. On Saturdays there were often biblical discussions, which Amy engaged in with great interest. On Sunday morning, she went for a walk.[47]

In January 2001 the retreat topic was the Sabbath, exploring the tradition that has been kept for thousands of years by Jewish communities and that Christians adopted. People in the Community acknowledged that it was hard to keep Sabbath, because many had demanding jobs as well as work inside the home. Yet they wanted to try to keep Sabbath. For about a year after that, several households from the Community held Sabbath suppers on Sunday evenings. But whoever was hosting prepared for people coming over. And some people attended even if they had spent the afternoon doing laundry, for example.

For Doug and Amy, that Community retreat inspired a commitment to Sabbath practice. For years after that they'd take either Saturday or Sunday as a day to do no work for their jobs or at home—no chores of any kind. Sometimes they went for a hike. Doug was still walking at that point with a pole he used for balance. He called it the Staff, in a biblical sort of way.[48]

Another Community practice learned from Judaism—seder meals during Passover—was troubling for Amy at first. The first time Amy attended a Community seder, in the late 1980s, she recognized the first part, recounting the liberation story from Exodus. The ceremonial washing of hands took the place of foot washing as is traditional on Maundy Thursday. Then there would be a transition in the liturgy, noting the first part had followed Jewish customs.[49] The second part was the Eucharist, with the preface, "We remember that on a Passover night two thousand years ago, Jesus gave a new commandment, which we now fulfill." The liturgy evolved through the years seeking to avoid supersessionism—the notion that Christianity replaces Judaism rather than God expanding the covenant. Yet the liturgy proclaimed, "We remember that in the fullness of time you sent your

47. Wind, in discussion with the author, October 2021.
48. Wind, in discussion with the author, October 2021.
49. Wind, in discussion with the author, October 2021.

child Jesus to live among us, who fulfilled and will fulfill all your promises." It also mistakenly called the Last Supper a seder.[50]

"The first few years I was kind of offended by it," Amy said. "It seemed like what now we would call cultural appropriation. I didn't have those words in those days, but it seemed like it was taking something and turning it into something that wasn't. And I can remember in the early years debating whether to go back. But then it kind of just grew on me." While someone else might have asked Community leaders to change the liturgy, that wasn't Amy's way of relating to people. She saw herself as a guest being invited.[51]

When Doug and Amy's son, Walter, was born in 1997, the Community threw him a welcome party. They wrote a liturgy with pieces analogous to a baptism while honoring Walter's Jewish heritage. As for infants who were baptized, they said, "we affirm that all children are born into community."[52] In Walter's case, they named three communities that he was part of at birth: "the tradition of the community of Israel," the Community of Christ, and the community of Mount Pleasant. The question for Doug and Amy was "will you raise Walter as a person of compassion, committed to the values of peace and justice, living a life of service to the community?" And the gathered said, "We take responsibility to support, nurture, and teach him as he grows." They renewed their own covenant "to bear each other's burdens, to assist in times of need, to share our gifts and possessions, to support each other in joy and sorrow, and in all things to work for the common good."[53]

For the welcome party, Margaret Ann knew a song about a man named Walter who waltzes with bears. She adapted the lyrics to be about a baby named Walter who sneaks out of his room and goes to the woods to dance. Everyone crowded into the living room of Doug and Amy's house, crooning, "wa-wa-wa-wa-wa-wa waltzing with bears / raggy bears, shaggy bears, baggy bears, too."[54] Instead of a baptismal certificate, the Community gave Walter a framed poster of a woodland scene, *The Bear Dance* by William Holbrook Beard. Written on it is, "Welcome to Wally from the Community of Christ."

With another interfaith couple, the Community took a similar approach of seeking to include each partner in whatever activities they wanted to be included. Andrew Wells-Dang spent two years in Vietnam, where he

50. "The Seder for Passover," Community of Christ, ca. 2000s, in the author's possession.

51. Wind, in discussion with the author, October 2021.

52. Baptism liturgies for children, 1994–97, in the author's possession.

53. Welcome of Walter Jonah Huron, 1997, in the author's possession.

54. "Waltzing with Bears," in the author's possession; Blood and Patterson, *Rise Up Singing*, 76.

met his wife, Giang Wells-Dang, and they moved to DC together in 2000. Giang grew up Buddhist but in a mostly cultural way. A few Community members were quick to educate the others on how to pronounce Giang's name—Zong—and sought to get to know her when she attended Community gatherings and retreats and occasionally worship.[55]

The Community didn't launch a formal interfaith dialogue but rather continued their pattern of sharing in each other's lives. Giang felt that she could be herself with Community people, sharing her ideas and background. Andrew and Giang didn't want something more formal engaging them as an interfaith couple at that time. Andrew once again valued Doug's example as a man a generation older, yet his and Giang's experience was different from Doug and Amy's in a crucial way. "One great characteristic about Buddhism is that it allows dual citizenship," Andrew said. Buddhism is a set of practices rather than theology. One can be a Christian, or worship with a Christian community, while still engaging the practices of Buddhism. Being with the Community was influential for Giang in giving her examples of "Christianity in action in a different way than she had experienced or thought of before."[56]

The Community also saw itself as extending welcome to people of diverse racial backgrounds. Yet there was still "exclusivity as opposed to inclusivity," Sandi said, around race and ethnicity. They had a robust sense of racial injustice, but it was outside of the Community. On the inside, members didn't openly address or collectively wrestle with the Community's own racial dynamics. Sandi said, "We have good intentions, but carrying through on them is really, really difficult."[57] By the time Sandi married John, who is Black, the Community had fewer Black people than it had in the early years in Dupont Circle. For their son, Cyrus, that smaller, majority-white group of people in Mount Pleasant was the only version of the Community he knew. To someone who didn't know the Community, he'd describe it as "this sort of hippie, very positive . . . very unusual take on what a church even is," he said. At the same time, it was a group of mostly "middle-class white folks."[58]

That was one of the first things Gail Taylor saw when she visited the Community. Gail, a biracial Black woman, arrived in the city in 1999 and looked for a church. She had seen the sign on the door while walking in Mount Pleasant and showed up for worship at the time stated. (Worship

55. Wells-Dang, in discussion with the author, December 2021.
56. Wells-Dang, in discussion with the author, December 2021.
57. Sandra Wojahn, in discussion with the author, September 2021.
58. Cyrus Hampton, in discussion with the author, September 2021.

actually started half an hour later. "They had changed the time of worship and they forgot to change the sign," Gail said.) "Inside the church, it was still very white, 1960s civil-rights-activism era," she said. People wore casual dress and sang folk-music hymns with guitars. She saw a few people she knew from DC activist events.[59]

Her childhood churches were mostly white, so she didn't have an experience of Black church worship in stark contrast with what the Community offered. "Everyone's trading things when they choose where to worship," Gail said. "For me it was important to find people who were wrestling with US foreign policy." The loss in the trade was that "the Community of Christ purported to be anti-racist but never was doing anything to be actively anti-racist."[60]

Joining the Bible study at Dora's house "really cemented my sense of being part of the Community." Like many in the Community, Gail likened it to a family rather than just a group of people who worship together. However, it took a decade for her to feel fully part of the family. "It's the kind of group that takes a long time to get to know, to feel like you belong." And even with a sense of belonging, "there's still a difference between me and the dominant culture."[61]

Similar to Gail, Sue Gaeta came to the Community with plenty of experience in majority-white churches. Sue, an Asian woman, was adopted as a child by white parents. And like Sandi, she saw racism being treated as a problem outside of the Community. "It was blatant to me that we never talked about racism really, except in a distant, distant way," Sue said. She arrived during the Obama presidency, a historical and cultural moment when some white people believed US society was post-racial. Mount Pleasant, where Sue lived at that time, remained racially diverse, especially on Mount Pleasant Street. "But you go into the big houses and it's almost all white folks," she said.[62] La Casa, originally one of those grand houses, had racially and culturally diverse groups in the space. But for the most part there was not a deeper interconnection between those groups and the two majority-white groups: the local government body called an advisory neighborhood council and the Community of Christ.

Sue had a broader perspective in the American religious landscape and the Lutheran denomination to which the Community belonged. Her parents were pastors in congregations in the Evangelical Lutheran Church

59. Gail Taylor, in discussion with the author, February 2021.
60. Taylor, in discussion with the author, February 2021.
61. Taylor, in discussion with the author, February 2021.
62. Sue Gaeta, in discussion with the author, December 2021.

in America Metropolitan New York Synod. Sue went to seminary and was ordained before she came to DC in the late 2000s. She worked in the national office of Lutheran Volunteer Corps, a program pairing participants with nonprofit social-justice-oriented organizations. "I don't feel like the Community of Christ was a whole lot different," she said, from people in "other mainline Protestant denominations who were trying to be good people."[63]

In the Community, the liturgy was the same as what she grew up with among "small rag-tag groups of Lutherans." They sang hymns from the same worship book with its solid green cover. Sue loved that there were several people who were theologically trained in different traditions. She valued the service leadership rotation giving space for many different voices. "It was refreshing because there was space for my leadership, but I didn't have to be the pastor there," she said. Two years after Sue and her husband, Richard, began attending, their daughter, Grace, was born. The Community—at that time an intergenerational mix from birth to eighties—provided lots of support.

Yet Richard, who is Puerto Rican and grew up Catholic, felt out of place because of his moderate-to-conservative political views. It was a new concept for him that Christians could be progressive—that people on the left of the political spectrum weren't all atheists. Attending worship together, and especially hearing what people said during homilies and the time for shared concerns and thanksgivings, Sue said, "led to conversation and me having to learn to better articulate what I believe and a vision for what the church could be in the realm of doing justice." At an early stage in their relationship, Richard and Sue learned about each other's different social, religious, and political perspectives—and that they both wanted to engage in conversation about them.[64]

Sue and Richard didn't find that same openness in the Community. People weren't necessarily on the same page politically, but they were usually in the same chapter. "There was this assumption that people would support the same things," Sue said. She and Richard agreed that the prayers shared during the open time in the service could become diatribes. Sue questioned whether people who disagreed on issues with the Community could feel welcome. She didn't know how much variety of views there was in the Community, because she didn't hear hard conversations about them. "That's the only thing that's going to make any change—learning how to listen to each other and articulate what we actually believe," she said.[65]

---

63. Gaeta, in discussion with the author, December 2021.

64. Gaeta, in discussion with the author, December 2021.

65. Gaeta, in discussion with the author, December 2021.

10

"A Collaborative Setting of Peer Ministers"

KIM KLEIN, A MOUNT Pleasant neighbor and friend, attended Community parties and Easter brunch as well as the occasional Sunday service. She saw it as a group that took action without anyone in particular being in charge. "One of the things I also was in awe of, as I got to know people, was how much they did," she said. She noticed a contrast between St. Stephen and the Incarnation Episcopal—"my traditional church"—and the Community. "Here was this place where you could just express what you felt," Kim said. "I was so impressed because there was no hierarchy. There was nobody telling you what to do."[1]

In the Community those who had the title of pastor or president didn't necessarily have more power. Decisions were sometimes made informally. If someone was going to a march, they'd announce it after worship, and whoever wanted to join them would, without the notion that the Community as a whole was supporting that cause or event. Perhaps less formality "was a weakness of the Community or lack of structure," David said, but he's not sure that it was. It reflected their context coming out of the 1960s, with the Civil Rights movement, antiwar movement, women's movement, and LGBTQ rights movement branching out into manifold organizations. Many in the Community "thought of ourselves as part of a movement as opposed to a structure or an institution," David said. "One of our visions was that the wider church should think of itself more as a movement rather than as an institution."[2]

1. Kim Klein, in discussion with the author,
2. David Anderson, in discussion with the author, March 2021.

From its start, the Community made decisions by consensus. It was written into the Community covenant, including a commitment to "encourage all those in the fellowship to participate fully in the decision-making."[3] Early on Community members developed a pattern similar to other groups practicing this method of decision-making: often a person or a few people at first vocally objected to the idea being discussed. As people who supported the proposal made arguments for it, the dissenters said something like, "I don't like this, but I can move forward with it."[4] This was a benefit of consensus: it was less likely to result in people feeling that there were winners and losers, since even if those opposed were in the minority, they still chose whether or not to accept the rest of the group going in a certain direction.[5]

The greater the trust was among the group, the more easily they reached consensus. The longer and deeper people were in relationship with each other, the more they could anticipate or at least understand each other's objections. The facilitator also needed to read the room well. "You have to be willing to be more blunt than most church people are at most church meetings, or it won't work," John Schramm said. For that reason, high turnover in a group made consensus difficult. It was also hard with a group larger than forty or fifty people.[6] During a period when they had closer to seventy adults participating in making decisions, they recognized that not everyone would speak. They recommended that Community-wide issues be discussed in small groups within a week or two of the monthly meeting, so that they could get closer to universal input.[7]

Periodically there were discussions about whether to keep consensus decision-making as a practice or switch to something like Robert's Rules of Order. One point in particular was at the same time as when, in the mid-1970s, the Community decided not to hire another pastor as an employee. Continuing with consensus decision-making felt appropriate to the approach they pursued moving forward—more of a tweak than a wholesale transformation—in which laypeople and the few ordained members would share the work of the church fully, without employees paid any kind of salary or benefits. The Community at that time was also half the size it had

3. Covenants of the Community of Christ, in Community of Christ Papers.

4. Schramm and Hayden, "Community of Christ"; Sandra Wojahn, in discussion with the author, September 2021.

5. Schramm and Hayden, "Community of Christ."

6. Schramm and Hayden, "Community of Christ."

7. Lisi and Hayden, "Good of Talking," 8.

been at its height, making consensus decision-making easier.[8] In 1995, the Community revisited its covenant and reaffirmed that sharing leadership and decision-making, encouraging all to participate, flowed from its central belief that each person has unique God-given gifts.[9]

Even though the Community had all the factors—small size, relatively low turnover, and high trust—the group didn't always reach consensus. "The way that usually is signaled is that somebody finally says, 'I still don't agree with most of you. And furthermore, I think we haven't gone into it thoroughly enough,'" Dunstan said. More than the disagreement, "that it hasn't been gone into thoroughly enough, that's the real signal that you don't have consensus."[10] Meetings were often very long. Sometimes, the Community arrived at iron-butt consensus, as some members put it. Yet often it was after passing the two-hour mark that all of a sudden a third way opened, Dorothy observed. The Spirit moved and all sides saw the issue differently. For the first few decades, Community parents brought their children to meetings, with varying levels of those children being able to occupy themselves on the sides of the room.[11] To Dora, "living with the frustration of open-ended discussions is worth every minute."[12]

There were also deeper tensions at times. In the mid-1990s Sandi, who had been part of the Community for more than fifteen years at that point, presented an issue to the Community for discussion and a potential decision. "I totally felt it was just sloughed off," she said. In the chuckles of a few people present, she heard, "Why would this be of concern?" and a judgment that she was a bit off-base. They moved on in the meeting. Sandi asked, "Well, will we ever come back to this?" They didn't.[13]

Long after she forgot the specific topic she raised and who laughed, Sandi remembered the hurt of feeling dismissed. Was there as much openness in power and decision-making as the Community thought it had? Was leadership shared in more than who was in charge of worship on Sunday mornings? Sandi wondered about several other people she had seen come to the Community for a while and not stay: did they have similar concerns as she had, which prevented them from being drawn further into Community life? While the Community wasn't rigid, it had a certain framework

8. David Anderson, in discussion with the author, March 2021.

9. "Covenant—Community of Christ, Draft—2 June 1995," in *Lenten Thoughts, 2006*, 4.

10. Schramm and Hayden, "Community of Christ," presentation at Holden Village.

11. Dorothy Pohlman, in discussion with the author, March 2023.

12. Dora Johnson, untitled selection in *Lenten Booklet 1995*, March 23.

13. Wojahn, in discussion with the author, September 2021.

that was established, even if it wasn't much talked about, let alone explained to newcomers. Some people had more power than others, without having been named to a particular leadership role.

Sandi stepped back from worship and being active in the Community. She didn't look for other churches during that time. She knew that for all its flaws, the Community's practice of power-sharing and collective decision-making was better than most. It built in people the capacity to take responsibility for decisions more so than a yes or no vote. "You just don't get that in most organizations, whether it be church, whether it be something else," Sandi said. In many congregations, people look to the ministerial staff to make a decision or "give more credence to the ministerial staff than they would to anyone else," she said. In contrast, she valued seeing everyone involved in struggling together with whether they could live with a proposal, even if it would be easier to go a different route on their own.[14] It was another example of the Community's collective self-examination.

After several months away to reflect and heal, Sandi returned to the Community. Beyond everything else, "I went back because it was still home."[15] Her son, Cyrus, observed that with Sandi's family of origin being geographically and politically distant from them, the Community was a distinct social circle where "you recognize everyone, you know everyone, you have a certain type of shared history with everyone." People had a bond they were continuing to work out in relationship.[16]

While the Community was a family in many ways, it also had leadership and shared decision-making in a way that most families don't. In the summer of 1996, the Community initiated a self-study and discussion of the future. The occasion was brought on by Walt (along with Korey and Krista) moving to Milwaukee for him to begin congregational ministry there. He formally resigned as pastor of the Community. He had taken on the position twenty years earlier mainly because the local Lutheran body wanted the Community to have someone in that role, even as the Community was lay led. In its discussion, Community members acknowledged that pastoral care had not worked well as shared ministry, and that practices such as taking the Eucharist to people who had missed Sunday service and visiting people who were hospitalized had fallen through the cracks. They debated, once again, whether they could afford to pay a part-time pastor, but a countervailing concern remained whether they could keep up with the bills for La Casa. Showing the continued influence of the Church of the Saviour,

14. Wojahn, in discussion with the author, September 2021.

15. Wojahn, in discussion with the author, September 2021.

16. Hampton, in discussion with the author, September 2021.

some wondered whether it was too easy to belong to the Community, and whether there was accountability. Dora asked whether they were fulfilling their early mission of eliciting and nurturing each other's gifts. Was shared leadership really working "or have we just settled?"[17]

Sandi named frankly the problems in their approach to shared leadership. She wrote in a public response to the group named as the Community's council at that time:

> The Community may have operated by consensus at one time, but it is certainly not the current process. In reality, we deal with consensus by default; we defer debate about our differences in perception even though the debate is necessary for true consensus. When some individuals express strongly held views, the Community "shuts down." Rather than confronting the issues and/or the "experts," we drop the topic. This inability to discuss and reconcile differences and arrive at true consensus is extremely destructive.[18]

The dynamic in the Community of Christ was in some ways similar to what was described in the essay "The Tyranny of Structurelessness." It was directed to activists in the women's liberation movement in the 1970s, but its insights apply more broadly. Jo Freeman wrote, "All groups create informal structures as a result of interaction patterns among the members of the group." They are formed even in groups that intend not to create them. Freeman continued: "Thus structurelessness becomes a way of masking power, and within the women's movement is usually most strongly advocated by those who are the most powerful (whether they are conscious of their power or not). As long as the structure of the group is informal, the rules of how decisions are made are known only to a few and awareness of power is limited to those who know the rules." It is necessary to select those who are granted authority by the group in order to hold them responsible for how they wield their influence, Freeman recommended. Further, "The group of people in positions of authority will be diffuse, flexible, open, and temporary." This allows leaders to be responsible to the group and for the group at large to make decisions.[19]

Just as the Community didn't always name who had power or give them an official role, it often practiced its values without talking about them.

---

17. "Self-Study and Discussion of the Future," 1996–97, in Community of Christ Papers; Larry Rasmussen, in discussion with the author, June 2020.

18. "Self-Study and Discussion of the Future," 1996–97, in Community of Christ Papers.

19. Freeman, "Tyranny of Structurelessness."

For example, in November 1985 the Community formalized the stance it already held affirming gay and lesbian Christians, through the group Lutherans Concerned. They also sent a donation "for carrying on the important work you do with those who must certainly feel rejected" by many who call themselves Christians, Valborg wrote as secretary-treasurer.[20] The decision felt like an easy one for the Community. The only debate was from those who wanted a strong endorsement of ordination and marriage for people in same-sex relationships. The Community received a certificate from Lutherans Concerned that said "Reconciled in Christ" and hung it on the wall in the main worship space.[21]

The challenge was, someone would need to know what that was or read the fine print. Rachel Haxtema, who attended the Community as a recent college graduate, was new to conversations among Christians "making such explicit connections between social justice and political issues with what was happening in the worship," including inclusion of LGBTQ people. She wished people in the Community had talked about what they believed about sexuality and inclusion, and why they believed it. "If you think of your church as a teaching community to help people understand theological or ethical values, I think we have to be a little bit more teaching-oriented towards people," she said. Articulating stances the congregation holds also reminds members of what's important and why the congregation does what it does.[22]

In June 2001, the Community began a series of meetings revisiting how it made decisions. Doug shared resources about the Quaker view of consensus. They noted that, as the Community had experienced many times, the goal was not unanimity. There can be dissent and yet people can find unity in a direction forward honoring values held in common. Similar to the Friends, the Community believed that anyone among them could be the source of God's leading and the Spirit's truth.[23] Dunstan named "respect for each other as the basis for consensus." He shared a quote from Isa 42:3,

---

20. Valborg Anderson to Lutherans Concerned, 13 November 1985, in Community of Christ Papers.

21. David Anderson, in discussion with the author, March 2021; John Stewart, in discussion with the author, April 2022; Reconciled in Christ certificate, November 3, 1985, in John and Bobbie Stewart's possession. Lutherans Concerned is now ReconcilingWorks: Lutherans for Full Participation and grants "Reconciling in Christ" certificates. https://www.reconcilingworks.org/.

22. Rachel Medema Haxtema, in discussion with the author, October 2021.

23. "Consensus and Decision-Making Discussions June–Nov 2001," in the author's possession.

of the Lord's servant who would not break "a bruised reed." Dunstan wrote, "Since we are all bruised, we all need that kind of respect."[24]

Amy, who was at that point in her career a mediator and arbitrator, facilitated the first two meetings in the series, on Sunday evenings. She summarized what she heard, including, at the first meeting, "almost universal dissatisfaction with the way Community decisions have come to be made in the last couple of years, especially the common practice of an issue being raised at the end of church and being dealt with in a '3-minute discussion.'"[25] She learned that their practice of consensus was deeply ingrained. "Early on the first meeting, where it was going on and on and on," Amy said, "I suggested that maybe we have some ground rules for limiting the discussion, or something like that. And Dunstan said 'hear, hear!' and everyone else recoiled in horror." Margaret Ann said, "That's not how we do it in the Community of Christ. We talk 'til we're done." Everyone else, other than Dunstan, agreed with Margaret Ann.[26]

People did not necessarily want more meetings, but they did want to thoroughly explore issues affecting the Community and give all voices a chance to contribute. Some saw an opportunity for time spent in decision-making to be more than merely business meetings, Amy wrote in her summary, "if people listen respectfully to one another, are open to considering each other's views and include 'spiritual discernment' as part of decision-making." The Community discussed how to re-affirm and clarify its core values, especially for newcomers, recognizing that no written description was readily available.[27]

The Community came to a consensus about consensus. Those holding the majority viewpoint committed to "striving to seek out and listen attentively to other viewpoints within the group, in the knowledge that the prophetic voice is sometimes at first in a distinct minority, and those in the minority striving to find a way to accept, if not endorse, the decision favored by the majority—based perhaps on the special trust we have in each other as members of the same Community." Unanimity would be welcome but not required; the goal instead would be a proposal that "(a) most favor, and (b) those who disagree can nevertheless accept in good conscience." Discussion

24. "Consensus and Decision-Making Discussions June–Nov 2001," in the author's possession.

25. "Consensus and Decision-Making Discussions June–Nov 2001," in the author's possession.

26. Amy Wind, in discussion with the author, July 2022. Confirmed with Margaret Ann Hoven.

27. "Consensus and Decision-Making Discussions June–Nov 2001," in the author's possession.

of an issue would continue as long as anyone thought it was still productive. The Community recognized that failing to meet time constraints for a time-sensitive decision is to decide against a course of action.[28]

One problem had been that there were no criteria to apply for what needed to be on an agenda for a monthly Community meeting rather than being a task that could be delegated to an individual or smaller group. After three meetings, the Community made a list about what topics would merit discussion at a Community meeting, including the pragmatic—such as location of the annual retreat and major building expenditures—as well as the spiritual: How would they live out Christian faith in the world? How could the Community live out its ecumenical identity? How could the Community encourage members in their inner journeys?

Dianne Russell—who held an official leadership title, in her words, "the president of this very lateral sort of structured organization"[29]—summarized the Community conversations. She wrote that "the ideal will be to continually anchor ourselves in the theological and spiritual grounding for the discussion, and to struggle with issues from a perspective of our faith." The Community affirmed that all could "bring the issues that burden us, that interest us, or that capture our imagination."[30]

In theological terms, the Community upheld the priesthood of all believers. "There's no one priest that we look to to tell us what the truth is or what the reality is," Dianne said. Every person in the Community was part of the priesthood for her. They had been her teachers; she had learned from the image of God that was in each of them. "They are part of how I've been able to learn and grow and stay centered in a way that allows me to be a good mother, to be a good partner, to be a good executive director, to be a good neighbor, to be good in the world," she said. "It has been really sweet and rare to be able to have that so alive and so present. I mean, it sounds great, like, the priesthood of all believers, but really having people be leaders and be priests to each other on a day-to-day basis, it has been so powerful."[31]

28. "Consensus and Decision-Making Discussions June–Nov 2001," in the author's possession.

29. Dianne Russell, in discussion with Christina Nichols and Martin Johnson, September 2016.

30. Dianne Russell, email message to the Community of Christ, July 15, 2001.

31. Dianne Russell, in discussion with Christina Nichols and Martin Johnson, September 2016.

Dianne's early years were on a farm in Ohio owned by her grandparents. Her mother's family belonged to the United Church of Christ, and Dianne was baptized in a UCC church. After her grandfather died when Dianne was eight, they had to move off the farm to a small town north of Shiloh. There she and her mother and siblings began attending a Lutheran church since there wasn't a UCC one. Her father, Ross, wasn't a churchgoer, but the pastor visited him while Ross was woodworking. After they got to know each other, the pastor asked if Ross would do some repair work in the church. Ross realized that a few of his friends from the American Legion, which was his primary social group, were already members of the church. "I have a very powerful memory of my dad being baptized and joining the church," Dianne said. "It made my mother so delighted to be able to share that with him."[32]

The pastor who was especially influential to Dianne was David Genszler, along with his wife, Barbara. They were from the East and had been living in Philadelphia and New York. Though culturally different, Dianne said, "he did a lovely job of relating to people in Shiloh in this little farming community." With the Genzlers' leadership, the congregation learned about global hunger and helped a Vietnamese refugee family settle in their area.[33]

The church, and Dianne's parents, taught the equality of all people. But then Dianne wanted to attend a high school dance with a friend who was Black, one of the few Black people in that area. "I was completely flummoxed when my parents said I couldn't go to dance with him," Dianne said. "I didn't have anybody to really turn to. So I hung out with Barbara and she talked me through what was close to a breakdown for me because I just didn't understand."[34]

Dianne excelled in athletics in high school and envisioned herself becoming a physical education teacher or coach. Then, during her senior year, a torn ligament injury ended her athletic activities and changed the course of her life. Instead of studying physical education at a state school, she visited Wittenberg, a Lutheran college in Southwest Ohio, and got a church scholarship that allowed her to attend the private school.

She majored in religion and sociology. As she prepared to graduate, she sensed a call to go to seminary. She was accepted into the Lutheran School of Theology in Chicago on a scholarship. But she felt she needed more experience of the world. She was passionate about social change and in college began to engage with policy issues to meet human needs. She signed up for Lutheran Volunteer Corps, which would involve a job

---

32. Russell, in discussion with the author, September 2021.
33. Russell, in discussion with the author, September 2021.
34. Russell, in discussion with the author, September 2021.

placement as well as community living for personal and vocational growth. She figured she could do that for a few years and then go to seminary. Moving to DC in 1982, among her job options was one with the Committee for a Sane Nuclear Policy, called SANE. She wanted to connect with the nuclear weapons freeze movement, and having that option in LVC confirmed for her that this was the right step.[35]

Though the days of school children hiding under their desks in bomb drills or family fallout shelters were over (at least for most people), those working at SANE were aware that the threat of nuclear devastation was still very real. The possibility that any city could be the next Hiroshima or Nagasaki was not remote. Network ABC broadcasted film *The Day After* on November 20, 1983, which was viewed by more than a hundred million people. It portrayed what the effects would have been of a nuclear attack on Lawrence, Kansas, and nearby Kansas City, Missouri. While the reality might have been even worse, it was realistic enough to terrify a lot of people. SANE was one of the organizations doing grassroots organizing across the country at the time, and the film increased public concern and involvement at the community level. Dianne was part of the field staff at SANE, whose work was grassroots advocacy and organizing local chapters.[36]

While Dianne felt a sense of purpose in her work, her parents were worried. Near the end of a visit to DC, they cornered her and told her she'd been misled. "We know you're excited about what you're doing, but you have to realize you're being controlled by the communists," they said. Dianne put a pause in that line of thinking and responded: "The people who are really influential in the peace movement are from the churches and from the synagogues. Those are the people who are deeply committed and who are leading the charge."[37] She worked with a few people affiliated with the Communist Party USA, but they were a small portion of the overall mass movement, and they didn't push their party line. Beyond them, communists were far from a unified front amongst themselves or with socialists. Furthermore, Dianne explained, her career choice was shaped by what she learned from her parents about participating in democracy and loving one's neighbors.[38] "I'm engaging people in helping to shape a foreign policy that

35. Russell, in discussion with the author, September 2021.

36. Duane Shank (deputy director of SANE in the 1980s), in discussion with the author, March 2022; David B. Cortright (SANE executive director in the 1980s), in discussion with the author, July 2022; Russell, in discussion with the author, September 2021; Maar, *Freeze!*, 144–145.

37. Russell, in discussion with the author, September 2021.

38. Cortright, in discussion with the author, July 2022; Russell, email message to the author, March 23, 2023.

is about living in harmony and justly distributing resources," she said. "It's because of what you taught me." Dianne's parents were taken aback. In their family, children didn't argue with their parents. Yet they returned to Ohio, and she remained in DC and in her job.[39]

The Lutheran Volunteer Corps house where Dianne lived was in Mount Pleasant. One of her housemates was a young woman named Mary Witt, whose father was a Lutheran pastor and connected to John Schramm, and Walt and Korey. She had grown up with an "incredible depth of understanding" about social justice and contemplation, Dianne said. Mary gave Dianne a 1978 book called *Embodiment* by James Nelson, about sexuality in a Christian perspective. Mary organized a group discussion of the book and Scripture, inviting a Lutheran volunteer who was out as a gay man as a speaker. "Mary played a really big role in opening me up to questions that were very, very alive inside of me that I had never let myself really explore that were about my own sexuality and being lesbian," Dianne said.

Mary also introduced Dianne to the Community of Christ. Dianne was impressed to find a place where they could ask and try out different ways of creating leadership that is held by multiple people. "I'd seen enough in the institutional church to know that people gave the pastor way too much power and had way too high expectations," she said. "Pastors also took that on for themselves as well." The Community "was not perfect, but power really was shared."[40]

Dianne was twenty-two years old and thought the older people in the Community, especially David and Dora, by then in their forties, were "cooler than cool." Gathering with a few dozen people felt like the small-group worship and prayer that Dianne encountered in college. She was familiar with the Prayers of the People in Lutheran liturgy and its nesting structure, praying for international and national church bodies, praying for the sick, and so forth. The Community didn't use that formula. Dianne was surprised that people didn't need it to open up to each other in a way that was heartfelt and unpolished. "The Spirit led us in those ways to pray with such intensity and integrity around our petitions," Dianne said. "I would walk away from worship feeling both challenged and elated."[41]

Another of Dianne's housemates was a woman named Dee Dee Risher. She was a year older and worked as the live-in LVC staff person. On a trip to DC with their campus minister, Dee Dee and a group of other college students stayed with Larry and Nyla Rasmussen, sleeping on their floor and

39. Russell, in discussion with the author, September 2021.
40. Russell, in discussion with the author, September 2021.
41. Russell, in discussion with the author, September 2021.

learning a bit about the Community. She found it to be a close-knit group, strongly based in its neighborhood. Dee Dee grew up in a Lutheran Church with highly formal liturgy, and she appreciated the creativity of how Community worship was shaped by those leading. While in DC, Dee Dee found her home at Church of the Saviour, while Dianne and Mary engaged in the Community.[42]

As is the hope with programs such as LVC, through her job at SANE Dianne found her calling. Dee Dee watched Dianne hone her skills in community organizing and training. Dianne was down-to-earth "in her theology and style of talking to people." Dee Dee realized that Dianne had a class consciousness that she lacked. Coming from a farm community in Ohio and being the daughter of working-class people gave Dianne a folksiness that was authentic. It was a tool she had and brought out to cross cultures and the different worlds people inhabit in the same country and even the same city. "I always think of the word *grounded* when I think of Dianne," Dee Dee said, "She is comfortable in her own skin."[43]

One weekend in 1984, Dee Dee drove her college friend Christina Nichols, who goes by Chris, to DC for some job interviews. She connected her to Dianne, who was no longer in LVC, but living in a different group house in Mount Pleasant. Dianne and her housemates invited Chris to dinner. When Chris arrived at the house, the door swung open and she heard a woman say, "Hi, I'm Dianne." Suddenly sparkling lights appeared in the air all around them and a voice spoke in Chris' ears, "This is the one! This is your soulmate, the one you will grow old with." The chemical reaction between the two of them continued with conversation over the shared meal. Dianne invited Chris back the next evening so she could meet more of the people in the group house, but coincidentally everyone else had plans. Chris and Dianne spent the evening cooking and talking. They still hadn't said out loud to each other that they were both lesbians. Chris hadn't moved to DC or gotten a job yet, but none of that deterred her. She was determined to be dating Dianne within six months.[44]

Dianne was running a grassroots campaign for SANE promoting propeace candidates in Daytona Beach, Florida, about ninety minutes from Chris's hometown in the middle of the state. It was near Disney World Magic Kingdom theme park, where Chris worked as a teenager. Chris hatched a plan. To her parents, she said she was coming to visit and to pick up some of her stuff to take back to DC. She timed it for the end of Dianne's campaign.

42. Dee Dee Risher, in discussion with the author, November 2021.
43. Risher, in discussion with the author, November 2021.
44. Christina Nichols, in discussion with the author, November 2021.

To Dianne, she said she could pick her up and take her to Disney World, where she had never been.

When the day arrived, Chris worked in a beach picnic and a swim in the ocean before the drive to her childhood home, during which they talked almost nonstop. A few blocks before they arrived, Dianne surprised Chris by blurting out, "I think I'm in love with you." Chris pulled over in a quiet place, and Dianne leaned in and kissed her. Chris felt her heart bursting with joy.[45] They walked around the Magic Kingdom the next day "in the blissful haze of early love."[46]

As they continued to learn more about each other, Chris appreciated Dianne's centeredness and deep faith. Chris was less certain in her faith, but she was a Christian and she wanted to worship with others. She grew up active in a Methodist church, where she was the youth group president and went to regional church activities in southern Florida. "Other than being a lesbian and knowing that the church actively rejected me, I had not rejected the church," Chris said. "I don't think God has created me as a mistake, and I don't reject my faith."[47]

Chris and Dianne were present but not out as lesbians when the Community discussed becoming "Reconciled in Christ" through Lutherans Concerned. Chris, raised Methodist, didn't know what it was or that it wasn't clarified for her until later that it would be affirming their relationship.[48] Once they were out, some people mixed up their names, "like we were interchangeable," as if to say, "Oh, the lesbian couple, one of them, Chris and Dianne, Dianne Chris, whatever." At the same time, she felt fully welcomed into the worship life and came to see the Community as a collection of broken people who were seeking healing together. "We are imperfect," Chris said. "But otherwise, why would we need Christ?"[49]

❧

After a few years in DC, Dianne arrived at the point when she planned to go to seminary. Did she still want to pursue pastoral ministry? She knew she felt called to community organizing and advocacy, which introduced her to the concept of training people toward social change. She was part of applying a

45. Nichols, in discussion with the author, November 2021; Russell, email message to the author, March 23, 2023.
46. Nichols, in discussion with the author, February 2023.
47. Nichols, in discussion with the author, November 2021.
48. Nichols and Russell, in discussion with the author, February 2023.
49. Nichols, in discussion with the author, November 2021.

grassroots organizing model that thoughtfully employed a method of teaching adults. Through roles in the peace movement and then the environmental movement, Dianne said, "I was doing God's work in the world."[50]

She realized that there were many paths to that sense of vocation. And yet there was another factor she weighed that straight people don't have to:

> The other thing, though, when I'm really honest about it, is when I came out as a lesbian and I looked at the institutional church at that point and where it was at in the eighties around its exclusion of gay, lesbian, bi, transgender, queer people. Chris and I fell in love and it was magic. And I wasn't going to threaten that by trying to become a pastor and fighting within a system that didn't make space for me.[51]

Deciding not to pursue seminary and ordination didn't diminish the variety of gifts Dianne gave in the life of the church. "It was delightful to be able to also do some of that work in a collaborative setting of peer ministers," she said. "It really helped ease the sting that the church wouldn't accept me."[52]

When Dianne and Chris married in May 1989, they asked their friend Dee Dee, who was gifted in crafting rituals, to officiate. They asked the Community to bless their union, and the Community came to consensus that it would. In La Casa the Sunday before the wedding, the Community gathered around Chris and Dianne and collectively spoke a formal blessing for the occasion.[53] For the meal after the ceremony, they handed out recipes ahead of time so that it felt less like an ordinary potluck and more like a communally catered event. Dee Dee "loved how Community of Christ showed up." Dianne's mother also attended, coming from rural Ohio—in some ways a separate world. "We introduced Dianne's mom and the whole room exploded in applause," Dee Dee said.[54]

A needlepoint hanging in Chris and Dianne's home near the front door has their wedding date and words from Ruth 1:16–17 that are embraced by many same-sex couples: "For where you go, I will go, and where you lodge, I will lodge. Your people shall be my people and your God my God." Together they welcomed two daughters. Chris gave birth to Lydia in 1994 and Dianne gave birth to Kaisa in 1996. They were both baptized in the Community.

Dianne's ministry gifts were the same gifts as in her grassroots work, and they gave her a pastoral bearing. "The same skills that made her a great

50. Russell, in discussion with the author, September 2021.

51. Russell, in discussion with the author, September 2021.

52. Russell, in discussion with the author, September 2021.

53. Nichols and Russell, in discussion with the author, February 2023.

54. Risher, in discussion with the author, November 2021.

organizer and organizational leader also would have made her a great pastor," Dee Dee said.[55] Members of the Community agreed, and over the years often turned to Dianne and Chris to provide a pastoral kind of listening and support in times of crisis and struggle.[56] Chris also became a liturgy leader, though she found it difficult at first to prepare a homily as well as other elements of the service, the hymns and a prayer of the day. "Most of us were willing to participate, but certainly not everybody," Chris said. "I thought, 'Well, we're all children of God. We are all called in some way to be part of the body of Christ. And I'm not bad at speaking publicly for my work. So I can learn to do this as part of the worship rotation.'" She appreciated the occasions when the Community offered training for each other on scriptural interpretation and how to lead with more confidence.[57]

Small group worship starting in the late 1960s and early 1970s, and the worship rotation after that, offered a place where anyone could find their voice and style of leadership. Yet especially for women in the Community, it was often not as simple as being given an opportunity to lead. Even Dianne struggled "as a woman in our society" to claim her power and gifts.[58] Barbara was part of the Community for twenty-one years before she "developed the courage to lead the service and to preach." Once she did, she grew in confidence and "found my legs as a Christian."[59] Hayley grew up with "this idea that interpreting scripture was not my job." It was a common idea for Catholic laypeople, but in a patriarchal context it came across more strongly for women and girls. Joining the Community in 1988, "in my mid-twenties, I was completely undone by the idea that I could preach," Hayley said, "to consider that I could have a theological voice." Yet for her the experience wasn't entirely an empowering one. "I don't think I ever stopped feeling like I wasn't enough in that space, because it felt like there were theological giants in our midst" and the ones who were men felt intimidating.[60]

While anyone could lead the service and preach, whether or not they chose to do so, the Community had a different standard for eucharistic celebrants. One needed to be ordained or at least have completed seminary training. "Some of us feel uncomfortable with just any of us serving communion," Dora told a reporter who featured the Community on the

---

55. Risher, in discussion with the author, November 2021.

56. One example: John and Bobbie Stewart, in discussion with the author, January 2021.

57. Nichols, in discussion with the author, November 2021.

58. Russell, "Living Humble," in *Lenten Thoughts, 2004,* April 6.

59. Hayden, *Lent 2009*, April 1.

60. Hoffman, in discussion with the author, September 2021.

Washington Post religion page in 1977.[61] When the Community had small group worship in the late 1960s and early 1970s, a group came to consensus that a lay person could celebrate the Eucharist in that setting. In the 1980s, with one Sunday service, the Community adopted a practice for when no authorized person was present: they read in unison, communally consecrating the Eucharist. They affirmed this as faithful to the intent of Christ and the traditions passed down through the Gospels.[62] If a woman was the worship leader on any given Sunday, she led the collective consecration of bread and cup. On several such occasions when Hayley was leading the service, "it always felt like I was breaking the rules when it happened, but I would reassure myself that the combined spirit of the group was powerful!"[63]

In early 2002, the Community looked around and realized that the four people who could celebrate the Eucharist were all older white men. (Several women from the Community went on to be ordained and pastor other congregations, including Wendy Ward in the United Church of Christ and Anne Yarbrough in the United Methodist Church.) The Community revisited all aspects of its practice and theology of the Eucharist. They again called on Amy, who had no stake in the decision, to share her gifts as a moderator. "It was so emblematic of who the Community of Christ was that they had a Jew facilitate all that," Amy said. She was surprised by the passion from people she knew for fifteen years at that point. But she heard no objections to a woman celebrating the Eucharist. More-debated questions were 1) what training they wanted celebrants to have, and 2) whether the bread and cup would be offered to people who were not Christian. The core people in the Community, whatever skepticism they might have, were all baptized. Newcomers and visitors might not be.[64] Initially the Community's covenant specified that "any baptized Christian who seeks to find in faith the Body and Blood of Christ at this table is welcome to share the Communion feast."[65] But they dropped that language after five years and replaced it in 1971 and 1995 covenants with affirmations that the Eucharist expressed and increased unity as the body of Christ.[66]

61. D'au Vin, "NW Group Shows Big Deeds," D8.

62. Kraus, "Friday Evening Worship," 11; Glenn, "Serving the Eucharist to the Community," 15, 20; Minutes of Community meeting, 29 April 1989, in Community of Christ Papers.

63. Hoffman, email message to author, August 8, 2022.

64. Wind, in discussion with the author, July 2022.

65. "Covenant of the Community of Christ," 21.

66. Covenant of the Community of Christ, 1 January 1971, in Community of Christ Papers; "Covenant—Community of Christ, Draft—2 June 1995," in *Lenten Thoughts, 2006,* unnumbered and undated pages near front cover.

The gathered came to consensus on points that could have divided other groups, but for them flowed naturally from decades of worship together. They wanted to continue the Eucharist, weekly, open to all who wished to partake, and celebrated by someone authorized for that role—and they were open to that being by the Community itself. There was a concern, though, that if the Community recognized individuals' call to celebrate the Eucharist without confirmation from some wider body, the Community could risk "becoming a sect," accountable only to itself. They returned to their grounding in the words of Scripture as the words that consecrate the elements in the Eucharist. Those words joined them with other Christians in two thousand years of tradition.[67]

In a statement on the Eucharist, the Community formalized its practices. The liturgy leader would welcome visitors at the start of each service and at that time, or when the celebrant prepared for distribution of communion, they would invite visitors to share in the bread and wine and describe how the elements were passed from person to person in the circle. The Community outlined the process for becoming a celebrant, which it would also follow for any future person who came into the Community ordained. The statement noted that the Community did not require its members to affirm the same set of beliefs, including about the Eucharist. Yet they did share the conviction that they were obeying Christ's command in memory of "his sacrificial giving of himself" and receiving "a foretaste of the banquet in the coming kingdom of God."[68]

For those considering becoming a celebrant, the Community asked them to ponder: Do you feel called to this kind of sacramental ministry in particular? Are you willing to participate in a clearness committee—a concept borrowed from the Quakers—to sit together in silence and sort through what it meant to be called? "The Community making that decision to invite people into eucharistic ministry, whether they were ordained or not, was probably one of one of our finest hours, as well as one of the most challenging," Dianne said. Duane Shank, who was Dianne's colleague at SANE, was now a lay leader in the Community and saw her gifts in both contexts. He asked if Dianne was considering becoming a celebrant. Dora also pulled her aside and wondered the same. Dianne appreciated the external encouragement but even more the internal confirmation that she had from the Spirit.

67. Amy Wind, summary of Community meeting on the Eucharist, 17 April 2002, in the author's possession.

68. "Statement on the Eucharist," June 2002, in the author's possession.

Dianne and one other woman, Joy Jones, began the process. They were each asked to take on an area of study related to Communion that they would research and write about, then talk about it with their clearness committee. Dianne's project was about Eucharist and the ecumenical movement: how Communion is viewed and practiced by the traditions in which various Community members had been raised.[69] Joy created an altar cloth and new liturgy for the Community and painted vines and flowers on the printed pages. She had a seminary degree but served a church that did not ordain women at that time. Celebrating the Eucharist amid leading a service with her liturgy culminated "a very healing process for me and gave me a sense of belonging in the Community that I had not felt in the wider church."[70]

As Dianne prepared, she watched ordained people in the Community more closely during the ritual. She asked Dunstan for his counsel. He told her that as long as she approached it prayerfully, taking the time to prepare herself, God would make her a channel to nourish the gathered body in the way that the sacrament is intended. In the weeks before the first time Dianne was the celebrant, she practiced all of the motions and recited all of the words. Still, she felt nervous. She prayed with Ps 19, that God would accept her words and the meditations of her heart. On that Sunday, as she began to speak, she felt the Spirit descend on her and the group. She knew in that moment "that the call was right and real."[71]

---

69. Russell, in discussion with the author, September 2021.

70. Joy Jones, email message to author, March 27, 2023.

71. Russell, in discussion with the author, September 2021.

11

"The Punk Show Is at Your Church?"

IN LA CASA, THE line between sacred and secular uses was porous. Beginning at age seven after my family joined the Community, I learned to know that space for worship, but also by playing hide-and-seek throughout the building. One summer I went to a day camp there run by a local arts nonprofit. As a teenager becoming politically active, I attended a meeting or two of the advisory neighborhood council, a local governmental body that met there. I went to a panel discussion about policing and human rights, and a screening of a documentary about homelessness. Not being a traditional church building also meant there wasn't a fellowship hall, so all of these gatherings were in the space that became our sanctuary. When not used in worship, the altar-on-wheels, liturgies, and songbooks were in a partially cordoned off corner.

Having had such eclectic experiences in the space, it seemed perfectly natural to me to also go to all-ages punk concerts at La Casa. The DC punk scene was shaped by rebels who very much had a cause, or rather causes, through the activist group Positive Force. Many punk shows were benefits for one social justice need or another. Other nearby venues for concerts included All Souls Unitarian and St. Stephen and the Incarnation Episcopal churches, and the basement of the Wilson Center, which was once a church and still looked like one. La Casa likewise showed its history, but in its case that was a private residence turned into a restaurant-nightclub turned into a community center. At night even the few panes of stained glass were not visible.

One of the organizers of the shows was Amanda Huron, who helped out with the Community youth group for a while. Like many preteens with their youth group leaders, I thought Amanda was the coolest person on the planet. Our youth group stopped meeting when our oldest member went to college. But Cyrus and I—who were part of the same high school friend group—continued to be influenced by Amanda's leadership through this blend of music and activism. And we came with our friends to La Casa on the weekends, to punk shows in the same room where we were both baptized. If a friend saw a flier first and I mentioned my relationship to the space, I got an incredulous response: "The punk show is at your church?"

After growing up with La Casa feeling like a second home, Amanda went to the Twin Cities for five years. She got involved in low-power radio in college. She returned to DC in 1995 and started working in various radio projects. She also reimmersed herself in the punk scene and she started playing in a band. They practiced in one of La Casa's basement rooms. She remembered growing up in the Community seeing the value placed on supporting members' dreams, whatever they were. Amanda's dream was to start a radio station.[1]

Amanda and her friend and bandmate Natalie Avery met with Doug, David, and Margaret Ann as the Community decided whether or not to let them broadcast from one of the upstairs rooms at La Casa. Officially, Doug and others are listed as founders who purchased a transmitter for the Mount Pleasant Broadcasting Club in 1998. The low-power radio station was "undocumented" like many of their neighbors, as Amanda put it. They named it Community Power Radio, commonly known as Radio CPR as it aided the neighborhood's artistic heartbeat. Radio CPR attracted a diverse group of people to host radio shows, representing many if not all of the cultures in the area it reached in Mount Pleasant, Adams Morgan, Columbia Heights, and Petworth. A few Community members tried their hand at it as well. Duane played blues music for his hour. Margaret Ann and David played folk and bluegrass.[2]

When Natalie moved to Mount Pleasant in the nineties, she thought longtime residents were "midwives and labor organizers" and the like. Then she attended an ANC meeting and started reading posts on the neighborhood email list. "We live in this neighborhood where people are really suffering because of poverty and disenfranchisement because of those Clinton-era welfare and immigration reform policies," she said. Meanwhile some of the white, middle-class people used coded, racist language, seeing their neighbors as the problem rather than working together to find solutions.[3]

1. Amanda Huron, in discussion with the author, September 2021.

2. Natalie Avery, in discussion with the author, July 2022; Amy Wind, in discussion with the author, July 2022; Huron, in discussion with the author, September 2021.

3. Avery, in discussion with the author, July 2022.

Seeking an antidote to that way of relating to marginalized people, Natalie and Amanda were inspired by a show they saw while on tour with their band bringing different performance styles together, called a cabaret. They thought it could showcase the many cultures of Mount Pleasant. They wanted to amplify other people's voices and not just have their own soapbox. They invited a mariachi band, a punk band, a soul singer, and a Vietnamese teenage poet. The first cabaret, at a local restaurant, went well, so they planned a second one. They then learned that a neighborhood alliance had agreements with many restaurants that if they refrained from hosting live music, the alliance wouldn't challenge their liquor licenses. So Amanda and Natalie moved the event to La Casa, with Christmas lights and checkered tablecloths to make the main space feel festive. Since it was a community center owned by a congregation, there was no liquor license to challenge (and no liquor served). Amanda and Natalie started having shows in La Casa regularly. They honored the noise ordinance and ended at 11:00 p.m.[4]

La Casa also hosted early meetings of a group called Stand for Our Neighbors, which pushed back on the way Salvadorans were treated in Mount Pleasant. It was a countervailing force to the neighborhood alliance, similar to the integrated Lincoln Civic Association that the Community was involved in during the early years in Dupont Circle. With Stand for Our Neighbors and Radio CPR, having space at La Casa was essential, Natalie said: "Neither of those things would have happened if meetings had to happen in private homes. You can't welcome people in the same way. It's different to come to a storefront than to come to a private home."[5] John Stewart and others in the Community enthusiastically supported Stand for Our Neighbors and continued opening La Casa's doors to the concerts.[6]

By the time Radio CPR set up in La Casa, it joined a decades-long parade of short-term and long-term renters in the building. To say that the groups varied widely is an understatement. There were Bible classes and birthing classes, drumming circles and dance workshops, meetings with police-community liaisons and meetings of prison abolitionist groups.[7] Instead of a church building that hosted neighborhood groups, La Casa was home to the Community and open to the neighborhood, as Natalie saw it.

4. Huron, in discussion with the author, September 2021; Avery, in discussion with the author, July 2022.

5. Avery, in discussion with the author, July 2022.

6. Stewart, in discussion with the author, May 2022.

7. Community of Christ Papers, Swarthmore College Peace Collection.

She was impressed by how Community members "thought about that place and let it be so many things to so many people."[8]

⁊⬥

The Community was doing all of this while the religious landscape around the United States was shifting to ask questions like those the Community asked for decades. In the late 1990s and early 2000s, groups of Christians in North America who were estranged by the culture wars of the 1980s began examining how modernity affected Western Christianity. Institutions such as seminaries and denominations arose in the modern period. What changes were necessary as the postmodern era began and churches moved from the center to the margins in society? The conversation among Christians came to collectively be called the emerging church movement. Many of the participants came out of conservative evangelicalism. Not everyone involved embraced the terms emergent or emerging church, but those became the common descriptions.[9]

Brian McLaren, arguably the most well-known pastor and author of this movement, emphasized that they were not seeking to distinguish themselves from traditional Christians, nor did they see themselves as superior.[10] McLaren noted that the Church of the Saviour, which influenced the Community at its outset, "anticipated and exemplifies many good qualities now associated with 'the emerging church.'"[11] They sought to bridge divides among Christians and to reach people not attracted to the traditional church and invite them into a deeper discipleship. They sought new ways to be faithful without creating new denominational structures. McLaren emphasized the value of institutions that preserve the values of their members. Yet each of those institutions "has to figure out what its wine is and what its wineskins are," he said. "Then we can look toward the future and let our traditions be living traditions."[12]

Another stream in this flow of renewal in Christianity was new monasticism. In his twenties in the 2000s, Jonathan Wilson-Hartgrove wrote down the vision of new communities growing "at the margins of church and society," he wrote. He connected their efforts to Dietrich Bonhoeffer's phrase "new monasticism" coined in 1935 to describe those taking the Sermon on

8. Avery, in discussion with the author, July 2022.

9. Francis, "Emerging Church," 3, 24, 33; McLaren, *New Kind of Christian*, 24–25.

10. McLaren, *New Kind of Christian*, 46–47.

11. McLaren, "Becoming Convergent," 3.

12. Kennel-Shank, "Author Connects," 2.

the Mount as a pattern for discipleship. The communities started in the 2000s were characterized by marks such as relocating to places powerful people had abandoned, sharing economic resources, peacemaking, and being invested in the place where they were living.[13] Caring for each other was their primary calling, Wilson-Hartgrove wrote. "The ministry of organizing childcare co-ops and shared meals, lending lawnmowers and scrubbing floors is every bit as important as preparing a sermon or working the soup line"[14] as the Community recognized since the 1970s. Also like the Community, new monastics engaged in "grassroots ecumenism," in contrast to a lot of the ecumenical movement in the twentieth century, which they saw as largely a conversation among mainline denominations. They found a way to live together without agreement on doctrinal questions.[15]

Bonhoeffer's *Life Together*, detailing his life in intentional community in the mid-1930s, was a crucial book for these younger Christians as it had been for older generations in the Community and elsewhere. The Community came back to it many times on occasions such as Lent 2005. We cherished insights such as this one, which my father, Duane, and I independently underlined in each of our copies from that Lenten book study: "Whoever loves their dream of Christian community more than Christian community itself will become the destroyer of every Christian community, no matter how honest, earnest, and sacrificial their intentions may be."[16]

Emerging church leaders and new monastics—which had many similarities without formal ties—had substantial overlap in their visions for faith communities. They were smaller, non-hierarchical, diverse in race and class (or at least seeking it), and engaged in each other's lives beyond Sunday morning, with some also sharing housing or some form of intentional community. Through authors such as McLaren and Wilson-Hartgrove and like-minded Christians, a new generation of young people were attracted to communities at the margins of the wider church. Several of those young people found the Community, and saw what it had created and sustained for decades to be in line with the new visions of church they were dreaming.[17]

For Emily Holman, the Community was a place where people were asking the kinds of questions she was, about what it means to be an ambitious

13. Wilson-Hartgrove, *New Monasticism*, 39.

14. Wilson-Hartgrove, *New Monasticism*, 138–40.

15. Wilson-Hartgrove, *New Monasticism*, 129.

16. Wilson-Hartgrove, *New Monasticism*, 26. This is his translation from the German in section 24; it does not vary substantially from the one in Bonhoeffer, *Life Together*, 36.

17. Francis, "Emerging Church," 43; Robert Francis, in discussion with the author, January 2022.

young professional while also wanting to go deeper in one's faith.[18] When she arrived in DC in 2002, she quickly met other young justice-minded people through mutual friends and began to engage in traditions then several decades old, like dance parties at group houses. After one particularly late night, Emily and others slept on couches and the floor rather than try to get home in the wee hours of the morning. Not many hours later, she woke to see one of the twenty-somethings who lived in the group house carrying her Bible and heading out the door. Emily asked, "Are you going to church?" It was Gail Taylor, and she was headed to Community worship. "Can I go with you?" Emily said, then, realizing how little sleep she'd had, "Not today, but another time." When she met people in the Community, "It was as if they'd known me my whole life from the very first moment." There were twenty to twenty-five people at that point. Emily saw the positives of the size. Instead of feeling like she had to put on a performance, as she felt she had to do in large churches, she showed the Community her "imperfect self—what God sees." Giving homilies was a stretch but a welcome one, and she learned a great deal from the Bible studies, she said. "As this 22-year-old with very little biblical history, because it was a small group, I was invited to ask questions even if they could have been looked at as stupid but they weren't."[19]

Yvette Schock encountered the Community first through the Order of Saints Martin and Teresa, an initiative of several Community members beginning in the 1970s. Following the Community's emphasis on disciplines, members took on Christian practices toward "being a peace church in a countercultural way," David said.[20] The order published a journal. People such as the college pastors at the Lutheran school Yvette attended read and disseminated it. "Dora was a peace-and-justice celebrity to me," Yvette said.[21]

Robert Francis was another of those young people. He had written his master's thesis on the emerging church as a new religious movement. He learned about how the post-World War II era saw the beginning of more new religious movements than any other time in US history. The 1960s in particular included questioning about the definitions people had been taught of God and where God is found. New religious communities emphasized service over doctrine and spirituality over organized religion. They sought liberation and were open to other religions. A lot of the critique from

18. Holman, "Ambition," unpublished homily in the author's possession, 12 February 2006.

19. Emily Holman, in discussion with Laci Barrow, Christina Nichols, and Martin Johnson, September 2016.

20. David Anderson, in discussion with Laci Barrow, Christina Nichols, and Martin Johnson, September 2016.

21. Yvette Schock, in discussion with the author, January 2022.

the emerging church in the late 1990s and 2000s was similar.[22] When Robert arrived at the Community of Christ, he found a living, breathing example of what he had read about in his research.[23]

Members of the Community who were long-time homeowners in Mount Pleasant offered new young people affordable housing. Robert moved into Duane and Ellen's basement apartment from the housing provided by the yearlong Sojourners program. Dora offered Yvette a room in her house,[24] where she had for decades offered the top floor to house renters and guests, often people who were working in social justice jobs for low pay. There were many "somebody who knows somebody" situations, Alicia said, "and of course there's always room at Dora's." She didn't charge more than $250 a month for rent.[25] Those arrangements made it possible for Robert and Yvette to live in the area. "Being in the neighborhood mattered so much for us, just to be able to walk to the Community of Christ on a Sunday morning and the potlucks," Robert said, "sharing life in the community."[26]

Yonce Shelton preceded Robert and Yvette as another of the younger people in this stream who were attracted to the Community. After working for a member of Congress on Capitol Hill and then going to seminary in DC, Yonce got a job as policy director of Call to Renewal, a coalition of Christian groups working to end poverty at the local and state levels. Yonce worked closely with Duane, a lay leader in the Community. Yonce and his wife, Johanna, called JoJo, were attending Sacred Heart, because JoJo is Catholic. But she didn't like the new priest who arrived in the Mount Pleasant parish in 2004. JoJo said to Yonce, "We're out of here. We're going to Duane's church."[27]

When they went, Yonce was surprised by the casual dress. He grew up in a "middle-of-the-road Methodist church in East Tennessee" where everyone dressed up for church. In the Community, he looked around at the jeans and T-shirts and even the occasional track suit and thought, "Wow, these people are funky." He also noticed the lack of a paid pastor, and the way laypeople in their homilies were talking about the upcoming election in fall 2004. They were edgy in a way that his home church didn't come close to, as it didn't talk about social justice.[28]

22. Francis, "Emerging Church," 34.

23. Francis, in discussion with the author, January 2022.

24. Francis and Schock, in discussion with the author, January 2022.

25. Alicia Koundakjian Moyer, in discussion with the author, September 2021.

26. Francis and Schock, in discussion with the author, January 2022.

27. Shelton, in discussion with the author, May 2022.

28. Shelton, in discussion with the author, May 2022.

While living in Mount Pleasant, Yonce and JoJo started a small group that met in their home. Robert and Yvette joined along with a few other younger people who were Christians. Fewer and fewer of their peers in the neighborhood engaged with any faith tradition. Many of the older adults in the Community were in that place a few decades earlier.

❧

Barbara was disillusioned with the church in her twenties. She was raised Catholic and valued the education she received from Ursuline nuns. "The nuns were secret renegades," she said. They told their students that Jesus was Jewish, that Black and white people are equal, and that all religions have knowledge of the divine. Through the sisters, "I met God, I learned about God, I learned how to honor God and feel God's presence."[29] Yet as a teenager Barbara felt doctrine was stale. And with pews burgeoning in the 1950s and 1960s, she often felt anonymous in the congregation. "The prayers of the people would begin with a prayer for the pope and a prayer for the bishop, and you go on down the hierarchy of all these colorful cardinals and then you would finally get to some situation in the world where there was famine," she said. She sat there and thought, "I didn't even know the bishop. How could I be invested in praying for him?" It didn't touch on her needs. "What about me? What about my mom?"[30]

She had attended Thomas Jefferson Memorial Unitarian Church while a college student in Charlottesville, Virginia. She appreciated the emphasis on peace and justice, but she wanted to talk about Jesus, she said. "I really missed any semblance of ritual, any echoes of my Catholic past." For about ten years she tabled the question of religion.[31]

In 1985, she was thirty-four and pursuing additional certification as a nurse when she met Dunstan at Northern Virginia Community College. Before long they became a couple. One Sunday morning Dunstan told her that he'd be attending his church at 10:30 a.m. and she was welcome to join him if she wished. "I flew out of bed," she said. As she walked in, seeing about thirty people in a semicircle, they appeared "like Christians in the catacombs," she said. "There was a wonderful sense of reverence that a church service was about to take place and that it was sacred. And I thought, you know, the drafty cold, leaky catacombs were sacred space. And

29. Barbara Hayden, in discussion with the author, September 2021.
30. Barbara Hayden, in discussion with the author, May 2020.
31. Barbara Hayden, in discussion with the author, May 2020.

so this modest inner-city all-purpose room is made sacred by this group of people."[32]

Soon she was there every Sunday when she wasn't working. "I had never heard preaching like that, and I was amazed that these were lay preachers," she said. "They engaged with the gospel so honestly and applied their life experiences to it and the challenges of the day."[33] She was grateful that the Community didn't let her, or anyone, hide in the pews. An active Christianity was expected of them. Barbara not only participated in worship but joined the Community in activities such as protesting apartheid outside of the South African embassy. The Community also knew how to celebrate together rather than being dour. "Churches need to make having fun more of a priority," in Barbara's view. "Even if life is full of grief and worry and hard work, it's still life, and God loves us," she wrote. The Spirit bids us to be full of life.[34]

In the 2000s, Barbara got involved in a group called Mount Pleasant Main Street, partnering with businesses to try to mitigate some of the worst effects of gentrification. She was the face of the Community of Christ to a lot of people in Mount Pleasant for a number of years.[35] They had to ask the question, "Who were we? A ragtag hippie remnant church, but we were going to do what we could do for as long as it lasted," Barbara said. "John Schramm called this 'necessary nonchalance.' Is it losing your ego maybe, giving up your life? It certainly meant we had no reputation to defend, no 'optics' to manage."[36]

Neighbors walking by La Casa or even coming inside for a meeting or concert, unless they knew someone from the Community, didn't think of the building as a place of worship. Even some owners and employees of the businesses on either side of La Casa didn't know that there was worship there. Aware of that, the Community decided to start letting its Christianity show at La Casa beyond the name and fish symbol on the sign designed by Rudy. They hoped that if the Community was more visible, people would visit on Sundays.[37] Barbara and Yonce led efforts to make the Community more known to its neighbors and beyond. They started by creating a website and redesigning a pamphlet about the Community placed near the front door.

32. Hayden, in discussion with the author, May 2020.
33. Hayden, in discussion with the author, May 2020.
34. Barbara Hayden, email message to author, August 18, 2021.
35. Hayden, in discussion with the author, September 2021.
36. Hayden, email message to author, August 18, 2021.
37. Minutes of Community meeting, 24 February 2008, in the author's possession.

Yonce wondered "what providing more leadership in the Community would look like and how it might help us take our witness and engagement with each other and the Mount Pleasant community to the next level." In 2008, he was in a graduate program in pastoral counseling and asked if he could work for the Community half-time unpaid. He could explore different ways to be pastoral and aid in spiritual formation. He proposed engaging the Community around discipleship disciplines as well as a "program on spirituality, vocation, and leadership aimed at emerging leaders," he wrote. "I have always come alive when helping emerging leaders (20ish) navigate the DC job scene in spiritual and practical ways." He asked the Community to help him discern his calling in a new way.[38]

Instead of the title of pastor, Yonce asked to be called choreographer of the dance in steps of change, referring to John Schramm and David Anderson's book about the Community's first five years. He developed a "'dance routine' (or, you might say, strategic plan) that synthesizes and articulates our many parts to help us see where we might go from here."[39] Yonce made up business cards and struck up conversations with other pastors and neighborhood activists. Neighbors respected that the Community had been around for forty years, but they weren't looking for a congregation, or at least not what they were picturing when Yonce invited them. A few came to visit. Families with children saw that there were few children or possibly none on any given Sunday. Another hurdle was the small size and configuration of the main space at La Casa that made it impossible to check the Community out in a low-key way.[40]

Music was also struggling at that point. Margaret Ann moved to her native Montana in the summer of 2004, along with her husband, David. Anticipating the loss of Margaret Ann's leadership, she and Sandi coordinated the Community to create a recording of the most popular songs they sang in worship. They turned it into a CD. It included "Oh Magnify the Lord," "Jesus, Show Me the Way," and "Lord, Listen to your Children." Sometimes on Sunday mornings, liturgy leaders played the CD for people to sing along with from their chairs.

In the midst of these conversations, the Community asked what they were willing to change. Yet some of what Community members, old and new, most appreciated about their worship—and what the young adults who had grown up in the Community valued as well—was not innovative to some prospective worshipers. Instead, it was strange. Not a lot of people

38. Shelton, email message to Community of Christ, January 25, 2008.

39. Shelton, email message to Community of Christ, January 2008.

40. Shelton, in discussion with the author, May 2022.

are looking for a different person preaching every Sunday, some with no training, Yonce observed. They didn't see evidence that people would beat down the door if only the Community changed in a particular way.[41]

A decade earlier, the Community explored its future viability in an extended self-study. Members recognized that twenty years into the future, half of the adults present at that time were likely to be deceased, living in a nursing home, or to have moved to another city for their retirement years. Twila Crawford, a newer participant who was closer in age to the longtime members, wrote, "to me there seems to be a comfortableness, without too many challenges, except concerning building repairs." She named the lack of racial diversity in the Community as an embarrassment. Chris and Dianne asked whether the Community was capable of doing outreach, and what the programmatic reason was to grow and stretch. It wasn't enough to seek to grow to survive.[42]

The Community wasn't alone in these questions. Amy Sevimli met with the Community a few times while working from 2008 to 2016 with the bishop in the metropolitan DC area in the Evangelical Lutheran Church in America, the denomination in which the Community was a member.[43] She developed young adult ministries and helped existing congregations who sought to attract young adults, working with dozens of ELCA congregations in the city and suburbs. She suggested adapting to each location. In some places, that might be more programs for families. In others, they might try meeting on weeknights or Sunday evenings. "What it boiled down to was sociological change, which most of the congregations were unwilling to make," she said. Another major factor for connecting with young adults for churches in any tradition, she observed, was having an engaged leader. The leader didn't need to be a hip, younger person. In fact, they were often middle-aged.[44]

At that time, Mount Pleasant "was thriving, young people everywhere," said Sevimli, who was in her thirties then. She met with young adults in DC and found that many saw the church as irrelevant or harmful, or they were ambivalent. Sevimli spent a lot of time apologizing on behalf of the wider church to people from many Christian traditions who had a painful experience as a child or teenager. As a result, they felt disdain for churches. For those who were coming back to or coming anew to a community of faith,

41. Shelton, in discussion with the author, May 2022.

42. "Self-study and Discussion of the Future," 1996–1997, in Community of Christ Papers.

43. Minutes of Community meeting, 24 January, 2010, in the author's possession.

44. Amy Sevimli, in discussion with the author, March 2023.

she observed that they didn't care how sophisticated the theology was in a church's sermons, and they weren't drawn to churches just because they were active in social justice. Instead, they asked, "Do I feel comfortable here, do I feel welcome here, do I belong here?"[45]

In the Community, longtime members were warm and welcoming. Yet new people had a hard time becoming part of the group in a deeper way. Alden felt like a newcomer in the Community for decades, though the Community "was considerably less cliquish than other groups I'd been a part of," he said. Trained as an anthropologist, he recognized that the history created during seasons of life shared with a particular set of people can't be replaced. He stayed because the Community retained the qualities he found attractive when he arrived in 1985. He learned to reinterpret Christian concepts he'd struggled with growing up in a missionary family. "I really appreciated having people who could share their knowledge and understanding of the old-time faith when the old-time faith had less purchase on me," he said.[46] He recalled a homily from Dunstan on Matt 5:48, "Be perfect, therefore, as your heavenly Father is perfect." Alden heard that often as a child and knew that he would never be perfect, no matter how hard he tried.[47] Dunstan told the Community that the Koine Greek word translated as "perfect" has a meaning closer to "whole," Alden thought, "Wholeness is something I could live towards."[48]

Rachel Haxtema, who came to DC in the early 2000s as a Sojourners intern, likewise was impressed by the Community but "felt a little bit like an outsider the whole time." She realized after attending for several weeks that she wasn't sure which people were partnered and who the parents of the children were, that families didn't necessarily sit together. "I saw that as a strength," she said, "a beautiful part of being so, so close knit." She also recognized the challenge of welcoming new people in a small community. "These people have known each other forever," she said. It felt like she was merely "along for the ride for a while."[49]

After years of coming to La Casa for Radio CPR and shows, Natalie started attending Community worship with her husband, Eddie Janney, and their two young children. Natalie and Eddie were both DC natives. She was baptized and confirmed at Holy Trinity Catholic Church in Georgetown,

45. Sevimli, in discussion with the author, March 2023.

46. Alden Almquist, in discussion with the author, December 2021.

47. Alden Almquist, in discussion with Martin Johnson, Christina Nichols, and Laci Barrow, September 2016.

48. Almquist, in discussion with the author, December 2021.

49. Rachel Medema Haxtema, in discussion with the author, October 2021.

and he grew up Episcopalian. They also went to Bible study for a while. Natalie loved the ritual shaped by an institutional history rather than people making it up. "I admired the way that Christian spiritual traditions were grappled with and were real anchors," she said. "But I didn't really have the same background with the Bible and theology or the same level of interest in pursuing it." The ages of their children weren't close enough to the few other children for them to have a meaningful connection. "There weren't really other people our age and stage of life," Natalie said. For Eddie, Community worship gave him a sense of peace "more than any other time during my week." Yet it was also apparent how much it had been shaped by "a certain generation," he said. They stayed for a couple of years and then continued trying neighborhood churches, not finding what they longed for.[50]

Most of those people had come of age in the same era, in the 1960s. "There was very little influx of new people who had staying power," Gail said. By this time, Gail had been in the Community for fifteen years. She saw the stories from the early years as being a creation story. "The creation story was very powerful but grounded in a certain time," she said. "The neighborhood, the church, and the people in the 2000s—that wasn't the time anymore."[51]

Changes in Mount Pleasant and adjacent neighborhoods that began decades earlier accelerated during the 2000s. Development increased around the new Metro train station in Columbia Heights. There were fewer group houses. Moving from an apartment to owning a home—as Community members did in the 1970s—was out of reach for many nonprofit workers. If the situation was bad for them, it was much worse for people whose incomes were below the poverty line. Bob led 140 organizations in the Coalition for Non-Profit Housing and Economic Development, which advocated for low- and moderate-income residents and small businesses as neighborhoods changed.[52] Bob and a colleague wrote in the *Washington Post* that when lower-income people are pushed into the suburbs for housing, it leads to higher transportation costs and affects the ability of small businesses to attract employees, "with adverse effects that ripple through the economy."[53] CNHED launched a campaign advocating for a "continuum" of affordable housing options during a time when nearly 50,000 families spent more than half of their income on a place to live. Bob wrote, "It may seem

50. Avery and Janney, in discussion with the author, July 2022.
51. Gail Taylor, in discussion with the author, February 2021.
52. 24Lanterns, "CNHED Tribute."
53. Masliansky and Pohlman, "Unhealthy Cycle," para. 2.

at times a hopeless task to address these needs, but God has not called us to solve the world's problems, only to respond."[54]

Bob was an exemplar of the ministry of laypeople that the Community embraced from the start: a Christian formed in the church yet out in the world, employing their unique gifts and abilities to meet human need. Under Bob's leadership, CNHED advocated for a housing production fund that is now among the strongest in the United States and an effective strategy for affordable housing.[55] Renata Eustis, a Lutheran pastor, summed up Bob's vocation: "Though he did not do it under a religious banner, he made the presence of God real by working for many people to have safe and dignified dwelling places. He incarnated God's love and care."[56]

                                         ❧

Bob knew when he was seven that he didn't want to be a farmer like his parents. There was too much dust. Bob was born in 1943 in Stanton, Nebraska, which had a population in the hundreds and educated its children in a one-room schoolhouse from first through eighth grade.

What fascinated Bob was numbers. He tracked the inventory of an imaginary grocery store, pretending the empty containers of household items were full again. Decades later, asked what brought him joy, Bob responded, "Spreadsheets."[57]

He met the woman he married, Dorothy, while working at his first post-college job in Chicago. As a date early in their relationship, they marched along with other protesters at the 1968 Democratic Convention. When tensions were escalating with police, Dorothy suggested they break off and go to dinner. Later they saw people who were tear-gassed splashing water in their eyes in the restrooms.

Bob, in the Navy Air Reserve and on a job track that could have led to extraordinary wealth as a partner in a major accounting firm, was inspired to join a different sort of fight. As part of the war on poverty, he signed up in 1969 for two years of community organizing in Jacksonville, Texas. After that, "he wound up in DC, battling for housing for poor people," wrote Doug, who became a close friend after they met in the Community. Bob started working for the DC government in the 1970s in the Model Cities

---

54. Pohlman, "Choosing the Good Fight," *Lenten Booklet 2011*, March 25.

55. Robert "Bob" Pohlman, August 10, 1943–April 26, 2018, in the author's possession.

56. Eustis, "Memorial Service for Bob Pohlman."

57. Doug Huron, eulogy for Bob Pohlman, May 19, 2018, in author's possession, 1; 24Lantern, "CNHED Tribute."

program. He then joined the DC Department of Housing and Community Development. He was director by 1988, when Mayor Marion Barry appointed Bob to be deputy mayor for finance. He entered that chief financial officer role again during mayoral transitions in 1991 and 1995. Bob and Doug connected around having held roles with a lot of responsibility, close to the top but also having to manage relationships with those who had more power and influence. Doug noted that while others believe their success is proof of how deserving they are, Bob regarded it with a sense of amazement.[58] While telling stories about being in the halls of power, he said, "And here I was, a farm boy from Nebraska!"[59]

Amanda worked with Bob at CNHED after she went to graduate school to study urban planning. She did research on housing policy to launch advocacy campaigns. He was a "down to earth, Midwestern, straightforward person" who knew everyone, especially those who had been in the DC government a long time. When he left the government for advocacy work for affordable housing, he had an "inside-outside analysis of how change happens," Amanda said. If they were lobbying the DC city council and there were protesters outside or occupying a building in the city, Bob's attitude was that it was necessary to have people in the streets pushing for more-radical policies. It made their policy requests relatively reasonable.[60]

In the Community, Bob was known for his humility. During a period when Bob was working for the mayor, Cathy Hays-Smith was part of the Community and lived near Bob, Dorothy, Kimberly, and Lindsey—and also taught at Lindsey's school. "Bob had a really powerful job and you'd never know it," Cathy said. During Sunday services he was simply one among the gathered, sitting in one of the metal folding chairs arranged in a semi-circle.[61] Gail worked with Bob on building maintenance at La Casa. They formed "a strong bond," relating as people who wanted to be behind the scenes rather than out in front. "Bob never quit working," Gail said. "He always wanted to do the right thing, I think, more than anything."[62]

Bob was one of the dozen or so people who put in hundreds of hours in care for La Casa: handling repairs and general upkeep as well as working with all of the groups that used the space. Barbara, one of the others who took on a lead role for a year or more, thought while the Community didn't necessarily defer maintenance, it was always conservative in spending

58. Huron, eulogy for Bob Pohlman, 1–2.

59. Eustis, "Memorial Service for Bob Pohlman," 1.

60. Amanda Huron, in discussion with the author, September 2021.

61. Cathy Hays Smith, in discussion with the author, March 2021.

62. Taylor, in discussion with the author, February 2021.

money on La Casa.[63] Perhaps it was an expression of its ambivalence toward the building. For decades, the Community periodically worried that owning La Casa had distracted it from its social mission. They discussed selling the building rather than "whining over building problems like all conventional churches do."[64] Here was another place where the Community held tensions.

Members did what they set out to do when they purchased La Casa and made it a place for ministry and mission—not only their own but that of other faith-based and neighborhood groups, organizers, activists, artists, musicians, and more. But this added to the usual work to maintain any building. Community members cleaned up after short-term use and navigated challenging relationships with long-term renters.

Sharing space also meant that they had less control over how it looked. The altar was on wheels and an art installation for a liturgical season wasn't an option. In 1989, some of the artists in the Community formed an "aesthetics group." Lois sparked it when she blurted out during announcements that their space was ugly and hindered her ability to worship. Korey and Hayley worked with Lois, and they redid the carpet and paint. In 2003, the shared kitchen—where pots on the stove weren't the only thing that simmered—got a $2,000 makeover to make it more warm and welcoming along with necessary replacements and repairs. Various rooms got facelifts over the years when vacated by renters.[65]

For more than a decade, the Community needed an elevator. After a stroke, Bobbie walked with a cane but could labor up the stairs. For several years when Doug came to services, people met him near the front door to help him move his legs up the stairs to the main space. While people chose accessible lodging for retreats, Doug could not get to the main room of La Casa, especially when he started using a powerchair. For a while Doug didn't go to worship, because it felt like too much trouble.[66]

In 2005, the Community finally began larger renovations. Its plan sought to "maximize accessibility at moderate cost." They explored installing a lift that would go to all levels, expanding the main space for meetings and worship, and making the building more energy efficient. Bob sought advice from his contacts in building renovation. In the end, the Community settled on a lift that went from the ground floor to the mezzanine-level gathering

63. Barbara Hayden, in discussion with the author, September 2021.

64. Minutes of Community meetings, January and February 1990, in Community of Christ Papers.

65. Minutes of Community meeting, 2 April 1989, in Community of Christ Papers; Hoffman in discussion with the author, September 2021; Sandra Wojahn, email message to author, March 23, 2023; Hayden, in discussion with the author, September 2021.

66. Wind, in discussion with the author, October 2021 and July 2022.

space, along with an accessible restroom and some cosmetic improvements. At that time the Community had twenty-six donating members. The Community took out a new mortgage on La Casa to add $110,000 to what it had in savings.[67]

As the Community worked on this project, in March 2008, an apartment building caught fire on the other side of Mount Pleasant Street. More than 200 people lost their homes in the five-alarm blaze. The Community joined a group of local congregations and organizations caring for the displaced, also offering its space and spiritual resources to neighbors. The next day, La Casa held a bilingual service. Those who gathered prayed for the victims of the fire and for those who were helping them, lamented with the psalms and acknowledged how faith is shaken by tragedy and suffering, and cried out *Kyrie eleison*—an ancient prayer from Koine Greek meaning "Lord, have mercy."[68]

Bob helped connect the tenants association to potential funders and other professionals who assisted with aspects of the process to buy and reconstruct the building. The association secured a $4 million loan from the DC government and worked with a national affordable housing organization to finance rebuilding the structure from the charred remains. The new apartments were 100 percent affordable, two-thirds of them rented by previous residents. The tenants, many of them from El Salvador, named their building Monseñor Romero Apartments after the martyred archbishop.[69]

At La Casa, new renters moved in after the renovations. Use of the building increased, benefiting many. A fair-trade store called Amani ya Juu moved into the space with windows to Mount Pleasant Street where the Sign of Jonah once was. Many Languages One Voice, an immigrant justice nonprofit, had offices in several of the eleven rooms. And the Community continued outreach efforts. On one late summer Saturday when the Mount Pleasant library had its open house, Dorothy and Ellen and Duane staffed a La Casa table with materials from Community, Amani ya Juu, and MLOV. A few people picked up the information.[70]

67. Minutes, January 29, 2006, and January 19 and March 16, 2008, in the author's possession; Bob Pohlman, "Request for Advice on Modifying and Modernizing La Casa," 20 April 2005, in the author's possession.

68. Sadon, "6 Years after Devastating Fire"; "Prayers for the Building Fire Victims," March 13, 2008, document in author's possession; Minutes of Community meeting, 16 March 2008, in Community of Christ Papers.

69. Hayden, in discussion with the author, May 2021; Dorothy Pohlman, in discussion with the author, March 2023; Sadon, "6 Years after Devastating Fire."

70. Minutes of Community meetings, 15 April and 16 September 2012, in the author's possession.

Having been nurtured by the Community, Yvette and Yonce each felt a pull to pastoral ministry, away from the faith-based advocacy and organizing work they had been doing. Yvette returned to parish ministry as pastor of an ELCA church in the Virginia suburbs where there was an opening. She and Robert, who married in December 2010 in La Casa as part of a Sunday service, moved there. Bill Wegener, one of the Community's named pastors, officiated.[71]

For Yonce, the Community was a good training ground. It gave him a chance to understand his own theology more deeply and to weave it into his whole life.[72] When Yonce left to become pastor of a congregation, he told the Community, "A major reason I am ready to take this step and feel able to help lead them is because of who I have become due to the Community of Christ's support, nurturing, example, and opportunities to lead and create."[73]

Yonce went to New Leaf, a church in the emergent stream in the near suburbs. The group of about twenty-five people in College Park, Maryland, had been a small group in Brian McLaren's church and wanted to try meeting as a church themselves. They didn't have an official daughter church relationship with McLaren's church but neither did they leave out of conflict with McLaren as pastor or the congregation, but rather came from a desire to lead a church in a different way. New Leaf had started seven years earlier and were meeting on Sunday afternoons in an Episcopal church building. Ten months after their founding pastor left, they were ready for a second pastor and hired Yonce.[74]

Yonce figured out that this group of mostly young adults and young families was struggling with whether to continue and needed help thinking through that question. At one point he thought, "Community of Christ and New Leaf should merge and bring that generational energy together." There wasn't a church similar to New Leaf in Mount Pleasant or adjacent neighborhoods. But College Park was far enough away that it was a logistic challenge, at least for the remnants of the parish model or the new monastic impulse to do life together. If the two groups had been closer geographically, Yonce would have told them, "Come on, people, this is a no-brainer." Instead, he helped New Leaf create a process for winding down.[75]

71. Francis and Schock, in discussion with the author, January 2022.
72. Shelton, in discussion with the author, May 2022.
73. Shelton, email message to the Community of Christ, February 11, 2013.
74. Shelton, in discussion with the author, May 2022.
75. Shelton, in discussion with the author, May 2022.

12

"Just One More Surprise"

MY LAST CONVERSATION WITH Dora was in January 2012. I lived in Chicago and was in DC to celebrate my father's sixtieth birthday. It was the sort of gathering Dora brought together often in the Community's five decades. But this time Dora didn't prepare a feast and enliven everything without pulling focus to herself. She sat on the side, weakened by cancer. Yet even then, her intensity of love and attention was still there. "I want to hear all about seminary," she said, motioning to the chair next to her.

That June, after the school year ended, I treated myself to an afternoon at the Art Institute of Chicago. My mother texted me to call her, so I stepped out into the sculpture garden. Dora died that morning. I sat on the stone stairs and wept. People taking their lunch breaks in the garden did what we do in the city for good and for ill: they walked right by, perhaps to give me privacy, perhaps not even noticing.

Returning inside, I sought out one of my favorite paintings, "Easter Mystery," by Maurice Denis from 1891. Women in the foreground, wearing black, bow down, one pressing her face to the earth. In the background, a group of people wearing white are visible through a stand of trees, headed toward a destination unseen. As I gazed at the painting and remembered Dora, words from 1 Cor 15:51–52 came to me, set to music in Handel's *Messiah*. "Behold, I tell you a mystery!" a baritone-bass voice sang in my mind. "The trumpet shall sound, and the dead shall be raised incorruptible, and we shall be changed."[1] A little earlier in the letter to the Corinthians, Paul compares our bodies to seeds, alluding to John 12:24–26 as Paul writes, "What you sow does not come to life unless it dies." That seed is not in the

---

1. Handel, *Messiah*, xvii, based on King James Version.

form that it will ultimately be: "you do not sow the body that is to be, but a bare seed," the apostle writes.[2] Our work, like our bodies, is perishable, but God will transform it into a form that is immortal. Therefore, our labor—all that we have done and left undone, all that we did imperfectly and all that pointed toward a wholeness it could not reach, none of it was in vain.

⁊⬤

During Lent each year, the Community engaged in collective self-examination, one of the hallmarks of its life together since the Book of Disciplines in the early years. Each person looked at their commitments and shortcomings in the life of faith, and shared with each other, deepening each of their reflections and opportunities for transformation. In the first year, 1987, Dora wrote as one of the editors, that instead of seeing Lent as a season of self-denial, it was for her "a time of amazement at Jesus resolutely moving toward the finish line—all the while knowing what the finish line was, but not knowing what was on the other side." Was it possible to understand even a little of what Jesus endured as he moved toward death? "I try to move more closely to this person Jesus. But mostly I wonder what it means to be that resolute."[3]

Holy Week was the most powerful time of the year for Alicia, Dora's daughter. Like the Lenten booklet, the Maundy Thursday, Good Friday, and Easter morning services were collective creations, she said. "That was the best thing that we did as a Community: to really center Easter and the message of Easter more than Christmas." After she returned to DC in the mid-2000s, she and Amanda—who have been close friends since their earliest years—contributed to a Good Friday service, performing "Were you there when they crucified my Lord?" with only drum and voice—causing the trembling the lyrics speak of, through its spareness.[4]

As Dora continued being a creator of the Lenten booklet, she saw it as a chance to review the past year. During a season when she was sorting through boxes of liturgies, homilies, and letters from the scattered in her basement, she reflected on all of her years in the Community since its first several months: "Sometimes the Spirit has rocked us; at times the Spirit has pained us; and at other times the Spirit has brought us to our feet to dance like Miriam danced."[5]

2. 1 Cor 15:37b NRSV.
3. Johnson, *Lenten Booklet 1987*, March 10.
4. Moyer, in discussion with the author, February 2021.
5. Dora Johnson, *Thoughts on the Lenten Season 2007*, March 28.

In 2010, Dora was diagnosed with pancreatic cancer. She shared the news with the Community, offering the essential medical details and promising updates. She counted the Community gathered and scattered as part of "a great support system," she wrote. At the same time, "I'd like to ask you all to please not hover. I feel fine and I seem to be functioning at pretty much full speed. Obviously, once the treatment starts, things will change, but I would like to have the freedom to maneuver in the best way I know how and ask for help when I need it."[6]

Two years later, she was still alive, which was unusual for someone with pancreatic cancer. The initial prognosis was that she would not live more than six months. Alicia attributed this to her mother's stubbornness. Dora befriended the nurses and other staff at the cancer unit, writing letters to the hospital administration to advocate for them because she didn't think they were being treated fairly. In the 2012 Lenten booklet, Barbara's entry shared her admiration for Dora's bravery while enduring suffering and facing death. "My life has been so comfortable; will I be able to fight as bravely as Dora is doing?" she wrote. "I'm beginning to see that God loves life and does not allow us to give it up easily."[7] Dora's submission was placed on Easter. In "After Death a Voice Said," by Henry Langhorne, the poet imagined that when we die, we surrender our souls and our energy becomes part of the oneness of all.[8]

Dora stayed fiercely independent until days before she died. She had remained at home as she wanted, and Community members sat with her individually and in small groups. Early one morning, after a quiet period as Alicia dozed nearby, Dora put her arms in the air as though she wanted to say something. Alicia called her brother, Martin, to the bedside and they each took one of Dora's hands in their own. "It was just the most beautiful spring day, and the window was open," Alicia said. A gentle breeze was coming in and out like breath. In one moment, it was an inhale into the room, "and on her exhale she went out with the breeze."[9]

๔

Lent 2013 was the first time the Community of Christ put together its Lenten booklet without Dora. The theme was "Traditions: Anchoring and Freeing." Dorothy Pohlman was introspective about her time in the Community. She

6. Dora Johnson, email message to a list of individuals, August 11, 2010.
7. Barbara Hayden, untitled selection in *Lenten Booklet 2012*, March 13.
8. Johnson, untitled selection in *Lenten Booklet 2012*, April 8.
9. Moyer, in discussion with the author, September 2021.

recognized that just as she learned new traditions in the Community, people who were newer to the Community weren't familiar with "how we've always done it" and may have been ready for a change. Dorothy wondered aloud how to find a balance "between defining ourselves so new people know who we are" and "being set in our ways." Being clear about the group's traditions allows newcomers to discern whether a community is a good fit for them. Even so, if the group is not open to new ideas, they resign themselves to stagnation. "As we examine our life and worship together during the coming months; as we address the fact that we are aging and our numbers are shrinking," Dorothy wrote, it was time to determine which traditions to keep and which to change.[10]

The Community entered a time of discernment. Dianne, who was president, invited the bishop of the Metro DC Synod of the Evangelical Lutheran Church in America, Richard Graham, to be part of reflection and re-envisioning in the summer and fall of 2013. The Community was a member congregation of the synod. He wrote a response to the Community, recognizing that its challenges were not unusual, for example the tension between caring for each other and welcoming new people. The Community began as a countercultural group in a time of turmoil, rejecting the hostility that many had toward urban life, he wrote. However, "much that was originally daring and adventurous has come to be taken for granted." Could the Community offer something new? And he named what Community members also saw. They lacked coordinated pastoral care. On Sundays there was inadequate accompaniment for those who needed help carrying a tune. He asked whether Community leaders could be more judicious "about voicing political opinions for the sake of visitors who may not share them" and if they could discuss task lists at a time other than announcements after worship.[11]

Managing the building as a community center was a lot of work. Tenants rented a total of seven rooms for $45,000, which covered the mortgage and the $31,000 annually for operating expenses—such as utilities, upkeep, insurance.[12] But among the fifteen to twenty regular attenders who remained, there wasn't a lot of energy to keep doing that work while also reinventing themselves and talking about their faith to their neighbors. At one Community meeting, Doug spoke up through his speech synthesizer:

10. Pohlman, untitled selection in *Traditions: Anchoring and Freeing, Lent 2013*, March 1.

11. Richard Graham to the Community of Christ, Autumn 2013, in the author's possession.

12. "Information about Community of Christ and La Casa," 24 April 2016, in the author's possession.

"We have to be realistic. We may have to close the church." Even Amy hadn't heard him say that before, and many in the Community looked shocked.[13]

Yet before long the Community began seriously talking about the transformation that was necessary. They acknowledged they weren't going to reach critical mass again. They talked about merging with another church, but no one presented options they wanted to explore. They knew of congregations that closed but continued Christian community life in some way, and they planned to talk to people from them. In December 2014, instead of Advent candle making or cookie decorating, the Community had Saturday evening meetings about how to proceed. In 2015, members reached consensus: it was time to close. "I was impressed and heartened by the near unanimity of people saying, 'OK, we've run our course,'" Alden said. "We had done what we knew how to do. And we all knew each other well enough to know what would come out in homilies."[14] They hoped to find a new owner that could use La Casa to continue work for peace and social justice as the Community had devoted itself to for decades. They set a goal to transfer the building by the end of 2016. Amanda, by then a professor of urban geography and history, estimated that La Casa was worth more than $1 million in 2016. The Community was "in the strange position of trying to figure out how to give away a valuable piece of real estate in the midst of a hyper-gentrifying city."[15]

꒰꒱

"The era of outsized wealth in Washington" began with the rise of lobbying. While the practice goes back to the first Congress in 1789, the "modern earmark" method of appropriating public funds for a private company or institution caused an exponential increase in registered lobbyists starting in the 1970s, wrote journalist Alec MacGillis.[16] After September 11, 2001, after a wave of contracts for the national security industry, well-compensated people flooded the city and suburbs.[17]

This population boom came to a centuries-old city without a lot of space for new housing. Since 1910, federal law has set limits on the height of

13. Amy Wind, in discussion with the author, July 2022.

14. Minutes of Community meeting, 16 November, 2014, in author's possession; Alden Almquist, in discussion with the author, December 2021.

15. Minutes, 1 November, 2015, in author's possession; Huron, "Dream Lives On," 26–27.

16. MacGillis, *Fulfillment*, 70–74.

17. MacGillis, *Fulfillment*, 77.

buildings so that the Capitol and monuments can be seen from around the city.[18] Historic districts such as Mount Pleasant created additional regulations for existing homes and potential future ones. Observing this trend in the 2000s, MacGillis wrote, "Real estate prices in metro Washington increased more than prices in any other city over the first decade of the century—more than New York, San Francisco, and Los Angeles."[19] In hundreds of thousands of households in DC without hundreds of thousands of dollars in assets, this influx of wealth was a bane and not a boon. A great deal had changed since the Community chose as its parish the economically struggling neighborhood of Dupont Circle and helped its neighbors buy housing. Or since it moved to Mount Pleasant in an era of integration and low-cost mortgages. Thus, the Community was deciding what to do with its property in a dramatically different context than congregations in cities such as St. Louis, Cleveland, or even Baltimore, less than an hour away.

કા

Mary Catherine Bateson, in her book about life after retirement, reflected on the 2007 closing of an organization started by her mother, the anthropologist Margaret Mead. "Just as people die, so do most institutions, and only by asking whether they have fulfilled their mission can we fully understand what the mission was."[20] Bateson worshiped with the Community while working with Dora and wrote the litany with the phrase "dance in steps of change." For fifty years, the Community danced those steps and here was one in a new direction. To Dianne, it was "in our dying that we became even more clear about the 'why' behind our spiritual life together and our desire for our ministries to live on in some core way" in a particular place.[21]

In a culmination of the parish model the Community started with in 1965—of tending to the wellbeing of all in an area without regard for whether they attend worship—the Community turned La Casa into a gift rather than a real estate transaction for maximum gain. The building was in good condition overall. The balance of the new mortgage the Community took out for the renovations in 2008 was at $65,000. Adding closing costs and associated taxes, the new owner would pay less than $100,000 for the building transfer.[22]

18. National Capital Planning Commission, "Heights & Views," para. 1.

19. MacGillis, *Fulfillment*, 79.

20. Bateson, *Composing a Further Life*, 112–13.

21. Huron, "Dream Lives On," 29.

22. "Information about Community of Christ and La Casa," 24 April, 2016, in author's

Community members approved by consensus the characteristics they sought in a congregation or other nonprofit: financial and administrative stability and plans to use the building long-term for its mission; and openness to allow use of the space for events and gatherings of other groups, including remaining members of the Community. A committee formed to move forward, starting with looking into whether any ELCA congregations wanted the building. Starting in fall 2015, they met and discussed possibilities with synod staff and pastors and laypeople from three congregations, for example to have ministries for youth in La Casa. In March 2016, the other churches encouraged the Community to move forward with a request for proposals, including one that the congregations might submit together. In April 2016, the Community invited twenty partner organizations, including the tenants at that time and ministries for which the Community provided volunteers or donations, to describe their work and how owning La Casa would enhance it. Other groups could inquire about submitting a proposal. The committee included Amy, Doug, Dianne, Gail, and Sandi, with Bob as chair. He combined prayerful openness to the Spirit's guidance with his background of work in government with competing bids for contracts. This time, the bidding wasn't in money but in demonstration of the ability to be good stewards of a resource.[23]

Among the six proposals the Community received was one from La Clínica del Pueblo. A Federally Qualified Health Center—which care for an underserved population—with dozens of employees and volunteers serving eight thousand adults and children, since 1983 it had been a refuge for people who fled from conflict-wracked areas of Latin America to Mount Pleasant and surrounding neighborhoods. La Clínica removed the language barrier that is present at many hospitals and clinics. With further waves of immigration because of the effects of globalization and the legacy of the wars in Central America, by the 2010s, "we were bursting at the seams," said Alicia Wilson, who was the executive director. The organization was looking for a space for all of its programs beyond medical care, one that didn't feel clinical. La Clínica found that many LGBTQ clients feared that doctors judged them. And survivors of domestic violence needed a location separate from the one where their abusers received medical care.[24]

possession.

23. Minutes of Community meeting, 4 October and 1 November, 2015; 6 February and 3 April, 2016, in author's possession; Huron, "Dream Lives On," 28; Doug Huron, eulogy for Bob Pohlman, 8.

24. Wilson, in discussion with the author, April 2022; Rachel Meyn Ugarte, in discussion with the author, April 2022.

As the Community interviewed its finalists for the building transfer, Suyanna Linhales Barker, La Clínica's chief of programs, was impressed by how tough the questions were. "The process was so transparent, not favoring anyone," she said.[25] Wilson appreciated the clarity of Community leaders on what was important to them and the aspects of their legacy they wanted to see continue.[26]

The Community chose La Clínica and transferred the building on December 10, 2016—International Human Rights Day. The building was filled with people from both the Community and La Clínica, who spoke about their dreams for the future in La Casa. As an expression of the values that guided the Community, the transfer "was both highly logical and deeply mystical," Amanda wrote. The day was in some ways like Community worship services over the decades, with singing, and tears of both joy and sorrow.[27] Sandi shared her thoughts as a longtime member of the Community of Christ and a board member of Life Skills Center, which was in La Casa for more than thirty years. The building helped people to fulfill their dreams and take pride in their abilities. As the Community let La Casa go to its next incarnation, Sandi told the new owners, "We look forward to hearing La Clínica's stories of the continued use of La Casa as a place that offers respect and dignity to all."[28]

Wilson and others from La Clínica recognized how emotionally fraught it was for the remaining Community members to give up the building they had stewarded for forty-two years. Yet they conducted all of the parts of the transfer in such a humane way, Wilson said, in contrast with previous experiences La Clínica had securing space through real estate brokers. Through owning La Casa, funders and donors saw the organization as more financially stable and strong. "We got to put a $1 million dollar asset on our books for $100,000," Wilson said. "Sometimes 'too good to be true' actually exists."[29]

The Community completed several steps to close as a formal body. The Community closed the nonprofit incorporated organization it held with the District of Columbia and resigned from the Evangelical Lutheran Church in America. The final acts included giving away $73,000 in "our remaining assets in our final benevolence gifts through a thoughtful and re-searched process to prioritize organizations that needed our support in the

25. Suyanna Linhales Barker, in discussion with the author, April 2022.

26. Wilson, in discussion with the author, April 2022.

27. Huron, "Dream Lives On," 29.

28. Sandra Wojahn, "Dreams and Life Skills in La Casa Dec. 10 2016," document in the author's possession.

29. Wilson, in discussion with the author, April 2022.

current political climate," Dianne wrote. She shared the full list of forty-two organizations, which included local and national groups, those working on housing, environmental justice, anti-racism, and support for immigrants, refugees, LGBTQ people, and others.[30]

❧

Margaret Ann Hoven and Oakley Pearson strummed guitar while others joined in singing the Appalachian Christian song "Will the Circle Be Unbroken." Rows of people gathered around them. Margaret Ann's alto, rich as comfort food, mingled with Oakley's baritone as they sang in the voice of one watching "the hearse come rolling for to carry my mother away."[31] Since the earliest centuries of Christianity, a metaphor for the church has been that of mother.[32] Two millennia later, here was a small community that raised and nurtured an unlikely group of people for five decades. Now the children had come back home to bury their mother and begin the journey of grief that is both solitary and shared.

All those who were scattered gathered into one body, weaving together a fiftieth anniversary celebration, reunion, and final retreat into one fall weekend in 2016. The Community returned to Claggett Center in Adamstown, Maryland, owned by the Episcopal Diocese of Maryland, where it often held retreats in the 1990s. They talked about the impact of the Community in their lives. Dunstan, the person who spent the most years as part of the gathered in DC, spoke of his life in terms of having three families: his family of origin, the Benedictine monastery where he was a monk and priest for eighteen years, and then the Community. "We all need a family of one kind or another—and a healthy family," he said. "There are a lot of unhealthy families in the world, but we need a healthy family. Your own blood family is one thing, but you need a community of some kind, of people that you can help, and they can help you."[33]

Doug took hours to type his response using his speech synthesizer. He told of having been raised Unitarian and cherishing his skepticism. Through four decades in the Community, he connected to a presence, a wholeness,

30. Dianne Russell, email message to the Community of Christ, September 3, 2017.

31. Carter et al., "Will the Circle Be Unbroken?" in *Rise Up Singing*, Blood and Patterson, ed., 98.

32. E.g. "Cyprian on the Unity of the Church," 80.

33. Hayden, in discussion with Laci Barrow and Martin Johnson, September 2016.

that transcended even the greatest sense of inner peace. He had powerful moments of finding grace.[34]

For Margaret Elsie, "the Community was incredibly formative." She was in her mid-twenties when she arrived in DC during the early months of the Community of Christ. The Community introduced her to a wider world beyond what she had grown up with, while being a haven of care during what was, for various reasons, an emotionally rocky time of her life, she said. "I got set on a path that has been positive ever since," Margaret Elsie said. "If that hadn't happened, I don't think I would've had nearly as good a life. I think I might very easily have gotten badly off track."[35]

At the retreat, Oakley talked with others who had sought a group similar to what they had in the Community. "In only a few instances were they able to find something similar in terms of community and supportiveness," he said. It reinforced "how unique the whole experience was and the whole idea was, and how amazing the people were that were involved in it." The retreat rekindled memories for Margaret Elsie of "all that we had in the Community that I have not found elsewhere," she said. She is part of an established church, yet feels it is "bound up in old things." She sees it in contrast with the Community's focus on most members living and serving alongside their neighbors in a square-mile area and committing to each other with a covenant that was regularly renewed. "It was a vital idea," Margaret Elsie said. "There was a lot of feeling that the church was really in movement about changing and becoming more relevant."[36]

When John Schramm, the founding pastor, preached at the final retreat, it was the first time many in the Community heard him, if they joined after the first decade. Religion has to make something memorable and manageable, he said. The tradeoff is, "as soon as you do that, you kill the spontaneity of faith."[37] He also spoke about the nature of community in all its messiness. He compared being in a community to being inside Noah's ark—if it weren't for the flood waters out there, we wouldn't be able to stand the smell in here.

In a casual conversation over lunch one day, John remarked that he never expected the Community to last as long as it did. In the first year of the Community's life, "I had said that it's OK for something to exist and then say goodbye to it when it's time to say goodbye. So it was kind of a prophecy

34. Author's memory; Amy Wind, in discussion with the author, October 2021.

35. Margaret Elsie Pearson, in discussion with the author, April 2021.

36. Pearson, in discussion with the author, April 2021.

37. Schramm, in discussion with the author, March 2021; confirmed the author's memory of the rest.

fulfilled." In contrast to "a church that becomes an institution," John said, the Community wasn't "set up for existing for a long time, it was set up to be relevant at the moment to what the needs of the community were"—both its members and the neighborhood around it. To Anna Mae, who joined the Community in its earliest months, outreach "was always central, whether it was taking turns cooking the meal at St. Stephen's on Saturday for hungry people, whether it was engaged in protest marches against the Vietnam War, you know, whether it was simply trying to be good neighbors and care for the people that were around us, which we did sometimes well and sometimes poorly."[38]

For the gathering time on the first evening, the planners created a ritual to honor each person present and those who were there in spirit. They invited each person to bring and place a small object representing themselves and others joining the celebration.[39] On a table in the main space were photos, of course. In one, three preteen girls are dressed as Magi; I was among them that year. The collective creation also held a potted plant, calligraphy done by Sally Hanlon with the words "Love never forgets," the Reconciled in Christ certificate showing that the Community welcomed and affirmed LGBTQ people, and an enormous set of keys to La Casa.

The room was filled with felt banners that graced the walls during Community worship, with messages such as "Share the Spirit," "A labor of love is the promise of peace," and "Sleepers Awake!" with a rooster for Advent. As Robin Pedtke walked into the gathering space and saw the banners, she was carried back to her early childhood, worshiping in the rented space in Dupont Circle where the Community started, with its dark clay-red floors. "It was a basement, but it was warm, fuzzy, and cozy," Robin said. "I looked forward to Sundays."[40]

There were strong women role models as her mother, Dorothy Pedtke, and her closest friends, including Dora, worked and worshiped together. "They were all professional working women and they were all moms and they were in the Community together," she said. The Community was one of the greatest influences in Robin's life. Concern for peace and justice "was such a big part of the Community's culture," she said. "It was an all-pervasive way of life." It affected the books in their homes, the commentary that children overheard while their parents watched the news, what they did on the weekends—going to a march when there was one (which in DC is often).[41]

38. Anna Mae Patterson, in discussion with the author, June 2021.

39. Logistics committee, email message to the Community of Christ, August 16, 2016.

40. Robin Pedtke, in discussion with the author, August 2021.

41. Pedtke, in discussion with the author, August 2021.

Her early Community life shaped her vocations as a mother and a physician. "It's in my practice of medicine that I'm a Community of Christ person, in the way I treat my patients," Robin said. She brought her family to the retreat because she wanted her children "to participate in the Community for their first and last time," she said.[42] Jaret Beane, Robin's husband, hadn't seen anything like the Community before. He grew up in an Episcopalian churchgoing family in West Michigan and hadn't connected much to that tradition as an adult. Robin and Jaret had made a promise to Father Theodore Hesburgh,[43] longtime president of the University of Notre Dame and member of the Civil Rights Commission. (There's a photo at the Smithsonian National Portrait Gallery of Hesburgh and Martin Luther King Jr. with linked hands at a Soldier Field rally in Chicago in 1964.)[44] Hesburgh became a close friend to Daniel Pedtke, Dorothy's father, when they were teaching at UND. Hesburgh officiated at Robin and Jaret's wedding. He made an exception to let them marry at Notre Dame, though Catholic churches usually require both people in the couple to be Catholic. Hesburgh told them, "I've spent enough time with both of you to know you and that you're walking in Jesus' path." But Hesburgh asked them to promise that they would have their children baptized into the Christian faith.[45]

They struggled with that promise when their children were born and grew past the years when they would usually be baptized in the Catholic tradition. Robin and Jaret had church-hunted near their home in Grand Rapids, Michigan, but the only place they felt at home was at Mass primarily for Dominican sisters—with no programs for children. They tried "a normal Catholic church with the normal dogma" so that the children could have religious education classes. They just didn't fit in there, and the children remained unbaptized.[46]

A core conviction for Robin is not holding prejudice towards other groups of people. The village raising their kids has a lot of diversity, Robin said. Her father was Muslim, and they chose godparents from all three of the Abrahamic faiths. They also have gay and lesbian couples in their lives. When they attend Mass during Holy Week or on Easter or Christmas, usually with Robin's mother, Dorothy, afterward they review what they heard and tell their children what they agree and disagree with, Robin said. Robin and Jaret especially remind their children that their vision of salvation

42. Pedtke, in discussion with Chris Nichols and Martin Johnson, September 2016.
43. Pedtke, in discussion with the author, August 2021.
44. "Champion of Civil Rights."
45. Pedtke, in discussion with the author, August 2021.
46. Pedtke, in discussion with the author, August 2021.

includes people of all backgrounds. They teach their children that if they follow what Jesus taught, if they speak and act as Jesus did, "you'll always do the right thing."[47]

At the Community's final retreat, Robin and Jaret found what they had longed for since they first married. This was a group of people who were "really following Christ as opposed to following the church," Robin said. She and Jaret turned to each other with the same idea: what if their three children were baptized among this gathered group of Christians?[48]

Twelve-year-old Dot, eleven-year-old Christopher, and nine-year-old Alex took the news of their baptism in age-appropriate fashion. They said, "That's cool, that's cool." They knew about their parents' promise to Father Hesburgh, who had died the year before, in 2015.[49]

A beloved hymn of the Community was John Ylvisaker's "I Was There to Hear Your Borning Cry." They sang it at memorial services and on ordinary Sunday mornings as well as at baptisms. In the lyrics, God speaks of remaining faithful to God's people throughout all the seasons of life. At the end, "I'll be there as I have always been / With just one more surprise."[50] At the final session—Sunday worship—of the Community's last retreat, there was the unexpected. Only a few people were in on it. Dianne, who was leading worship, told the gathered, "Oh, by the way, we have one more thing this morning." Dunstan, who had been part of making Catholics such as Dorothy Pedtke feel more fully welcome in the Community, would baptize her grandchildren: Dot, Christopher, and Alex. Everyone applauded. Dunstan came to the front of the worship space, and said, "OK, let's get this place organized."[51]

Robin had a complex mix of feelings, as she often does with religion. Yet she wasn't holding tension in her body, waiting for the concepts she disagreed with to come out during the service that she'd have to explain to her children later. She didn't feel any of the dissonance that she usually does in a church. She was relieved that she didn't have to hold herself and her children as different from other worshipers. She belonged in this gathered body, where she had received her first communion, and now Dot, Christopher, and Alex did, too.[52] "It was very moving for us, and renewed our belief, and solidified our convictions as followers of the way of Christ," she said.[53] "Now

47. Pedtke, in discussion with the author, August 2021.
48. Pedtke, in discussion with the author, August 2021.
49. Pedtke, in discussion with the author, August 2021.
50. Ylvisaker, *Borning Cry*, 522.
51. Dunstan Hayden, in discussion with the author, May 2021.
52. Pedtke, in discussion with the author, August 2021.
53. Robin Pedtke, email message to the Community of Christ, November 29, 2020.

we could send our kids out in the world as legitimate Christians." To Jaret, the baptism was "powerful and perfect." They were "finally bringing the kids into the fold, finally giving them a group of people like them," he said.[54]

"It turned out to be such a joyous time for everybody," Dunstan said. "I'm so glad we did it."[55] Amid the joy, Robin and Jaret longed for this kind of faithful community beyond that weekend, in the city where they live. Robin wondered, How could they find people who have a life together like the Community did?

To Alden, "having that final retreat where the founders showed up— that was one of the memorable experiences of my life in the city," he said. "When our numbers were that large, the old spirit was there." Having the baptisms "at the swansong of a group" was dramatic and spectacular. "It was a salute across generations to the spirit of our group."[56]

The interdenominational institutions of the twentieth century had waned from their height, but here—even as one expression of grassroots ecumenism was ending—was hope for a unity that comes from the Spirit of Christ embracing us all. Anna Mae saw the baptisms as the children "being welcomed into the household of faith and being made a part of the continuity of the Community of Christ."[57] At the end was another chapter beginning in a story much longer than any of our lifetimes.

54. Pedtke, in discussion with the author, August 2021; Robin Pedtke, text message to author, August 24, 2021.

55. Hayden, in discussion with the author, May 2021.

56. Almquist, in discussion with the author, December 2021.

57. Anna Mae Patterson, in discussion with the author, May 2021.

Epilogue

WALKING AROUND MOUNT PLEASANT, Adams Morgan, and Columbia Heights is the closest I come to X-ray vision. I see through the present into four decades past. Beneath gleaming new high-rises, there are gravel-covered empty lots. Historic buildings where a studio apartment starts at $1,700 a month are the former homes of immigrant families and other low-income neighbors.[1]

On a sunny day in April 2022, I walked in the area where several Church of the Saviour ministries are located. Some were going through changes, but Christ House was the same as ever. Men in wheelchairs gathered outside around the sculpture of Jesus kneeling to wash feet. One smoked a cigarette as we all enjoyed the sun. Across Columbia Road, the Potter's House was renovated a few years earlier, giving the coffee shop a more open feel and letting in more natural light. It remained a nonprofit, and the bookstore retained its social justice bent. There were large balloons with a six and a two—Potter's House was celebrating its sixty-second birthday. In line to order lunch, my mind went back to a moment in my childhood, standing next to my father and looking forward to a meal of mac and cheese, greens, and cornbread. In the cozy, dimly lit space, we ate among neighbors who didn't pay for the meal if they couldn't afford even the modest price.[2]

The feeling of historical X-ray vision was heightened when I went inside La Casa for the first time since 2016. In the main space, La Clínica del Pueblo had a training for staff on caring for oneself while caring for others. I saw underneath to Community of Christ worship, a few dozen people in a semicircle of folding chairs. I heard Margaret Ann Hoven and my father, Duane, singing in harmony while the rest of the Community made a joyful noise. I saw the space full for punk concerts. And I saw the DJ we hired for an after-party following my wedding in 2007. Barbara made paper garlands

1. For example, the Argonne Apartments, "Stylish Floor Plans."
2. The Potter's House, "Our Story," para. 7.

223

with photocopied photos of me and Josiah, and Dora ran out for more beer when we needed it.

In the present-day health and action center, a computer and conversation lounge for the Empodérate program occupied a room that held Sunday school, Life Skills Center activities, and for a few years a fair-trade store. Upstairs, I learned about La Clínica's healthy cooking classes in the kitchen where we finished preparing dishes for Community meals. Sally Hanlon, who was an interpreter for La Clínica for many years, died in 2017 and yet she was still present, in a photo on the wall, in the memories of all the people she worked with at La Clínica, and in all the ripples that moved outward from her life of struggle for justice and the dignity of all people.

Catalina Sol, director of La Clínica, said of Mount Pleasant, "If you've been here a long time, you can see the layers. It still feels like a place where the history of our community is not just visible, but real."[3] From the new location, La Clínica staff continued the practice of going out into the streets to promote public health and connect with neighbors. "Really the community is our patient," said Rachel Meyn Ugarte, chief development officer. "If one group isn't healthy, then the whole community is sick." LGBTQ Spanish speakers created a place of belonging through the Empodérate program. Many of the trans-Latinas came to the United States after their families disowned them because of their identity. For those who made a gender transition, they spoke of it as a homecoming. La Casa represented that home in a physical space.[4]

When another program, Entre Amigas—for women who know "between friends," as its name says, that it is a support group for domestic violence survivors—began meeting in La Casa, they loved that it had a kitchen. Women brought tamales, or ingredients for them to prepare the food together. Around a one-hour session on mental health and self-care, they sometimes spent five hours in the building connecting with each other. With child care provided, the children played throughout the building[5] like those of us who grew up in the Community did decades ago.

La Clínica kept La Casa open to justice-oriented groups that don't have their own space, for example day laborers organizing to advocate for their rights. Spanish-speaking groups began meeting in the main room more than they did when the Community owned it and handled requests

3. Morley, "Mount Pleasant Miracle." This quote influenced the metaphor of X-ray vision.

4. Rachel Meyn Ugarte, in discussion with the author, April 2022.

5. Alicia Wilson, in discussion with the author, April 2022.

for space.[6] La Clínica also installed a more-welcoming door: the old one confused many visitors to the Community over the years and was heavy even once someone found it.

As I stood at the threshold of that new door, I looked over once more at the lab on one side of the ground-level space, where people are tested for sexually transmitted infections. Then I looked to the other side, through the Empodérate lounge to the storage room connected to it. A few steps led down into the windowless space. In the Community, we called it the tomb all year long, a reference to an Easter morning ritual to start worship. We gathered around the door to that darkened room, and someone looked in and proclaimed, "He is not here. He is risen!" Now that tucked-away room provided privacy for one-on-one counseling for those who are receiving results from tests. Someone who received a positive diagnosis of HIV would then be connected to treatment, resources, and community in the Empodérate lounge where rainbows covered the walls and furniture. They emerged from the tomb released from the power of death into new life.

≈

Across Mount Pleasant Street is Past Tense Yoga Studio, where Alicia became coowner in 2022. It's on the second floor of a building, above a pharmacy that has been there for decades. The studio windows have a view west to La Casa and beyond that to the sunset on clear evenings. Alicia sees this part of her work as "creating a new kind of community right across the street" from the building where she spent much of her childhood in Community worship and gatherings.[7]

Dora's house—where she hosted over the years Sunday evening worship, Community meetings, holiday meals, Bible study, and so many parties—became Alicia's home, along with her husband, Justin, and daughter, Isadora. Alicia turned the basement into a studio where she taught yoga for several years and then began a craniosacral and massage therapy practice. She started studying Eastern philosophy in her thirties. She earned certification to teach yoga, not as a fitness class but incorporating Buddhist and Hindu thought.[8] Leading meditation on one occasion, she began with a Sanskrit chant for peace.

---

6. Wilson, in discussion with the author, April 2022.

7. Alicia Koundakjian Moyer, email message to author, March 14, 2023.

8. Moyer, email message to author, March 14, 2023; Moyer, in discussion with the author, February 2021.

A few years after her mother died, Alicia began to create a bridge between her understanding of the goddess, which is central to her spirituality, and "new understandings of Mary Magdalene and how Christianity can also have that divine feminine as its core," she said. "That's the piece that I wish I could talk to my mom more about." Growing up in the 1970s and 1980s, "I definitely felt like the Community of Christ was very masculine," she said, even as "my mom was a matriarch." People sometimes used female or gender-neutral language for God while reading Scripture or sharing homilies, but it wasn't consistent. Women did most of the cooking for shared meals.[9]

Alicia valued that the Community was led by laypeople, who modeled for her the practice of speaking to the group about faith and spirituality and finding they had more to say than they thought they did. It prepared her to care for people who aren't going to church but are bringing the same kind of needs to yoga and meditation classes. "I've had to step into the shoes of someone who guides people spiritually," Alicia said. "I'm uncovering a voice there for myself that feels very natural." Alicia finds that a lot of people come to yoga hungry for something they can't quite name. "I can't talk about God, per se, in really explicit terms," she said. "But there is this desire that I'm feeling from people to go to that depth and to uncover something sacred in the movement itself. And so, it's a huge part of my work now to lead people to feel their sacredness, starting with the body and then going through all the layers."[10]

Alicia led a group called Magical Mornings, which met by video conference after the COVID pandemic caused lockdowns beginning in March 2020. She wrote to participants: "We have all fallen for that teacher at some point who tells us we need what they have in order to be happy. But I am not that teacher. I am here to tell you you already have everything you need. You always have—kind of like Dorothy's ruby red slippers—you just might not have realized or remembered." The point of practicing meditation is not to get better at meditating, she wrote. "We are practicing to get better at being present for our lives."[11] Dora taught Alicia to literally stop and smell the flowers when they walked past particularly fragrant yards.

One of the Magical Mornings with Alicia was "Woo Woo Wednesdays" in which she got more religious. She drew on her study of Hinduism and Buddhism, while also offering poetry and personal reflections to the multicultural group composed of people from different faiths and those

9. Moyer, in discussion with the author, February 2021.

10. Moyer, in discussion with the author, September 2021.

11. Moyer, email message to Magical Mornings group, March 17, 2022

who are spiritual but not religious. "Everything has a beginning, a middle, and an end," Alicia told the group. "We need to break that idea that the end is worse than the beginning."[12]

≈

Chris asked her wife, Dianne, how she would advise someone who wanted to start a worship community like the Community of Christ. Dianne translated the question as "What has been the secret sauce for the Community of Christ?" Her answer was "the people who have come and this real intentionality about allowing each person to be who they are and to bring the gifts and talents that they have to the Community." In the process five years prior that they asked themselves what was core for them, "we came back over and over again to worship. Worship was really the central place where we were able to both worship God but also be with each other in a way that was intentional and that was focused and that fed us both in a sense of spirituality, but also in a sense of how do we go out into the world in a way that allows us to be what God or Jesus would have us to be in the world, to be love in the world?" She distilled her advice into two points:

1. Figure out who you are, what you want to be, and what principles guide your community.

2. Ask how you can engage and involve people in such a way that you start to really understand their needs as well as the gifts and talents they can bring to the community at large, but also to this community that's gathered.[13]

To Barbara Hayden, while the Community ended as a formal entity registered with a denomination, the spirit behind it could not die. "The Community of Christ idea is not new, is porous, and is available in whatever community," she told the gathered at a party to send off her and Dunstan as they left DC and moved to a retirement community. Barbara feels bad for people who think they'll never find the same kind of community again. "It's like saying 'I can only have water in Mount Pleasant.' The water is everywhere. The Spirit is everywhere."

---

12. Moyer, email message to author confirming spoken statement, June 2, 2021.

13. Dianne Russell in discussion with Christina Nichols and Martin Johnson, September 2016.

Bibliography

Aaseng, Rolf E. "A House for 10 Children." *The Lutheran Standard* 8.13 (June 25, 1968) 4 pp.

Anderson, David Earle. "Doing the Disciplines." *Stance* 3.7 (May 1969) 2.

———. "Ecology Is Where It's at." *Stance* 4.2 (February 1970) 3.

———. "An Editorial Adieu." *Stance* 2.2 (July 1967) 3.

———. "In Closing." *Stance* 3.11 (August 1969) 23.

———. "Looking toward Denver." *Stance* 3.9 (July 1969) 2.

———. "Marilyn's Gone." *Stance* 4.1 (December 1969) 2.

———. "Mission and Economic Interdependence." *Stance* 4.10 (December 1970) 7.

———. "Our Thing in the City: Community of Christ." *Greater Works* 9.12 (December 1968) 30–39.

———. "Remembering the Reformation." *Stance* 2.12 (October 1968) 3.

———. "The Quest for Community." *Stance* 1.7 (September 1966) 1, 6.

———. "Some Call It a Day That Will Live in Infamy. I Just Call It My Mom's Birthday . . ." *Facebook*, December 7, 2021. https://www.facebook.com/permalink.php?story_fbid=pfbidopdA7gd1tvMRWWa2YfFULPphpGZMfprZ2NjRqhz8erFGgZtFTGkU65gBhjmop6wZdl&id=1411930238.

———. "Stance: An Introduction." *Stance* 1.1 (March 1966) 1, 3.

———. "Tom Luke Torosian." *Stance* 7.2 (Summer 1973) 4.

———. "The Tragedy and Absurdity of Colonialism." *Stance* 3.12 (September 1969) 3.

———. "Welcoming Dunstan." *Stance* 4.8 (October 1970) 2–3.

Anderson, David E., and Walter B. Scarvie Jr. "Small Group Liturgies." *Liturgy* (May 1978) 5–11.

Anderson, Judith. "Group Ministry, Lay Style." *Stance* 4.6 (Summer 1970) 11.

———. "Summer Program." *Stance* 3.9 (July 1969) 9–10.

Anderson, Margaret. "A Time to Look." *Stance* 6.4 (August 1972) 7–8, 12.

———. "Whither the Sign of Jonah?" *Stance* 2.5 (January 1968) 1.

Anderson, Valborg. "Calling." *Stance* 5.5 (June–July 1971) 11.

———. "Community: Minority Report." *Stance* 6.7 (January 1973) 5–6.

———. "Dateline: December 8." *Stance* 4.10 (December 1970) 2.

———. "Dear Rosemary." *Stance* 5.6 (August–September 1971) 8, 10.

———. "I've Got the Circle on My Mind: Some Rambling Thoughts on Community—with a Proposal." *Stance* 4.10 (December 1970) 5–7.

———. "One Man's Answer." *Stance* 4.10 (December 1970) 3.

———. "A Phoenix Shall Arise." *Stance* 2.10 (August 1968) 9, 14.

———. "Shall We Share Our Shepherd." *Stance* 5.3 (April 1971) 4.

——. "Strictly Personal." *Stance* 14.1 (Summer 1984) 18.

——. *Thoughts, Faith, and Friends: Poems 1967–1994.* Washington, DC: A & D, 1994.

The Argonne Apartments. "Stylish Floor Plans Designed for Your Comfort." https://www.theargonne.com/washington-dc/argonne/conventional/.

Asch, Chris Myers, and George Derek Musgrove. *Chocolate City: A History of Race and Democracy in the Nation's Capital.* Chapel Hill, NC: University of North Carolina Press, 2017.

Associated Press. "Explaining AP Style on Black and White." *AP News,* July 20, 2020. https://apnews.com/article/archive-race-and-ethnicity-9105661462.

Bateson, Mary Catherine. *Composing a Further Life: The Age of Active Wisdom.* New York: Knopf, 2010.

——. *Composing a Life: The Age of Active Wisdom.* New York: Atlantic Monthly, 1989.

——. "Strangers and Pilgrims." *Stance* 1.6 (August 1966) 1, 4.

Bellah, Robert N., et al. *Habits of the Heart: Individualism and Commitment in American Life.* Reprinted with a new preface. Oakland, CA: University of California Press, 2007.

Bernard, Diane. "It Was Created as a Refuge for Needy Kids. Instead, They Were Raped and Drugged." *Washington Post,* May 18, 2019. https://www.washingtonpost.com/history/2019/05/18/it-was-created-refuge-needy-kids-instead-they-were-raped-drugged/.

Bethge, Renate. "Bonhoeffer's Family and Its Significance for His Theology." In *Dietrich Bonhoeffer—His Significance for North Americans,* by Larry Rasmussen, 1–30. Minneapolis: Fortress, 1990.

Bettenson, Henry, and Chris Maunder, eds. *Documents of the Christian Church.* 3rd ed. New York: Oxford University Press USA, 1999.

Bibeau, Donald F. "The Dangling Conversations, or: The Community Revisited." *Stance* 2.5 (January 1968) 2.

——. "Dissent." *Stance* 1.11 (January 1967) 1, 4.

——. "Learn Baby, Learn!" *Stance* 2.3 (September 1967) 2.

——. "The Meeting of White and Red." *Stance* 3.12 (October 1969) 7–8, 12.

Blood, Peter, and Annie Patterson, eds. *Rise Up Singing: The Group Singing Songbook.* Bethlehem, PA: Sing Out, 1992.

Bonhoeffer, Dietrich. *Life Together; Prayerbook of the Bible.* Edited by Geffrey B. Kelly. Translated by Daniel W. Bloesch and James H. Burness. Minneapolis: Fortress, 2004.

Braaten, David. "A Blooming Idea." *Washington Star,* February 1972. In Community of Christ papers.

Brockell, Gillian. "She Was the Only Member of Congress to Vote against War in Afghanistan. Some Called Her a Traitor." *Washington Post,* August 17, 2021, https://www.washingtonpost.com/history/2021/08/17/barbara-lee-afghanistan-vote/.

Carper, Elsie. "Adams-Morgan Chancery Sites Voted." *Washington Post,* April 11, 1967, B1. ProQuest Historical Newspapers.

Carter, A.P., et al. "Will the Circle Be Unbroken?" In *Rise Up Singing: The Group Singing Songbook,* edited by Peter Blood and Annie Patterson, 98. Bethlehem, PA: Sing Out, 1992.

Center for Applied Linguistics. "Our Founder." https://www.cal.org/who-we-are/our-founder.

Center for Justice and Accountability. "Client: Dr. Juan Romagoza Arce." https://cja. org/what-we-do/litigation/romagoza-arce-v-garcia-and-vides-casanova/clients/ client-dr-juan-romagoza-arce/.

Cherkasky, Mara. *Mount Pleasant*. Images of America. Charleston, SC: Arcadia, 2007.

Cleage, Albert B., Jr. *The Black Messiah*. 1968. Reprint, Trenton, NJ: Africa World, 1989.

Cole, Hazel, and Grady Cole. "The Tramp on the Street." https://digitalcommons.library. umaine.edu/mmb-vp/5680.

Community for Creative Non-Violence. "History of the CCNV." http://www.theccnv. org/history.htm.

"Community Notes." *Stance* 2.3 (September 1967) 6.

"Community Notes." *Stance* 2.4 (December 1967) 6.

Community of Christ. "Our History: W. Grant McMurray." https://cofchrist.org/ history/.

Community of Christ Papers, 1965–2016. Swarthmore College Peace Collection, Swarthmore, PA.

"Contributors." *Stance* 1.6 (August 1966) 3.

"Contributors." *Stance* 2.12 (October 1968) 21.

"Contributors." *Stance* 3.4 (February 1969) 8.

"Conversations at the Sign of Jonah." *Stance* 2.4 (December 1967) 5.

Cosby, N. Gordon. *By Grace Transformed: Christianity for a New Millennium*. Chestnut Ridge, NY: Crossroad, 1999.

———. *Seized by the Power of a Great Affection: Meditations on the Divine Encounter*. Edited by Kayla McClurg. Washington, DC: Inward Outward, 2013.

"Covenant of the Community of Christ." *Stance* 3.11 (August 1969) 21.

Cox, Harvey. *The Secular City: Secularization and Urbanization in Theological Perspective*. Rev. ed. Princeton, NJ: Princeton University Press, 2014.

Currie, Bettie. "What Does It Mean to Be an Ecumenical Congregation?" *Stance* 8.1 (Advent—Christmas 1974) 5–6.

D'au Vin, Constance. "NW Group Shows Big Deeds Grow from Small Seeds." *Washington Post*, October 7, 1977.

Day, Dorothy. *The Long Loneliness: An Autobiography*. San Francisco: Harper & Row, 1952.

DeFerrari, John. *Lost Washington, D.C.* Charleston, SC: History, 2011

DenBoer, Daphne. "That Last, Best Prayer." *Stance* 1.5 (July 1966) 1.

Devers, Dorothy. "Introduction to the Third Edition." In *Journey Inward, Journey Outward*, by Elizabeth O'Connor, n.p. Washington, DC: Potter's House, 1999.

Diaz, José "Chico." Interview by Patrick Scallen. December 15, 2017. Mount Pleasant Riot Oral History Project. https://digdc.dclibrary.org/islandora/object/ dcplislandora%3A42730.

Dobbins, Alexander. "Just a Reminder." *Stance* 4.3 (March 1970) 13.

Eisenhower, Dwight D. *Mandate for Change, 1953–1956*. Vol. 2, *The White House Years: A Personal Account*. Garden City, NY: Doubleday, 1963.

Eustis, Renata. "Memorial Service for Bob Pohlman, John 14:1–6." May 19, 2018, in the author's possession.

"Excerpts from the Statement of the Lincoln Civic Association on the International Center." *Stance* 1.2 (April 1966) 2, 4.

Fautz, Betty. "Lincoln Civic Association." *Stance* 2.5 (January 1968) 3.

Ferguson, Charles. "An Advent Psalm." *Stance* 2.4 (December 1967) 4.

———. "Paul's Letter to the Community of Christ." *Stance* 1.6 (August 1966) 1, 6.

Flannery, Austin, ed. *Vatican Council II: The Conciliar and Post Conciliar Documents.* Northport, NY: Costello, 1975.

Francis, Robert Donald. "The Emerging Church as a New Religious Movement: A Case Study in the Negotiation of Continuity and Change." Master's thesis, University of Chicago, 2006. In the author's possession.

Freeman, Jo. "The Tyranny of Structurelessness." https://www.jofreeman.com/joreen/tyranny.htm.

"FYI." *Stance* 2.12 (October 1968) 3.

Gerassi, John. "Introduction." In *Revolutionary Priest: The Complete Writings and Messages of Camilo Torres,* edited by John Gerassi, 3–56. New York: Vintage, 1971.

Glenn, Bert. "Serving the Eucharist to the Community." *Stance* 13.4 (Summer 1983) 15, 20.

Green, Penelope. "An Anthropologist's Take on Homemaking: At Home with Mary Catherine Bateson." *New York Times,* August 25, 2010. https://www.nytimes.com/2010/08/26/garden/26bateson.html.

———. "Mary Catherine Bateson Dies at 81; Anthropologist on Lives of Women." *New York Times,* January 14, 2021. https://www.nytimes.com/2021/01/14/books/mary-catherine-bateson-dead.html.

Grigg, William. "House Unit Hears Foes of Chancery Enclave." *Washington Star,* February 15, 1967. Newspaper clipping in Community of Christ Papers.

Handel, Georg Frideric. *Messiah.* Edited by Friedrich Chrysander. https://www.free-scores.com/download-sheet-music.php?pdf=24052.

Hayden, Dunstan. "Economic Interdependence." *Stance* 6.7 (January 1973) 13.

Hennelly, Alfred T. *Liberation Theologies: The Global Pursuit of Justice.* Mystic, CT: Twenty-Third Publications, 1995.

Hilfiker, David. *Not All of Us Are Saints.* New York: Ballantine, 1996.

Huck, Gabe. "The Community of the Empty Garbage Can: Some Notes Toward a Different Ministry and Structure." *Stance* 4.9 (November 1970) 7–8.

Huron, Amanda. "The Dream Lives On: How to Give Away Your Church—and Fight Gentrification at the Same Time." *Sojourners* 50.7 (July 2021) 24–29.

Huron, Doug. Homily in the Community of Christ. Washington, DC, February 2, 2003. In the author's possession.

———. Eulogy for Bob Pohlman. Christ Lutheran Church, Washington, DC, May 19, 2018. In the author's possession.

———. "Putting the Burden Behind Us." *Stance* 9.2 (Spring 1979) 5–6, 8.

———. "Race." Unpublished essay, ca. 2017–18. In the author's possession.

———. "Second Sunday in Lent." Homily in the Community of Christ. Washington, DC, March 11, 2001. In the author's possession.

———. "Second Sunday of Easter." Homily in the Community of Christ. Washington, DC, April 23, 2006. In the author's possession.

———. "Third Sunday of Advent." Homily in the Community of Christ. Washington, DC, December 16, 2001. In the author's possession.

International Bonhoeffer Society—English Language Section. "Statement Issued by the Board of Directors of the International Bonhoeffer Society." *Religion News,* February 3, 2017. https://religionnews.com/2017/02/03/statement-issued-by-the-board-of-directors-of-the-international-bonhoeffer-society/.

Jezer, Marty. *The Dark Ages: Life in the United States 1945–1960*. Boston: South End, 1982.

Johnson, Alicia. "A Normal Day at Church—for the Community of Christ." *Stance* 14.1 (Summer 1984) 10.

Johnson, Dora. "FLOC's Half-Way House." *Stance* 2.2 (July 1967) 1, 5.

———. "For the Archives." *Stance* 5.1 (February 1971) 7–9.

———. "Here We Are: Slightly Overwhelmed." *Stance* 9.1 (Advent 1978), 5–6.

———. "The House on Montague Street." *Stance* 2.5 (January 1968) 1, 6.

———. Shared word in the Community of Christ. Lent ca. 1977, in Community of Christ Papers.

———. "Some Hesitations." *Stance* 1.11 (January 1967) 3, 6.

Keating, Kathleen. "Community Is—." *Stance* 1.11 (January 1967) 6.

Kennel-Shank, Celeste. "Author Connects Anabaptist and Emergent Movements." Interview with Brian McLaren. *Mennonite Weekly Review*, April 21, 2008.

———. "U.S. Lutheran Seminary Returns Rare Manuscript to Greek Orthodox Church." *The Christian Century* 133.26 (December 21, 2016) 14–15.

Kernan, Michael. "Mitch Snyder, the Wayward Shepherd." *Washington Post*, January 11, 1984. https://www.washingtonpost.com/archive/lifestyle/1984/01/11/mitch-snyder-the-wayward-shepherd/a9b99828-5953-4f4b-b890-072e193130e6/.

Kifner, John. "Armenian Genocide of 1915: An Overview." *The New York Times*, n.d. https://archive.nytimes.com/www.nytimes.com/ref/timestopics/topics_armenian genocide.html?simple=True.

Klonowski, Bob. "Community Sketches: Dora Johnson." *Stance* 8.1 (Advent—Christmas 1974) 11–12.

Koundakjian, Yevnige Berejiklian. "ZORYAN Institute Yevnige Koundakjian." *YouTube*, April 14, 1989. https://www.youtube.com/watch?v=bmVqlzRfrac.

Kraus, Bonnie. "Friday Evening Worship." *Stance* 6.2 (June 1972) 11.

Legal Defense Fund. "*Brown v. Board* and the 'Doll Test.'" https://www.naacpldf.org/brown-vs-board/significance-doll-test/.

Lenten Booklets (alternately titled *Lenten Thoughts* or *Thoughts on the Lenten Season*). 27 vols. Washington, DC: Self-published, 1987–2014.

"Lincoln Civic Association Urges 'People' Consideration before Senate Committee." *Stance* 1.2 (April 1966) 1, 5.

Lisi, Tom, and Dunstan Hayden. "The Good of Talking." *Stance* 4.9 (November 1970) 8.

Livezey, Lowell W. "Church as Parish: The East Harlem Protestant Parish." *The Christian Century* 115.34 (December 9, 1998) 1176–77.

Lokken, James. Review of *Lutherans and Catholics in Dialogue IV: Eucharist and Ministry. Stance* 5.4 (May 1971) 19–20.

Maar, Henry Richard, III. *Freeze! The Grassroots Movement to Halt the Arms Race and End the Cold War*. Ithaca, NY: Cornell University Press, 2021.

MacGillis, Alec. *Fulfillment: Winning and Losing in One-Click America*. New York: Farrar, Straus & Giroux, 2021.

Maney, Ann. "The Story of FLOC." *Stance* 7.2 (Summer 1973) 16.

Masliansky, Nechama, and Robert Pohlman. "An Unhealthy Cycle Triggered by Unaffordable Housing." *Washington Post*, July 5, 2011. http://www.washingtonpost.com/opinions/an-unhealthy-cycle-triggered-by-unaffordable-housing/2011/07/05/gIQANePm7H_story.html

Markey, Eileen. *A Radical Faith: The Assassination of Sister Maura*. New York: Nation, 2016.

Marty, Martin E. *Righteous Empire: The Protestant Experience in America*. New York, Dial, 1970.

McArdle, Lois. "Cutting the Umbilical Cord." *Stance* 3.12 (September 1969) 7.

McBride, Jennifer. *The Church for the World: A Theology of Public Witness*. New York: Oxford University Press, 2011.

McClurg, Kayla. "Introduction." In *Seized by the Power of a Great Affection: Meditations on the Divine Encounter*, edited by Kayla McClurg, ix–xi. Washington, DC: Inward Outward, 2013.

McDannell, Colleen. *The Spirit of Vatican II: A History of Catholic Reform in America*. New York: Basic, 2011.

McLaren, Brian. "Becoming Convergent." https://emergent-us.typepad.com/emergentus /files/becoming_emergent.pdf.

———. *A New Kind of Christian: A Tale of Two Friends on a Spiritual Journey*. San Francisco: Jossey-Bass, 2001.

Merry, Stephanie. "'Just Like Korea Is the Forgotten War, the Pentagon Is the Forgotten 9/11.'" *Washington Post*, September 5, 2016. https://www.washingtonpost. com/lifestyle/style/just-like-korea-is-the-forgotten-war-the-pentagon-is-the- forgotten-911/2016/09/05/049e3e52–713c-11e6–9705-23e51a2f424d_story.html.

Milius, Peter. "U.S. Is Revising Chanceries Plan." *Washington Post*, February 16, 1967. ProQuest Historical Newspapers.

Miller, Steven P. *Billy Graham and the Rise of the Republican South*. Philadelphia: University of Pennsylvania Press, 2009.

Morley, Jefferson. "The Mount Pleasant Miracle: How One D.C. Neighborhood Quietly Became a National Model for Resisting Gentrification." *Washington Post*, January 25, 2021. https://www.washingtonpost.com/magazine/2021/01/25/mount-pleasant -washington-dc-gentrification/?arc404=true.

Mosher, Lydia. "Black Power Christianity." Review of *The Black Messiah*, by Albert B. Cleage Jr. *Stance* 3.3 (February 1969) 14, 17.

Mosher, Peter. "Signs of the Times." *Stance* 3.11 (August 1969) 15.

Musuta, Selina. "Looking for Mount Pleasant's Live Mariachi Bands?" *DC North*, July 2007.

National Capital Planning Commission. "Heights & Views." https://www.ncpc.gov/ topics/heights/.

National Coalition for the Homeless. "Remembering Mitch Snyder." https://www.nation alhomeless.org/news/RememberingMitchSnyder.html.

Nees, Tom. "What's in a Name?" https://www.communityofhopedc.org/whats-name.

Nelson, Angela. "History of Bipolar Disorder." https://www.webmd.com/bipolar-disorder /history-bipolar.

O'Connor, Elizabeth. *Call to Commitment: The Story of the Church of the Saviour, Washington, D.C.* New York: Harper & Row, 1975.

———. *Journey Inward, Journey Outward*. Washington, DC: Potter's House, 1968.

Pacatte, Rose. "Blase Bonpane, 89, Peace and Human Rights Activist, Dies in Los Angeles." *National Catholic Reporter*, April 16, 2019. https://www.ncronline.org/ news/blase-bonpane-89-peace-and-human-rights-activist-dies-los-angeles.

Paka, Vincent. "Churchless Congregations Growing." *Washington Post*, May 31, 1969.

Patterson, Anna Mae. "The 'X' and 'Y' of Christian Mission in the Lincoln Civic Association." *Stance* 1.1 (March 1966) 1–2.

Perriello, Pat. "Exploring Christian and Jewish Connections at Easter." *NCR Today* (blog), April 10, 2017. https://www.ncronline.org/blogs/ncr-today/exploring-christian-and-jewish-connections-easter.

The Potter's House. "Our Story." https://pottershousedc.org/history.

Rasmussen, Larry. *Dietrich Bonhoeffer—His Significance for North Americans.* Minneapolis: Fortress, 1990.

———. *Moral Fragments and Moral Community: A Proposal for Church in Society.* Minneapolis: Fortress, 1993.

"Rev. A. Thomas Murphy Jr., Founding Pastor, Youth Advocate, Fire Chaplain, Dies at 85." *OBX Today*, August 18, 2020. https://www.obxtoday.com/the-rev-a-thomas-murphy-jr-founding-pastor-youth-advocate-fire-chaplain-dies-at-85/.

Riddle, M. B., trans. "Didache." Revised and edited by Kevin Knight. https://www.newadvent.org/fathers/0714.htm.

Romagoza Arce, Juan. "No Safe Haven: Accountability for Human Rights Violators in the United States, Before the Subcommittee on Human Rights and the Law." https://www.hrw.org/news/2007/11/14/no-safe-haven-accountability-human-rights-violators-united-states.

Romagoza, Juan. "A Tortured Path to Justice." *Post Magazine*, August 18, 2003. https://www.washingtonpost.com/wp-dyn/articles/A64158-2003Aug15.html.

Ruether, Rosemary Radford. "From Competition to Community, with Some Remarks on the Liberation of Women." *Stance* 5.6 (August–September 1971) 7–8.

———. "Going Away: Perspective from the Left." *Stance* 4.7 (September 1970) 13–14, 17.

———. "The Latin American Church from Medellín to Puebla." *Stance* 9.3 (Summer 1979) 6, 14.

———. *Mary—The Feminine Face of the Church.* Philadelphia: Westminster, 1977.

———. "Motherearth and the Megamachine." In *Womanspirit Rising: A Feminist Reader in Religion*, edited by Carol P. Christ and Judith Plaskow, 43–52. San Francisco: HarperSanFrancisco, 1992.

———. *My Quests for Hope and Meaning: An Autobiography.* Eugene, OR: Cascade, 2013. Apple Books.

———. "The Myth of the Community of Christ." Special "community" issue, *Stance* 3.11 (August 1969) 11–12.

———. "The Piety of Political Repression." *Stance* 4.7 (September 1970) 11–12, 17.

———. *Women and Redemption: A Theological History.* Minneapolis: Fortress, 1998.

Ruether, Rosemary, et al. "A Call for a Group to Explore a New Human Perspective." January 10, 1972. In Community of Christ Papers.

Runck, Bette. "The Community of Christ Tutoring Program." *Stance* 2.5 (January 1968) 3.

"Ruth Schumm Dies." *Washington Post*, June 26, 1988. https://www.washingtonpost.com/archive/local/1988/06/26/ruth-schumm-dies/15a4e32b-8cae-4fa4-bdcc-2976902da7f5/.

Sadon, Rachel. "6 Years after Devastating Fire in Mt. Pleasant, Tenants Set to Return in Fall to Rebuilt Home." *Washington Post*, May 7, 2014. https://www.washingtonpost.com/local/six-years-after-fire-deauville-tenants-move-closer-to-returning-to-their-rebuilt-home/2014/05/07/d337c3b0-caf8-11e3-a75e-463587891b57_story.html.

Scarvie, Walter B., Jr. "The Adiaphoristic Principle: Its Role in the Roman Catholic and Lutheran Consultation on Eucharist and Ministry." Paper for a class at Catholic University of America, 1973. In Community of Christ Papers.

———. "The Crisis of Belief and Liturgical Integrity: Toward Establishing a Theological Principle for Safeguarding the Christian Character of Contemporary Liturgical Forms." Paper for a class at Catholic University of America, December 1971. In Community of Christ Papers.

———. Homily in the Community of Christ. Washington, DC, August 4, 1996. In Community of Christ Papers.

———. "I Hear You Saying." *Stance* 9.5 (Fall 1979) 9–10, 16.

———. Lecture series on aspects of the liturgy. Washington, DC, 1973. In Community of Christ Papers.

———. "Life's Meanings, Rite's Meanings." *Liturgy* (August–September 1975) 214–17.

———. "What Language Shall We Borrow?" 1975. In Community of Christ Papers.

Schramm, John. "Community of Christ: An Experiment with Flexible Servanthood." *This Day* (September 1966) 15–21.

———. "For Love of Children." *Stance* 1.9 (November 1966) 1, 6.

———. "Restructuring the Community: A Proposal." *Stance* 1.10 (December 1966) 1, 5.

———. "Shared Responsibilities." *Stance* 5.5 (June–July 1971)

———. "Theological Issues confronting the Urban ministry." Paper presented at the American Lutheran Church's Conference of Inner City Ministries, June 1969. *Stance* 3.10 (August 1969) 4–5.

———. "Throwing the Brick." *Stance* 4.9 (November 1970) 5.

Schramm, John, and David Anderson. *Dance in Steps of Change: The Story of the Community of Christ, Washington, D.C.'s Answer to the Tensions that Challenge the Church Today.* N.p.: Thomas Nelson, 1970.

Schramm, John, and J. Dunstan Hayden. "Community of Christ in Washington, DC." Presentation at Holden Village, Chelan, WA, 1978. In the author's possession.

Schramm, John, and Mary Schramm. *Things That Make for Peace.* Minneapolis: Augsburg, 1976.

Schramm, Mark. "Shared Word." *Stance* 3.12 (September 1969) 6.

Schramm, Mary. "Death Wish/Wish Dream." Special "community" issue, *Stance* 3.11 (August 1969) 7.

———. *Gifts of Grace: Discovering and Using Your Unique Abilities.* Chelan, WA: Holden Village, 2000.

———. "Gifts of Grace." Presentation at Holden Village, Chelan, WA, June 10, 2004. In the author's possession.

———. "A Letter to Jenny Moore." *Stance* 3.2 (January 1969) 13–14.

———. "More from the Store." *Stance* 3.9 (July 1969) 8.

———. "The Scattered and the Gathered." *Stance* 1.6 (August 1966) 5.

Schudel, Matt. "Douglas B. Huron, Lawyer Who Won Landmark Workplace Bias Cases, Dies at 75." *Washington Post*, June 13, 2021. https://www.washingtonpost.com/local/obituaries/douglas-b-huron-lawyer-who-won-landmark-workplace-bias-cases-dies-at-75/2021/06/13/10d51f06-cbc3-11eb-81b1-34796c7393af_story.htm.

Schumm, Ruth. "Home Buyers, Inc." *Stance* 2.2 (July 1967) 1, 5.

———. "Home Buyers." *Stance* 2.5 (January 1968) 5.

———. "Home Buyers' President Says." *Home Buyers Happenings* 1.1 (November 1968) 1.

———. "Introducing Our First Family." *Home Buyers Happenings* 1.1 (November 1968) 1.

"Second Report of the Process Committee." *Stance* 7.1 (March–April 1973) 14–15.

Shelton, Elizabeth. "Selling the Green: The Greening of the City." *Washington Post*, March 5, 1972. ProQuest Historical Newspapers.

Sierra Club. "Rudolph Wendelin: Designer of the 1964 John Muir Commemorative Postage Stamp." https://vault.sierraclub.org/john_muir_exhibit/stamps/rudolph_wendelin.aspx.

"Sign of Jonah: An Introduction." *Stance* 1.11 (January 1967) 5 .

Sims, Laura. "Creative Non-Violence in Community." *Stance* 5.3 (April 1971) 7–8.

Smith, Sam. *Captive Capital: Colonial Life in Modern Washington*. Bloomington, IN: Indiana University Press, 1974.

Staff of *Stance*. "An Editorial Introduction." Special "community" issue, *Stance* 3.11 (August 1969) 3–4.

Streitfeld, David. "Mount Pleasant Under Glass: In a Gentrifying Neighborhood, Must Classes Always Clash?" *Washington Post*, July 15, 1988.

Stringfellow, William. *A Private and Public Faith*. Grand Rapids, MI: Eerdmans, 1962.

St. Stephen and the Incarnation Episcopal Church. "A Brief History of the Parish." https://www.saintstephensdc.org/history.

Sweeney, Jon M. *Light in the Dark Ages: The Friendship of Francis and Clare of Assisi*. Brewster, MA: Paraclete, 2007.

Tentler, Leslie Woodcock. *American Catholics: A History*. New Haven: Yale University Press, 2020.

Torosian, Tom Luke. "Reassurance." Homily in the Community of Christ, Washington, DC, November 11, 1973. In Community of Christ Papers.

———. *Someday Yonkers: An Armenian-American Odyssey*. Self-published, 2012.

Trueblood, Elton. "Introduction." In *Call to Commitment: The Story of the Church of the Saviour, Washington, D.C.*, edited by Elizabeth O'Connor, ix–xii. New York: Harper & Row, 1975.

24Lanterns. "CNHED Tribute to Outgoing Executive Director Bob Pohlman." https://vimeo.com/110284546.

University of Chicago. *Chicago Manual of Style*. 17th ed. Chicago: University of Chicago, 2017.

University of Notre Dame. "Champion of Civil Rights." https://hesburgh.nd.edu/fr-teds-life/champion-of-civil-rights/.

The Veterans of Hope Project. "Rev. Dr. J. Archie Hargraves." https://www.veteransofhope.org/veterans/rev-dr-archie-hargraves/.

Walton, Ellie, dir. *La Manplesa: An Uprising Remembered*. Washington, DC: independent documentary, 2021.

Ward, Wendy. "Plants for the Elderly." *Stance* 6.7 (January 1973) 14.

———. "Through a Glass Lightly: Oblique Theological Refractions." *Stance* 9.5 (Fall 1979) 13–14.

———. "Tom Torosian Talks." *Stance* 8.1 (Advent—Christmas 1974) 7.

Washington, James, ed. *A Testament of Hope: The Essential Writings and Speeches of Martin Luther King, Jr.* San Francisco: HarperSanFrancisco, 1991.

Webber, George W. *The Congregation in Mission: Emerging Structures for the Church in an Urban Society*. Nashville, TN: Abingdon, 1964.

Wendelin, Rudolph. "A Probable Submission for Journal St. Martins & Theresa." Unpublished draft, 1988. In Community of Christ Papers.

———. "Trinity Sunday." Homily in the Community of Christ, Washington, DC, May 28, 1994. In Community of Christ Papers.

West, Hollie I. "Three Samaritans: The Soft Voices of Washingtonians Who Have Chosen Another Way." *Washington Post*, December 21, 1980.

Wheaton, Philip E. *Faithful Community: Campesino Vision of the Kingdom of God History of the Christian Base Community in Jiñocuao, Nicaragua*. Washington, DC: EPICA, 2005.

Whiteside, Haven. "A Search for a Responsible Future: An Interview with Haven Whiteside." *Occasionally Speaking: A Supplement to Stance* 9.4 (September 1979) 17.

Wild, Mark. *Renewal: Liberal Protestants and the American City after World War II*. Chicago: University of Chicago, 2019.

Willmann, John B. "High-Rise Living Area Grows in Dupont Southwest." *Washington Post*, April 22, 1967. ProQuest Historical Newspapers.

Wilson-Hartgrove, Jonathan. *New Monasticism: What It Has to Say to Today's Church*. Ada, MI: Brazos, 2008.

Wojahn, Sandra. Easter homily in the Community of Christ, Washington, DC, April 7, 1985. In the author's possession.

Ylvisaker, John Carl, comp. *Borning Cry: Worship for a New Generation*, Waverly, IA: New Generation, 1992.

Subject Index

activism for social justice, 20, 39–43, 69–70, 133, 137–38, 143, 146–49, 155–56, 192–93, 205

Adams Morgan, 14, 93–94, 150, 192, 223

Advent, 113 (photo), 129, 163, 213, 219

Almquist, Alden, 112 (photo), 132–33, 202, 213, 222

Almquist, Nancy, 132

American Lutheran Church, 4, 11, 15, 57, 76

Anderson, David Earle, as lay leader: 20, 69, 76–77, 85–88, 99, 102, 120, 122–23, 156, 165, 173–75, 183, 192, 196; family of: 40, 45–46, 91, 120, 153, 200

Anderson, Valborg, 44–48, 67, 70, 77–78, 82, 90–91, 94, 104, 110 (photo), 148, 153, 178

anti-globalization movement, 155–56, 215

Armenian people, 27–30, 80–81

arts in activism and worship, 96, 119, 138, 206

Avery, Natalie, 192–94, 202–3

baptism, 4–5, 72, 85, 87, 129, 135, 169, 188, 220–22

Bateson, Mary Catherine, 5, 8, 74–75, 118–19, 214

Beane, Jaret, 117 (photo), 220–22

Benedict, Don, 16

Bibeau, Donald "Don," 66–67, 85

bivocational ministry, x, 1–2, 77

Bonhoeffer, Dietrich, 17, 194–95

Catholic Worker movement, 1, 137, 145, 147

Catholics, 3, 16, 58–73, 75, 94, 99, 107–8, 127, 139–50, 154, 158, 187, 197–98, 220–21

children in communal life, ix, 18, 30–34, 53, 69, 102–6, 118, 121, 125–26, 175, 202–3

children's faith formation, 2–5, 18–21, 32–33, 49–50, 58–61, 105, 113 (photos), 118–35, 169, 202, 219–22

Christ House, 2, 121, 145–46, 223

Church of the Saviour, 2, 12–17, 33–34, 49, 65, 93, 121, 145–46, 156, 176–77, 194, 223

church planting, 11–18, 21–25, 95–96; pastoral transition in, 82–85

civil rights, 20, 23, 30–32, 37–39, 42, 68, 79–80, 127–28, 157–59, 171

Cleage Jr., Albert, 41

closing, church or organizational, 80, 212–27

coffeehouse ministry, 14, 20, 55–56, 223

Cold War, 19, 156, 182–83

communes, 84, 102–4

Community for Creative Non-Violence, 146–49

conflict, congregational, 82–85, 162–65, 176–77

consensus-based decision-making, 56, 165, 174–80, 186, 188–90, 213, 215

Wilson, Alicia, 138, 144, 215–16, 224
Wind, Amy, 159–62, 167–70, 179–80,
     188–89, 213, 215
Wojahn, Sandra, ix, 116 and 117
     (photo), 126–130, 170–71,
     174–77, 200, 206, 215–16

women in church leadership, 70,
     89–90, 129, 187–90, 226

Yarbrough, Anne, 85, 103–5, 120–21,
     125, 158–59, 188
youth group, 131–33, 191–92